MĀL

Private and Public School Partnerships: Sharing Lessons about Decentralization

Dedication

This is dedicated to Jim, Chris, Todd, Elizabeth, Tommy, Michael and Baby Cakes so that their children and their children's children will find that their public school will emulate the type of schooling found in this book.

Private and Public School Partnerships:
Sharing Lessons about Decentralization

Jean Madsen

 Falmer Press

(A member of the Taylor & Francis Group)
London • Washington, D.C.

UK Falmer Press, 1 Gunpowder Square, London, EC4A 3DE
USA Falmer Press, Taylor & Francis Inc., 1900 Frost Road, Suite 101,
Bristol, PA 19007

© J. Madsen 1996

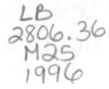

LB
2806.36
M25
1996

First published in 1996

10-17-96-1943352

**A catalogue record for this book is available from the British
Library**

**Library of Congress Cataloging-in-Publication Data are
available on request**

ISBN 0 7507 0536 1 cased
ISBN 0 7507 0537 X paper

Jacket design by Caroline Archer

Typeset in 10/12pt Garamond by
Graphicraft Typesetters Ltd., Hong Kong.

*Printed in Great Britain by Biddles Ltd., Guildford and King's
Lynn on paper which has a specified pH value on final paper
manufacture of not less than 7.5 and is therefore 'acid free'.*

Contents

Contents

Contents

Acknowledgments

In writing this book, I would like to thank the three schools who took part in this project. Each school allowed me the freedom to talk to their participants and went out of their way to meet my requests. Even after the data was collected, these schools continued to embrace my involvement in their lives. Many return visits and discussions with the principals helped to shape the nature of this research. I personally want to thank Mrs Kathy Betz, Dr Barb Fulton and Ms Barbara Clewell for allowing me into their schools. They sanctioned this study without fear of how this might impact their school community. They were very kind in allowing me the time to have an interactive dialogue. These women were wonderful principals who cared deeply about schooling and their willingness to share their vision with me. I feel very fortunate that I was able to find these schools and how they have influenced my understanding of private schools. Being a public school proponent, I learned that we need to reduce our prejudices and be open to the pieces of the quilt called schooling.

During the collection and writing phase of this project, I was a faculty member at Fontbonne College. This institution provided me with release time and the support necessary to complete this project. My thanks go to Dr Judy Failoni, Sister Rita Schmitz and Sister Joan Lescinski. Dr Jean Wasko patiently did the editing and the cutting to bring this book to closure. Mary Andrews was so kind to put up with the major editing that she often spent long weekends and nights doing this instead of being with her family. Others who assisted with this project include David Wilson (PC Innovators) with computer support, and Kathy Stenner, Randy Taylor and Wendy Gornall who transcribed tapes, located research and read pieces of the manuscript. They were wonderful and a life savor when I needed them.

The last touches of this book were completed at the University of Wisconsin-Milwaukee. This institution provided the resources to complete this book. Cathy Nelson finished the final edits and the many last minute changes. She did them so willingly. There were people who read several chapters towards the end of this project that also need to be recognized: Rick Reitzug, Bill Kritek, Gail Schneider, Linda O'Neil and everyone else. Jim Cibulka willingly gave up much of his time to let me bend his ear during the early and last phases of this book.

There were many researchers in the field that I would like to thank for their support and encouragement. Pat Bauch and Mary Anne Raywid were very helpful at AERA sessions in putting the pieces of the pie together. Mary Anne sent me in the direction of the community literature and provided great feedback. Pat was a great friend in letting me talk about how to outline this data and what were the connections between public and private schools. She was helpful along with Ellen Goldring and Phil Woods.

When I moved to Milwaukee, with most of my things in boxes and a deadline to complete this book, I was fortunate to find many helpful relatives and friends. The Fontbonne students who helped me pack this research and guaranteed its safety. I want to thank Mary Rands who so quickly had the computer up and running. She made it possible to find some stability even with the boxes. The Stroms (Kelly, Hogan, Beth and Karl) were the best movers who put my really big furniture into a small apartment and provided closure on my living arrangements. Finally, to my sister Joan Madsen who has the best sense of direction and could locate the School of Education and my apartment so I could find my way to the computer to complete this project. Without these individuals, this move would have greatly impaired the writing of this book.

Finally, I need to thank my family for their never-ending support. My mom and dad who tolerated another round of 'I can't, because I have to finish this book.' when I was really needed at home for their needs. They were always there for me, so I hope they understand. Being public school proponents, it was difficult for my family to understand the reason for this book. However, they were supportive and we often had good discussions about choice. Thanks, Jin, John, Jim and Joan for being a supportive family.

Finally, I really want to thank Malcolm Clarkson. He has defined so much of my work. What a pleasure to have such a delightful editor who believes in your conceptualization and writing ability to improve schools. He is a credit to the field of education by being visionary and not limited by the number of sales.

Thanks to all who supported this project. The intent is not to take sides, but to begin the discussion of how we can consider partnerships for educating all children.

List of Figures

Foreword

The issue of governance has emerged as an important consideration in the education reform movement. Governance is significant, at least potentially, because it shapes or influences many features of the schooling enterprise, which in turn may affect institutional performance. Governance includes ownership of the school, the role of it's board, relationships of the board with parents and community, forms of accountability between the board and the community, and related matters. Governance, in turn, shapes the roles, rights, and responsibilities of administrators, teachers, and students.

Recent developments in organizational theory, rooted in conceptions of organizational culture, as well as the work of 'new institutional' theorists, have reasserted the importance of governance. Earlier theories tended to de-emphasize the degree to which changes at the level of governance are capable of penetrating to the level of the organization's day-to-day operational performance. For example, Talcott Parsons' functional theory of bureaucracy posits a disjuncture between institutional, managerial, and technical levels of the organization. The theory provides an explanation for why the behavior of teachers, working in isolated classrooms, has been so impervious to a variety of efforts to reform teaching. Similarly, Karl Weick's portrayal of educational organizations as 'loosely coupled' led to the same conclusion. By contrast, much of the literature on powerful organizational cultures begins from the opposite premise, that it is possible to mobilize an organization to work together in a common direction.

These recent advances in organization theory, some propelled by 'popular' theorists such as Tom Peters, Peter Drucker, W. Edwards Deming, Ted Gaebler, and David Osborne emphasize the value of decentralizing authority, delineating clear missions, a customer orientation, competition, flexibility, accountability, and other themes. In efforts to restructure governments, among them schools, the call for *privatization* has included efforts to abandon some functions, sell off others, contract with private firms to handle certain functions, promote more entrepreneurial activity by governments, and so on. Efforts to 'privatize' public schools, such as contracting, creating charter schools, and private school choice, have proven to be very controversial in the United States. Similar controversies have occurred in Great Britain over grant maintained schools, City Technology Colleges, local management of schools, and other efforts by Tory governments to create a new national system of schooling. Despite the controversy, school privatization activities continue in both countries.

In the present volume, Jean Madsen addresses one piece of this large question of decentralization and privatization. She examines closely the operation of several independent schools to determine what, if anything, is distinctive about these responsive models of privatization. She then considers the implications of these findings for redesigning public schools.

The governance arrangements in these schools appear to have much to do with the emergence of distinctive school communities. The nature and roles of a board of trustees are examined. The picture that emerges is of boards which are quite successful in shaping the mission of the school. There is much to be learned here which may have application to councils in locally governed public schools and even to school boards in public school districts. For example, there is little systematic evidence that site-based management in public schools in the United States has been successful. Part of the problem seems to be in defining the role of local councils or committees. What is their function, who should the council represent, and how should members be selected and held accountable? How do such boards work with the principal, teachers, parents, and the broader community? These are some of the practical issues which are examined in this book.

Another important topic of the book is the leadership and management of independent school principals. The breadth of the principal's role in these settings is apparent, extending to fund raising and development, fiscal management, recruitment, and public relations, as well selection of staff. Further, effective management requires not controlling others but empowering them. Beyond the nice-sounding rhetoric it evokes, a participatory leadership style poses considerable role strains for principals. The book helps us understand in a concrete way some of the obstacles, perhaps dilemmas, which have to be faced if we are serious about redesigning public schools to be more responsive to a variety of audiences. Empowering people to accomplish shared goals requires a variety of complicated managerial strategies, including goal setting, joint problem solving, and consensus-building.

Hence, Professor Madsen captures an empowerment process which is not entirely problem free. It is challenging not simply for principals, but also for those who are empowered, such as teachers and parents, who must learn new responsibilities and balance more commitments on their time. Not all of these challenges were resolved in these schools, and probably never will be. For example, a higher degree of responsiveness to parents on the part of the school administration is viewed with alarm by some teachers.

A strength of the book is a focus on comparisons among the three schools. The schools have somewhat different histories and contexts. Yet they have achieved remarkably similar organizational cultures. The author's detailed descriptive analysis gives the reader a very clear picture of how this convergence in school effectiveness in the three settings has occurred. Yet, differences also are highlighted. For example, at one school the decision not to encourage parent participation at the governance level seemed to create problems which were not experienced in the same magnitude at the other two schools.

Professor Madsen also offers insights concerning some of the big themes in the school privatization debate. Her findings make it clear that while markets may facilitate the emergence of a different organizational culture in these schools, it is the mission orientation of the school which is a critical dynamic enlisting the loyalty of the members of the school community, including teachers, parents, and students. She shows the various ways in which this mission orientation shapes each school's effectiveness.

It remains an important, unanswered question whether the exemplary characteristics of these schools, e.g., mission adherence, strong board govern-ance structures, parent organization, strong administrative leadership, and a professional community for teachers, can be transposed to the public sector. Professor Madsen raises this concern herself. At its core, her analysis lays out clearly what public schools would have to 'look like' if they were to be restruc-tured. She cannot answer, given her data, what it will take to achieve such a transformation in the public sector. To be sure, she cautions against overly simplistic calls for privatization which assume that markets automatically trans-form schools. At the same time, her evidence is unmistakable: the need to be competitive makes these schools mission oriented and encourages them to be responsive and accountable. Her conclusions lead us to what may be the most important question of all: How can this system of incentives be injected into the public schooling enterprise in order to achieve the transformation that is long overdue?

James G. Cibulka

Rationale for Privatization

The restructuring movement, as it unfolds, represents an attempt to reinvent schooling. One idea, spawned by the movement, involves dissolving the educational bureaucracy and allowing individual schools to compete in the marketplace (Murphy and Hallinger, 1993). The concept of school privatization which promotes competition as a way to foster improvements in public schools leads to the decentralization of schools (Chubb, 1988; Clune and White, 1988; Elmore, 1988; McNeil, 1988; Sizer, 1984). Although deregulation is only a theoretical tenet at present, it promises to become a viable option for school improvement. With the public sector eyeing privatization as a means to improve education, private schools, already competing in the marketplace, are being viewed with great interest.

For the last three decades, the bureaucracy of public schools has been criticized as inefficient and ineffective. Policy-makers, taking the lead in defining the agenda for school reform, created a series of legislative policies. The first wave of these reform policies, known as the 'excellence' movement produced a series of prescriptions for improving the teaching profession. These top–down legislative mandates left many educators feeling powerless to enact change. The second wave, known as the restructuring movement, resulted in returning authority to schools by changing the governance structure to increase the educator's role in decision-making. Many districts developed site-based management which allowed schools greater autonomy in improving their delivery of services (Elmore, 1990; Murphy, 1992; Raywid, 1990). However, this governance reform was fraught with many problems of defining full authority to schools. The constraints of site-based management, for example, made school autonomy difficult to achieve. As a result, school decentralization has become the focus for the third wave. Proponents of school decentralization call for radical change in governance or privatization to create opportunities for schools to reorganize their organizational structures within a competitive environment. With such deregulation on the horizon for school reform, additional study is needed to establish models of autonomy that public schools can emulate.

Because data suggest that private schools outperform public schools, there is renewed interest in studying the benefits of competition and shared governance found in these settings. In fact, plans to privatize public schools are quickly rising to the forefront of the decentralization movement (Guthrie, 1990). Several privatization models include a voucher system that allows tax dollars to flow to any school. Other strategies involve developing the availability of alternative schools (Chris Whittle and his Edison Project), and implementing the charter school movement that allows schools to opt out of district control (Murphy and Hallinger, 1993). Another approach to privatization allows private investment firms to take over districts considered academically deficient. These private management organizations, hired by districts, try an array of educational strategies often spending their own money to improve student achievement. McCarthy (1995) believes the privatization movement may signal a new role for public schools based on corporate involvement in the schools. While these privatization alternatives are being tested, schools still do not have a decentralized model that guides them into self-governance where schools must compete for students.

In addition to enjoying the benefits of autonomy and shared governance, private schools involve their participants in cultivating a school ethos based on community principles. By being responsive and sharing authority, private schools establish a cultural linkage that invites a cultivated social order founded on norms, values, and traditions. Competition among private schools forces these settings to be responsive to the needs of their constituencies. The success of privatization rests on the school's ability to discern what parents need and how they can support parents. Private schools are prosperous because they can determine what mission and package of services will attract parents to their school. In order to retain parents, private schools must be flexible and open for change. The notion of privatization is based on the premise of consumer empowerment that allows parents the opportunity to have voice and vote in the school's practices. School privatization establishes a market culture that is flexible, innovative and relevant to the needs of students. Shared governance enables parents to contribute to the educational system and gives them a choice that insures their commitment to the school.

Why Study Privatized Contexts?

The movement to privatize public schools encourages educators to closely examine their private school counterparts. Private schools which are self-governed, mission driven, and responsive offer a model of school autonomy for public schools to emulate. Private schools, in order to survive, develop a clear sense of mission and a mechanism for accountability to insure the quality of services they provide. Because each school is dedicated to its mission, it establishes a communal organization where participants develop an affiliation and an allegiance to the privatized setting. Privatization benefits schools because it insures that these settings are accountable or parents have the option of leaving. Parents will choose a particular school because they feel it will provide schooling on their terms. As public schools study their private school counterparts, they will find characteristics that will define the reforms necessary to improve public schools (Newmann, 1993; Sergiovanni, 1994a).

Privatized settings can be a model for public schools to decentralize in order to create ownership.

The intent of this book is to study the nature of privatization as it relates to public school improvement. This book examines how three elementary independent private schools remain self-sufficient by competing for students though their educational program. Decentralization requires that these independent schools focus their energies in order to stay competitive, mission driven, and innovative. Retaining students requires that these privatized settings address the needs of their constituencies. The governance structure in these settings equalizes power among participants. Each school becomes aggressive through its commitment to long range planning and its sensitivity to the marketplace. Independent schools create an interdependence among the participants that leads to a voluntary community where there is commitment, respect, and trust. Parents support these settings because they have input in determining the nature of schooling.

Independent schools, with their self-governance, can serve as prototypes for public schools to pattern. These privatized settings receive no state aid so they must compete for students. According to Kane (1986, 1989), independent schools are free to define their mission and are limited by the conditions of the marketplace. These schools can be diverse ranging from boarding schools to 'second chance' schools for students who have failed in other settings. Although each school has a specific mission that defines its educational program, these schools are similar in their organizational structures. Independent schools are self-governed by boards of trustees consisting of parents, former school parents, alumni, and community participants who administer the school's interests and financial viability. These schools have considerable authority in defining curriculum, selecting teachers, and determining the number of students.

Parents can select an independent school for the type of educational program that meets the needs of their children. Parental choice forces independent schools to be true to their mission and responsive to their constituencies if they wish to retain students and attract new recruits. Independent schools are mission driven more than market driven. Through mission adherence, independent schools focus on their intent and how students benefit from their program. The interaction between mission and long-range planning then leads to ongoing improvement and student retention. Due to the increase of minority children, these schools are accepting the challenge of responding to a more ethnically diverse student population. Independent schools must become more responsive to families of color if they are to remain open. As the movement for choice impacts the marketplace, independent schools must strive to define their niche. Mission for adherence requires independent schools to examine their practices closely and remain flexible and innovative. Accountability to parents for mission adherence and quality student outcomes forces independent schools to scrutinize their delivery of services.

By studying independent schools, we can understand how privatization impacts the quality of education in these settings. These autonomous settings can serve as prototypes for schools that are innovative, mission driven, and reactive to their competition. This competitive environment challenges these schools to establish a community committed to the same educational goals. In privatized settings, when parents choose a particular school for their children, they are more likely to be connected to the school as an affirmation of their choice. Students also take school more seriously when parents select schools that meet their needs. Finally, teachers are more committed because they have a supportive relationship with parents. When teachers' goals for students replicate parents' goals, the school becomes a mutually supportive atmosphere for improved academic achievement and a commitment to educational success.

Organization of Chapters

The premise of this book is to present ways that public schools can emulate many organizational characteristics of private schools. Because independent schools have a unique shared governance structure, they are more adaptive and responsive to their participants. These settings have been known to create an ethos of 'social capital' where participants have a strong affiliation to the mission of the school. There are cultural linkages that tie the school to participants with shared values, mutual trust, respect, and interdependence. The context of privatization involves solving problems and working collectively for the good of the whole. Independent schools give important lessons to assist public schools with school governance and strategies for improvement.

Much of the book reports on the success of three independent elementary schools organized to attract and retain students. These are quality private schools, recognized within the community for an outstanding educational program that provides students with successful learning experiences. The schools are similar in their organizational arrangements which involve boards of trustees and parent organizations. The schools differ in mission adherence, placement in the metropolitan area and years of service to the community. The book examines how the organizational structures in these settings empower parents and teachers to participate in curriculum design, long range planning and policy-making. It provides insights into the professional community created among the faculty at these schools. The teachers thrive in their settings where they encourage collaboration through teaming with colleagues and autonomy in defining professional development opportunities. The principals' leadership and management contributes to the high standards that give these schools their reputation for excellence.

The initial chapter begins with a general look at privatization with an introduction to the particular schools identified in this study. Thus, the first chapter provides the theoretical underpinnings for understanding the nature of privatization and its potential for developing a strong cultural linkage to its participants. The chapter also includes a review of the literature on the difficulties with site-based management and explains the rationale for schools to be more autonomous and privatized. In addition, the criteria for selecting the private schools and the methodology for this study also are presented. Finally, the chapter concludes with a detailed profile of each independent school to give the reader an understanding of similarities and differences in mission adherence. The schools are located in a metropolitan area with many educational choice options for parents. Given this competitive environment, this provides the background for understanding how these schools remain self-sufficient and mission driven in order to retain parents.

Chapter 2 provides an understanding of the organizational structure of each school which involves a board of trustees composed of parents, former school parents, alumni, teachers, and community members. Because each school is autonomous in defining its own mission, the schools vary in their procedures for defining board committees, long range planning, and parent participation. Each school fosters a participatory management, limited bureaucratic authority, and equalized power sharing through the board structure. Board members are identified by a nominating committee for their expertise and knowledge. Board members do not represent a constituency of parents but are identified for their ability to solve school problems. Each school has different procedures for selecting board members, but the determining factor for school representation is the board member's expertise and the ability to contribute collaboratively to the school. Each school differs in their lengths of board terms and the number of parent representatives. Finally, the chapter examines the important role that the parent organization plays in providing financial and emotional support for the school.

Chapter 3 gives information about the important leadership and management role the principal plays in administering a private school. Independent school principals wear many hats. A private school principal is a collection of superintendent, personnel director, and public relations expert rolled into one administrator. Each principal directs her leadership toward realizing the school's mission and long range plan in its day-to-day practice. Each principal responds to the needs of parents while balancing her authority with the concerns of the other participants. These principals weigh the wants and needs of individual parents with the collective commitment to the mission. A private school principal creates coalitions for change and acts as political negotiator in leading the school toward a school improvement agenda. Only visionary leadership and participatory management insure that the school retains its identity and practice of schooling.

Chapter 4 gives insights into why teachers are committed and feel efficacious about their ability to enhance student learning. Each private school has a professional community of teachers who work as a collective 'we'. These teachers are encouraged to remain current in their practices through the development of their own professional growth. Each principal establishes structural conditions that allow teachers opportunities to exchange and collaborate in team teaching settings. Teachers are willing to attempt innovative teaching techniques and disclose personal inadequacies in dealing with student problems.

Teachers believe in their ability to make a positive contribution to student learning. High morale among teachers results from their opportunities to determine their own curriculum and instructional practices. This strong teacher commitment and efficacy, fosters the school's 'client orientation', and its desire to improve student achievement. Teachers are given opportunities to participate in the board governance structure which allows them to influence their working conditions. However, privatization is not without its problems. Teachers express concern with the amount of time required for preparing lessons, working with colleagues who have management differences, and responding to parents' concerns. Teachers also worry that their principal is too solicitous to parents, thereby, undermining their own authority.

The issue of choice is explored in Chapter 5 as parents define their role in supporting their school. Parents who were interviewed explained the selection process that they used to find a school for their children. Retention they noted, depends upon the school's ability to implement its mission, the principal's and teachers' support, and their own feeling of ownership with the school. Parents feel the school responds to their needs throughout their child's progression through the grade levels. Each school provides a consistent support to help parents with managing discipline, teaching independence, and identifying secondary schools. Parents also feel that their school's governance structure solicits their input into the decision-making process. Teachers, parents, and principals work collaboratively together to meet the emotional and academic concerns of students.

Chapter 6 defines how students view their relationship with their school. Because each school has a strong mission adherence, there is a consensus among parents and teachers about what students should learn, how they will interact and how their behavior will reflect the school's philosophy. Students remain at the school because of the caring teachers and the school's commitment to their learning. They believe their school prepares them for the rigors of secondary schools through its strong academic and behavioral expectations. Articulate about their school's mission, students embrace the tradition of what their school represents within the community. Students feel that their teachers show them respect as they stimulate learning. Teachers take calls from their students at home, because they appreciate the students' commitment to learning. Students clearly enjoy learning in their privatized setting.

The last chapter shows how all schools can benefit by emulating the practices found in independent schools. Autonomy and mission adherence forces privatized settings to evaluate the way they provide schooling leading to an ongoing school improvement agenda. Each private school cultivates its traditions even as it directs its efforts in retaining students through innovative practices. The organizational structure of independent schools empowers families and school participants. Each school has a board structure with full authority in defining its mission and a long range plan. To administer these schools, the principal must be willing to adopt a participatory style which leads to an equalization of power. Teachers and administrators work collectively to implement the school goals and respond to parents' concerns. Commitment to the educational program leads to an interactive relationship between the school and parents. Parents remain loyal because the school is committed to improving and willing to listen. Teachers have considerable freedom in defining their own professional development and working in teams where they support each other in common endeavors. Students feel the school has their best interests at heart and view the school as a caring place.

The model of the independent school has much to offer public schools as they begin their transition to radical decentralization. Independent schools function autonomously according to their mission and focus their vision in order to attract and retain students. Privatized settings establish an environment where all participants are encouraged to provide support to enhance the quality of schooling. The responsibility of maintaining a quality school rests with the participants. Parents and teachers work collectively to share the burden for improving student learning. Controversy is reduced because no one constituency has more power than another. The school environment works as a voluntary community with a common agenda and a commitment to student learning.

For many decades independent schools have proven successful in their self-governing and organizational structure. This study of privatized schools offers compelling evidence that mission adherence and long range planning play a role in school improvement. These privatized settings, motivated by competition, are shaped by sound educational practices that attract and retain families. To avoid reinventing the wheel, schools undergoing decentralization should study independent schools as models of decentralization. Independent schools emulate an 'entrepreneurial spirit' and sound educational practices that solidify school improvement.

Chapter 1

Defining the Context for Privatization

From Site-based Management to Privatization

The 'excellence movement' resulted in policies that prescribed educational reform from the top down. These state legislative mandates, considered 'safe' in their approach, aimed to improve educational outcomes by improving the teaching act. This 'excellence movement' focused quite specifically on fixing the people and not the organizational structure of schools. The 'excellence movement' was seen as the standards-raising for school improvement (Murphy and Hallinger, 1993). Analysis of the 'excellence movement' revealed that the conventional public schools of the mid-1980s with their standardized, highly regulated environments were ill-suited for school reform. The restructuring movement in the 1990s took a bottom–up approach for school improvement that called for districts to modify the structure of educational decision-making and realign the balance of authority among teachers, administrators, and parents. This early movement, known as site-based management (SBM), meant more than just delegating authority to lower levels of the system. Within the SBM movement came the call for greater accountability in conjunction with the return of more authority to the schools.

Chapman (1990) defines school-based management as a form of educational administration where decision-making occurs at the local level. Site-based management is a business derivative of decentralization and participatory decision-making. The intent of the site-based management is to improve student performance by making those closest to the delivery of services — teachers and principals — more autonomous, resulting in their being more responsive to parents' and students' concerns. Many educators thought site-based management would give them greater flexibility and trust in decision-making and make them more responsive to their public. While in some cases site-based management did not appear to be a stimulus for school improvement, many parents and teachers did feel positive about their involvement in the school decision-making process. However, there are many illustrations of where site-based management principles were implemented very poorly.

Hannaway's (1993) study of two districts implementing a site-based management plan revealed that many of the concepts tended to undermine the schools' concerns about curriculum and teaching. While teachers traditionally work in isolation, the SBM movement required them to work in a participatory manner that was foreign to them. Her study discovered that innovative governance structures must consider technical demands such as curriculum and teaching. Clear objectives and a uniform philosophy of instruction create a common thread that gives teachers a sense of mission and ties to the educational program of the school. Teachers in decentralized schools must have commonly defined goals that everyone shares, and they need to feel efficacious in how those goals will be implemented into the curriculum and in their teaching.

Hill and Bonan (1991) studied several suburban systems that had implemented site-based management policies. Their research indicated five major conclusions: (1) Although SBM focuses on individual schools, its success depends upon the success of the entire school system; (2) SBM requires a basic reform strategy not just a connection of reform programs; (3) under SBM, schools need time to develop their own distinctive features; (4) SBM requires a degree of accountability that will not interfere with the intent of autonomy; and (5) SBM should be based on parental choice to create product differentiation in educational mission. They believe efforts to control schools at the district level make schools more accountable to higher authorities rather than to the constituencies that they serve. Deregulated schools must take the initiative in responding to students' and parents' needs and must become competent organizations and not clones of bureaucratic regulated models.

While many schools in the United States claim to implement SBM, very little decision-making is truly decentralized. In most cases SBM is only a subset of the various types of decisions that are made at the district level. Thus, some districts may decentralize budget decisions but may maintain control of personnel and curriculum concerns. Other SBM plans give some autonomy about trivial issues like school safety, parent involvement, and career education. The illusion of autonomy based on SBM is often constrictive because the district office retains the final authority or limits the range of decision-making (Bimber, 1993).

Clune (1993) notes that presently educational policy recommends a more ambitious approach in improving student achievement through a centralized strategy of a state mandated curriculum and student assessment. He believes that by having a more centralized approach to school improvement defeats the intent of site-based management. Local districts are unable to implement their own curriculum policies because they have to carry out a state-mandated curriculum. While some districts may be given greater autonomy through new site-based policies, the State undermines their power through state curriculum mandates (Madsen, 1994).

The State department of education plays a pivotal role in allowing greater flexibility in state regulations. Many state agencies seem to welcome legislative mandates as an excuse to use their authority to regulate behavior and allocate resources as they see fit. Madsen (1994) notes that the State department has what is known as the 'Ivory Tower Syndrome'. The State department of education makes sweeping state regulations to be implemented into local schools for which they may be neither necessary nor relevant. State departments of education like to regulate schools to ensure uniformity, thereby preventing schools from having greater autonomy and flexibility with school improvement programs. Weiler (1990) believes that the sharing of the State's power affects two key conditions for the maintenance of state authority: (a) the need to maintain control of district decision-making, and (b) the need to assure the reproduction of existing social relations with the help of the educational system. Both of these concepts are in direct conflict with the 'sharing-of-power' notion of site-based management that allows for greater flexibility in allocating resources so districts may exercise greater latitude in responding to their needs.

Anderson and Dixon (1993) believe that despite the shift of authority from the State to the local level, preliminary results indicate continued conformity to state mandates. Their research of SBM reveals that high schools in their study were moving to more stringent and control-oriented policies involving student conduct. The high school management council instituted permanent expulsion policies while ignoring concerns about curriculum, equity issues, and major restructuring. Their study reveals that participation in site-based management does not guarantee an equitable voice for its diverse constituencies. These researchers reveal that class and race play an important role in the SBM movement. Middle class parents are related to schools through the social discourse of language while many poor parents are excluded from the participatory process. For site-based management to effect fundamental change, power must be equally distributed among all participants, not just a few.

Malen, Ogawa, and Kranz (1990) conducted a study of site-based governance councils in several districts, which revealed that teachers and parents did not wield significant influence on major decisions. The study suggests that parents and teachers exert less power than administrators on decisions made by councils. Thus school-based management generates involvement into the decision-making process but does not truly empower its participants when it comes to making policy. There is little evidence to suggest that school-based management truly affects structural changes needed to improve schools. However, site-based management may open lines of communication between the school and district. As a result, principals may be able to alter their role and facilitate open communication with parents and teachers. When school councils are allowed to function they take on an advocacy role for their school. This advocacy allows parents the opportunity to create an awareness of their needs and voice their concerns to the districts. However, they still have no vote in school decisions.

Site-based management, as we have seen, does not necessarily allow for all voices to be heard. Typically site-based councils represent individuals who are like-minded resulting in stricter standards for behavior. These standard-raising policies do not address organizational or governance concerns. Site-based management implies that curriculum, personnel, and budget decisions be made at the building level. However, there is considerable variance across school settings regarding who makes the decisions at the building level. School advisory councils are a way to obtain input from teachers, parents and local businesses. However, it is unclear how much authority site-based management allows in these settings.

A synthesis of research findings raises many concerns about site-based management. Although many educators view site-based management positively, some researches have not generated favorable reviews. While one particular theory states that site-based councils will empower teachers, parents and others, research indicates that administrators retain their dominant position by controlling the flow of information. It also indicates that participation in site-based councils does not necessarily influence policy making. Site-based management was also seen as a way to energize the organizational structure of the schools by improving motivation and morale. While morale improves in the early stages of implementation, school personnel often become frustrated and lose enthusiasm due to constraints of resources and limited input in the governance structure. Site-based management was also expected to improve long range planning and allow for greater flexibility and innovation. Since many of the advisory councils tended to focus on discipline issues and not curriculum concerns, opportunities for school improvement were minimal (Clune and Witte, 1990). Because the term, school site-management, defies a precise definition, implementation was difficult and unsuccessful.

The Nature of Marketization and Privatization

After a decade of state reforms, problems in implementing site-based management, and varied attempts to improve student achievement, a new tactic — privatizing public schools using marketing principals — offers some promise. Research on the performance levels of public versus private organizations reveals that privatized contexts perform significantly better at lower costs than do public agencies (Savas, 1987). These favorable experiences have led governments to experiment with broadening the role of the private sector. Privatization works because it allows government to separate the roles of provider and producer. Furthermore, privatization has been effective because it empowers consumers by giving them choices among different providers of service. Privatization forces organizations to consider the wishes of consumers, to use resources efficiently, and to create innovative and marketable programs. Privatization and district-wide choice offers a more effective delivery of educational services.

Privatization has been defined in many different ways. Cooper (1989) defines privatization as a way to foster competition between the State and non-public school sectors and between schools within sectors, in order to stimulate improvements and innovations; to bring private funds and local initiatives into education; and to offer a wide range of schools (philosophies, types and values) to parents in order to allow them to select the schools they prefer. Hannaway and Carnoy (1993) view privatization as individual schools (whether publicly owned, privately owned and secular or privately owned and religious) which would operate with equal access to public resources and independent of public control in a free market for educational resources. Comprehensive choice, on the other hand, involves providing public school funds to parents so they can purchase educational programs offered by multiple providers. Allowing parents to use their education taxes to pay for tuition at private schools constitutes a kind of contracting out for educational services. Both comprehensive choice and privatization allow for parental choice among public schools which fosters competition among schools as a way to stimulate school improvement. They also promote making schools individual units, responsive to attracting and retaining a fee-paying (through either tuition or tax credits) student clientele.

The privatization movement is based on the 'market economy' concept. The intent of privatization is to make schools responsive to their clients and accountable for the delivery of services. The introduction of more competition and the enhancement of parental choice is essential to improving schools. The school privatization movement means competing for students, marketing a product, organizing efficiently, and developing a clear school mission (Beare and Boyd, 1993). Universal education without the constraints of public school regulations and a market-oriented competition will create an incentive for school improvement (Savas, 1987). Savas (1987) believes that to begin the privatization of schools is to introduce competition by allowing parents a choice in selecting public schools and forcing those schools that are ineffective to go out of business or make modifications for improvement. Savas also believes that private schools may 'save' public schools because they model the responsiveness needed to change the organizational structure of schools.

James Coleman *et al.* (1982) bolster the case for vouchers and tuition tax credits. Coleman found that private high schools provide a better education than public high schools and offer greater economic and ethnic diversity. Yet, Cooper (1989) believes that total privatization is highly unlikely because of the demand for universal educational services for all children. However, he also states that a little capitalism and privatization may challenge the basic tenets of the public school system. It may force schools to be more responsive to their clients' needs and react to national concerns. Naismith (1994) defines four main features of a demand-driven market system in which schools might remain competitive. (1) Schools would become autonomous in their financing and dependent on parent support. (2) Parents would participate in selecting the educational program for their needs using a voucher system. (3) The State would relinquish its governance over the supply and demand of school closings. (4) The State would strengthen quality control mechanisms to prevent schools from falling below acceptable standards and provide technical support for improvement.

Chubb and Moe (1988) believe that private schools create an involvement that allows them to be more autonomous and mission driven. Private school principals' autonomy is greater in the areas of curriculum, instructional methods, discipline, hiring and firing. Privatization allows a school to develop a mission that creates an environment where everyone works collectively. The school is consumer driven so it responds to parents by remaining innovative. Teachers are encouraged to remain current in their field and contribute to maintaining the quality of the school. Privatization is based on the premise of creating a community of learners who must work collaboratively to retain its membership. The work of Chubb and Moe is significant because they believe that market-driven schools are better because they are not governed from a centralized authority.

Problems of Privatization and Choice

Because the free-market concept of school privatization is only a theory at this point, advocates believe that choice is the panacea for all educational concerns and that only a free market can improve schools and stimulate children's learning. Although the benefits of privatization are still unproven in the literature, there is strong belief that competition for students can improve schools. However, there is little proof that choice will necessarily lead to better student outcomes. Paulu (1989) states that choice in school privatization can bring about structural changes to schools by encouraging individuality, fostering competition and accountability, improving educational outcomes, reducing the drop-out rate and improving parent satisfaction and involvement in the schools. Cookson (1992) notes that not all school choice policies imply complete deregulation of public schools. Controlled choice allows parents to choose from several public schools that have specific educational missions. He also notes that some schools, reduced to mom and pop educational stores, struggle to retain students from year to year in response to the whims of the marketplace. He also implies that some schools will be great while other schools will be poor. Cookson also questions how privatized schools will be monitored in a decentralized context.

In their criticism of self-managed schools in England, Smyth and others (1993) suggest that increased competition among schools creates a hierarchy of unequally funded schools. In a competitive market, schools already advantaged will have substantial leverage over poorer, less developed schools. Smyth believes that by deregulating schools the State is shrinking in its responsibility for providing quality outcomes for all students. Competition creates greater inequality because those with financial resources can leave while those remaining are trapped in ineffective schools. Principals would become more like 'entrepreneurs' than managers of school reforms. Schools within a competitive environment may cut corners rather than providing services for students.

Downes (1994) argues that the self-managing school philosophy in England is based on a culture of 'competitiveness and possessive individualism'. Critics argue that 'marketing' should not be viewed as an effort to persuade reluctant purchasers to buy a product but as an opportunity to meet the needs of customers. However, questions arise regarding these customers. Are they students or parents? Defining parents as consumers raises further questions: Are the parents engaged in their children's education, or do they rely on the school to perform its role? Schools cannot always control their 'marketing' since word-of-mouth among parents is a major tool. Yet, they have a responsibility to match the professional message to the product.

Wells' (1991) study indicates that families do not always choose schools on the basis of academic excellence but on the basis of racial affiliation. She discovered that many urban African American children often selected neighborhood schools even though these same children knew that the white schools were better. Parents of these same children, feeling powerlessness and alienation from their children, often deferred to their wishes. Thus, choice will not always be the solution for disadvantaged children. Brown (1992) believes that choice will foster conservative political ideology that will promote school prayer and religious overtones. He also states that choice may lead to social inequalities because the 'haves' are already informed, and no effort will be made to educate the 'have nots'.

Issues of equity in terms of school privatization have been debated in the literature for many years. There are those critics who believe that privatization, which allows for choice, will stratify society on the basis of race. However, under the current public school system we still continue to have inequalities in funding public schools. A stratified school system exists even now following several desegregation cases that have not succeeded in improving racial distribution and equity.

Benefits of Privatization

On the other hand, researchers who favor privatization argue that such choice will improve schooling opportunities for all children. Slaughter and Schneider (1986) examined four private elementary schools and discovered that middle class African American parents selected private schools for their children because they perceived that these schools would assist them in achieving the educational goals they had for their children. Many of these same parents believed that the public schools that surrounded them were of inferior quality. These African Americans also felt that the academic push was more rigorous at their private school than at the public school. Schneider (1989) believes that most public schools have policies that make it impossible for poor minority parents to achieve parity in their children's education in comparison to other children in other districts. Equitable schooling, it would seem, can only be assured if parents have choice.

Yet, there is considerable literature to suggest that minority parents are unable to make wise educational choices. As a result there is concern about legislating parental choice policies for alternative schooling. However, many studies (Bauch, 1989; Boykin, 1986; Bryk, Holland, Lee, and Carriedo, 1984; Cibulka, O'Brien, and Zewe, 1982) reveal that minority parents are responsible

decision makers. Poor parents also are willing to make great financial sacrifices because they believe that private schools will be responsive to their children's needs. Private schools also foster greater accountability for academic
achievement for minority children due to their organizational characteristics
and value structure. Issues of choice for minority families are governed by
certain 'consumer strategies', and poor families may need education to make
appropriate choices (Bauch, 1989).

With time many poor parents will become active consumers who can
make informed decisions about the school needs of their children. It can be
proven that when poor families make choices, they act very much like nonpoor
families and become active participants in their school. Coleman, Schiller,
and Schneider (1993) note that African American and Hispanic parents who
are quite disadvantaged in terms of income and education showed strong
response in selecting schools for their children. The privatization of schools
allows these parents to choose freely the kind of education they want for their
children. As a result, these families get more schooling for the tax dollars they
spend.

The Community Aspect of Privatization

Choice is not the only benefit that comes with privatization. The ethos of
private schools leads to the development of a community. Everyone supports
the mission of the school through the curriculum and parental involvement
activities. The school has well-defined boundaries that permeate its policies.
Private schools work together to create a sense of ownership developing a
bond of commitment and collaboration; these schools have considerable
autonomy from state regulation and greater flexibility in responding to their
constituencies. Cibulka (1989) views private schools as having an internal self-
regulation that allows school participants to develop community by defining
their own needs and resolving their own problems. This type of freedom from
state regulation gives schools the opportunity to develop a community that can
meet the needs of its constituencies.

Michaelsen (1989) believes that the market approach to schooling will
lead to consensus and community needed to prepare children to live in a
pluralistic democracy. Competition among schools will result in the development of personal autonomy. Under a radical decentralization of schools, those
who value personal autonomy will develop schools that can model the importance of autonomy and democracy. Children gain personal autonomy through
meaningful parent involvement, which cannot be achieved given the present
system. Giving children access to inexpensive private schools would facilitate
the kind of parent involvement that fosters personal autonomy. Public schools,
because of their diverse student population, have little consensus about school
goals while private schools create a community that exerts a coherent force
guiding the conduct of families, students and staff. Michaelsen (1989) believes

schools that have shared values and similar goals for their children will encourage parents to take responsibility for their children's education in ways that are consistent with their values. Michaelsen (1989) also notes that privatization supports the values of a democratic society by empowering parents in the educational process of their children. Clayton (1994) shows that grant-maintained, self-governed schools in England worked with parents to define their school, and developed principles that were responsible for connecting the family to the mission of the school. These decentralized settings emulated characteristics of independence, responsibility, and accountability. Schools developed their own ethos and character to respond to the needs of their students.

Several studies of Catholic schools at the elementary and secondary level (Bauch, 1989; Bryk, Lee, and Holland, 1993; Bryk *et al.*, 1984; Cibulka *et al.*, 1982; Erickson, 1989) indicate the organizational characteristics and value orientations of these schools are beginning to be reflected in the restructuring movement. Bauch (1989) believes that many families choose Catholic schools not only for religious reasons, but because these schools are perceived as accepting cultural differences, and showed more empathy for individual students' needs. Cibulka and his colleagues (1982) discovered that small Catholic elementary schools were very effective because of the strong institutional leadership, shared values and similar goals for the school, and the clarity of the mission that permeated the school curriculum.

A study of several Catholic high schools by Bryk *et al.* (1993) suggests that the public schools might take lessons from these schools. Catholic schools serve as models because they are able to achieve high levels of academic achievement, provide a more equitable environment with regard to race and class than the public schools, and maintain a high level of student and teacher commitment. The above-mentioned study indicates that Catholic schools function on four foundational characteristics: a delimited technical core, communal organization, decentralized governance, and an inspirational ideology. The academic structure of the core curriculum is based on a set of courses required for all students. As a result there is an equal social distribution of achievement. Low achieving students are required to study the same content, but they are given resources to achieve satisfactory progress. The communal organization of Catholic schools provides opportunities for face-to-face interaction between students and faculty. Shared academic experiences and school events create a special bond among parents, teachers and students. Teachers are more than just subject matter specialists, they take an interest outside the classroom. These teachers are a very collegial group inside and outside the school who take responsibility for students' learning. These Catholic high schools are decentralized giving principals greater autonomy, and making them more sensitive to clients and responsive to the market forces. The inspirational ideology of Catholic schools is based on the tenets of the Catholic doctrine that tends to guide the organizational structure. It is this ideology that shapes the members' actions giving them shared values and making sense of their work and teaching.

Catholic schools can be regarded as privatized contexts due to minimal constraints of state regulations. These institutions are often characterized as a communal organization with considerable autonomy in managing themselves at the building level. Participants in these settings collectively agree on the same educational goals for students and all work collaboratively for the common good. Erickson (1989) believes that the Catholic schools' communal strength is best understood through the specific benefits they produce. Membership in Catholic settings evokes a commitment that is at the core of this community and fosters participation by those connected to the school. Proponents of privatization argue that only those schools that are organizationally structured to be autonomous evoke parent participation and foster collaboration among their participants.

Coleman and Hoffer's (1987) comparisons of private versus public schools tracked sophomores from 1980 to their senior year. They discovered that sophomore students attending Catholic schools had a higher achievement level than their public school counterparts. After controlling for socioeconomic background and differing levels of achievement, they still found private school students increased their achievement by one grade level. The study attributes this increased achievement to the important role that private schools play in establishing a community with its own 'social capital', where parents and schools support their children during their school years.

Rationale for this Book

Decentralization alone cannot ensure commitment without common-sense practices that combine local empowerment, participant decision-making and effective communication. Moving from a centralized to a decentralized structure involves more than a cosmetic change. Reducing class sizes, using heterogeneous grouping rather than tracking, converting teachers into team players and making formerly autocratic principals into collegial supporters will not produce the benefits of self-governance. It is the development of community that reinforces commitment and competence that can provide leadership for organizational improvement (Newmann, 1993).

The intent of this study is not to dispute the relative merits of private versus public schooling or to determine which institution better serves the needs of its constituencies. The purpose of this book is to show how three elementary independent schools are responsive to their constituencies and establish a collaborative environment that stimulates student achievement. Studying private schools that are established communities will provide important lessons that all schools might want to emulate for school improvement. Independent schools define their niche in the marketplace and attract parents who want their children educated in a particular fashion. Independent schools do not compete on the basis of the quality of the education that they offer; rather, it is the mission of these schools that attracts and retains students.

Quality evolves over time as the school implements its mission. Ongoing school improvement becomes a part of the mission.

Those who argue against choice and privatization because of issues of equality of opportunity and the public good of education are unclear in their arguments. One only has to examine previous state mandates and interventions that have failed to improve schools and to recognize the significant research that supports the market concept. Choice allows everyone equality of opportunity to seek schools that provide an efficient delivery of 'public good'. Private investment in public education should not be viewed as diminishing 'schooling in a democratic society'. A new relationship is forming between public education and private companies to create a new alignment of the American economy, and we need to rethink what is public education (McCarthy, 1995).

The movement toward privatization is not a simple matter; attitudes have to be changed and new skills are needed to work in these deregulated settings. Coalitions of policymakers and educators must work together to develop legislation for the privatization movement. Schools must be redesigned to maximize choice and competition among these settings. Each school must be perceived as an individual setting that can be self-governed to define its educational mission and solve its own problems with the support of its constituencies. The challenge of school decentralization is to equalize power so both parents and educators can participate in decision-making. A school partnership can provide an education that is consistent with the fundamental beliefs of both constituencies.

If the school privatization movement appears to be the wave of the future then we need to have a better understanding of the organizational structure of privatized schools. These model institutions establish their educational mission and develop goals accordingly, are responsive to their constituencies, compete against other schools in recruiting and retaining students, empower teachers to make curriculum decisions that are responsive to the goals of the curriculum and provide leadership that can establish a collaborative community to facilitate a parent/educator partnership. The relative merits of private versus public must not be the issue as all schools move closer to a responsive model of self-management.

Methodology

A case study approach was used to analyze the organizational structure of three elementary independent private schools. Merriam (1988) defines a case study as an examination of specific phenomenon such as an institution to produce interpretive data rather than to test a hypothesis. The study involves an explanation of a context, and this method is appropriate to situations where it is impossible to separate the phenomenon's variables from their context (Yin, 1989). The intent of this research endeavor was to become involved in independent private schools to understand the nature of the setting and the way the participants in the study interact among themselves and with their constituents. This type of methodology assumes there are multiple realities and functions as an exploratory and inductive process.

Several qualitative methods were used to collect and analyze data for this study. Within-site and multi-site (Miles and Huberman, 1984) qualitative methods were used to analyze the schools included in this study. Three independent elementary schools (grades pre-kindergarten through sixth) from a large metropolitan area in the Midwest with a high proportion of religious private schools and other independent private schools were selected. Independent schools are schools of choice that develop their own mission statement and educational program; include staff who are like minded and cohesive; have a coherent mission or an agreement on educational goals among the groups associated; show concern with interpersonal development as well as academic progress; and define roles flexibly, creating collaboration among administrators and staff. Independent private schools are decentralized and deregulated from state requirements allowing these institutions to determine enrollment capacity, designate class size, and select teacher and curriculum programs. These independent schools were identified because they seemed to emulate many of the characteristics of the decentralization movement. These schools were deregulated and self-managed and with a focus on accountability to attract and retain students.

The study was completed over an academic year from September 1992 to June 1993. Participant observation, interviews and document analysis (Guba and Lincoln, 1981) were the primary methods of data collection. Classroom observations were used to analyze classroom interactions between the teacher and students, the use of questioning related to class assignments and behavior management techniques. Observations were done in each classroom including the specials (art, music, physical education, social studies, science, foreign language, etc.) for one day a week for a period of approximately two to three hours per day. The classroom observations occurred over a period of a school year. In the first eighteen weeks, observations were completed in the mornings while in the second eighteen weeks the observations took place in the afternoon. Notes from the observations were transcribed onto notecards and analyzed according to the criteria mentioned earlier.

Teachers, parents, students and administrators were interviewed to gain additional insights into the school (see Appendix). The investigator for this study developed questions based on observations and attendance at school functions. The interview portion of this study occurred about mid January. Parents, teachers, students, and administrators were interviewed in that order to understand the interactive relationship between the groups. Administrators were last. They were interviewed when the observations and interviews were completed. A sample of participants were asked identical questions posed by the investigator. The questions were developed based on the investigator's observations. Questions were posed to the participants who were requested to elaborate on the area of inquiry. All interviews were taped and transcribed. Data from these interviews were categorized into various areas based on similarities of responses. Similar responses were grouped collectively to interpret themes that became apparent in the interpretation process. A total of thirty-two parents, twenty-eight teachers and all administrative staff members at each of the schools were interviewed. Thirty students at each of the sites were placed into small groups and questioned about their feelings about the school and about how content they were with their school. Most interviews lasted approximately an hour to two hours. Much of the interview data from all the school participants was used to characterize general perceptions among the teachers, parents, students and administrators.

In addition, school communication such as letters to parents, agendas for meetings, school publicity, newsletters to parents and board/faculty minutes were analyzed. Documents from the three sites represented a natural source of information that provided additional insight. The documents were used to verify information and to assess the level of communication to parents. Notes to the parents were classified as relating to school information, board meeting notices, fundraising and social activities. Teachers' communication to parents was analyzed to indicate the types of activities that were occurring in the classroom and the level of parent involvement. The level of communication ranged from highly sophisticated mailings to notes left on the tables for parents. School correspondence was an important aspect of school responsiveness in communicating its mission to its participants.

The investigator for this study also attended faculty, board, staff, parent and board subcommittee meetings to gain additional insights about the three schools. The investigator gathered notes from the meetings and used agendas and minutes to substantiate data verification. Notes from meetings were reviewed and categorized according to themes and impressions and then put into summary statements. Data from similar types of meetings were crosslisted with other sites to document similar findings in each of the three sites. Data were then classified according to interpretations then generalized into the findings. Information from various school committees were interpreted to substantiate the link between the nature of privatization and the school's ethos.

Data Sources

Selection of Sites for the Study

Independent private schools were identified for this study because of their adherence to self-governance and their communal culture, which is noted in the restructuring literature as essential for improving schools (Newmann, 1993; Sergiovanni, 1994a). One of the many reasons parents may select an independent private school for their child is the opportunity to match the type of school with their child's abilities and their own philosophy of education. Independent schools are noted for their ability to market themselves in relation to their school mission. These schools share power, leaving their participants with a sense of ownership. There is a degree of mutuality where the process of listening leads to a responsive dialogue. Because the school's organizational culture is based on mission adherence and shared goals, there is an interdependence resulting in a collaborative environment for change. Parents support the school by adhering to its mission. The school continually reflects on its mission resulting in an ongoing vision for its existence. The context of privatization requires these settings to define their mission every five years and solicit parents in this process.

A large metropolitan area was selected for this research endeavor because of the high percentage of independent schools, religiously affiliated private schools and public magnet schools. This highly competitive arena leads to strong opinions about choice options and creates many alternatives for parents. Opportunities for choice in this large metropolitan area create a highly competitive atmosphere that requires independent schools to develop a sophisticated sense of mission and innovative programs.

This metropolitan area has the highest number of independent schools per capita in the nation. There are approximately twenty-five independent private schools in The Metropolitan Confederation of Independent Schools, an organization that provides collaborative support and leadership to independent school educators and serves as a clearing house for administrators' and teachers' needs. Independent private schools in the area belong to this organization only if they are accredited by the Independent Schools Association of the Central States, an accreditation process recognized by this State. At the elementary level preschool-sixth grade there are fourteen schools and at the secondary level (7–12) there are nine. There are two preschool-high school programs that provide an entire educational program for children. Due to the market considerations these schools, located over an entire metropolitan area, vary in tuition and financial expectations. A large number of independent private schools are located in wealthier portions of the metropolitan area. Most independent private schools compete against quality suburban public schools in recruiting students. Several independent schools in the area do provide for special needs children with severe learning or behavioral problems. These schools are usually segregated special education settings. There are also several inner city independent schools that serve predominantly African American children. One of the inner city independent private schools has an Afrocentric curriculum and provides many outreach programs for African American parents.

Competition for independent schools also comes from the religious affiliated private schools. This metropolitan area has a high proportion of Catholic, Lutheran, Jewish and other denominated Christian schools that serve many of the religious sectors located throughout the community. Most of the Catholic schools are tied to parishes, but there are high schools that are considered independent from local parishes. The Catholic schools are located in both the city and suburban areas and vary in tuition costs. The Catholic Education Office notes they educate approximately one fourth of the school-age population. There is a strong tradition for single sex schools among the Catholic high schools. Many non-Catholic families send their children to these parochial schools because of the discipline and rigorous educational program. There are also many Jewish and Lutheran elementary and high schools competing in the vicinity for students, but these do not have the following found in the local Catholic schools.

This metropolitan area is also involved in a city-county voluntary desegregation plan to provide greater equity for the predominantly African American school-age children attending the city public schools. The intent of the plan was to integrate 15,000 African American children into sixteen predominantly white suburban school districts. In order for the plan to succeed, major fiscal incentives encourage the suburban districts to participate. The desegregation plan also includes the development of voluntary magnet schools to create a racial balance within the city schools. These schools are presently undergoing major facility and curriculum enhancements to attract students from the county. Also, the metropolitan public schools are completing major capital improvements to ensure equity among the city and county schools. After many years of resistance the plan is still being implemented. While the suit was enacted in 1983, by 1996 there are still many issues left unresolved (Colton and Uchitelle, 1992).

The independent private schools for this study were identified on the basis of their competitive placement against other quality private and public schools; years of operation in the community; minority recruitment and scholarship opportunities; nonreligious affiliation; parent involvement in the governance structure; and innovative practices at the elementary level (such as peer and cross-age tutoring, cross-discipline activities and multicultural activities). The school's location greatly affected the selection process. Schools for the study had to be located in the metropolitan area where they had to compete against other quality independent schools, highly regarded public schools and/or innovative city magnet schools. Such competition was necessary to identify how these schools perceive their marketing niche to attract students. Two schools in this study, Appleman and Bakersfield, were located in suburban areas where they compete against several other well known independent elementary private and quality public schools, and religiously affiliated private schools. The other school, Crestview, was situated in the downtown area of the city. Its competition was from other religious and independent schools and public magnet schools. Crestview also had to deal with a court ordered desegregation program that allowed African American students the opportunity to attend quality suburban public schools. Independent schools were sought out because parents had many choices near their homes and selected their school on the basis of mission rather than location or religious affiliation.

The school's years of operation within the community was a determinant for the school to be considered for this study. The schools had to be established for at least five years which indicated their ability to remain open and establish a presence in the community. The schools selected had been in existence for a varied number of years to give the investigator an opportunity to understand the developmental process private schools use to survive in the marketplace and the length of time it takes to develop a school's ethos and educational program to implement its mission.

The oldest school in the study was Appleman. In existence for seventy-five years and considered an icon in the metropolitan area, it was known for its quality and traditional program. Appleman School was highly regarded for its strong mission adherence that focused on a rigorous traditional program. The second oldest school was Bakersfield with a thirty-year tradition of a Montessori program for toddlers through the sixth grade. Bakersfield School did not have the historical presence like the Appleman School. This school is just beginning to be recognized as a solid educational program that is becoming a competitor among the other more prestigious elementary private schools. The third school, Crestview, has a six-year history of providing a school program for working parents in the downtown area. Crestview, a newly formed school, is establishing itself within the community as a rigorous academic and arts program for working parents. This school is experiencing problems with financial stability and retention of families.

Schools were selected through discussions with parents in the metropolitan area and through the investigator's knowledge of other independent schools from sources such as local newspapers and magazines. Working as a parent might, using word of mouth from other parents or considering the location of the school, the investigator generated a list of independent schools to make on-site visits. A total of thirteen independent schools were contacted about their possible participation in this study. On-site observations were conducted to meet with school personnel to determine if their school met the established criteria regarding competition, minority population, parent participation in governance, and innovative practices. Classroom observations were made to verify innovative practices; the commitment to minority recruitment was determined by the number of minorities attending the school and the number of multicultural projects at the school; and the percentage of parent representation in the governance structure of the school was investigated. The initial thirteen schools were identified mostly by the competitive element which is cited in the privatization literature as a way to improve schools. Elementary schools were identified because there was a better fit with the criteria, and the competition for students was more aggressive at the elementary level. All three elementary schools were forced to compete actively for students and maintain an innovative mission. Parents selected these schools because of mission, high secondary placement rates, and academic preparation of students.

The following is a brief description of each independent school in order to highlight their differences and similarities. Information was collected from

observations of the school, interviews with school participants, school publications and documents and local newspaper articles.

School Profiles

Appleman School

The Appleman School has been in existence for over seventy-five years. It
recently celebrated its rich tradition by promoting a gala that identified some
of its more distinguished alumni. A history of the school was written just for
the event and given to all alumni and current families. The school has retained
its heritage of tradition through consistency of its leadership and curriculum,
retention of teachers, and long range planning.

In 1962 Appleman School decided to move from its city location to the
suburbs as the metropolitan area continued its westward expansion. An analysis of parents' addresses indicated that 67 percent of the students were living in the county. By moving the school's location, Appleman would have a
greater opportunity to attract more students to the school. The school has
remained in its present location and has undergone several renovations to
remodel the facility.

In the mid 1980s the school experienced a change in management in
order to be more responsive to its parents' needs. Under the direction of this
new leadership the school has undergone a capital campaign building program,
changed the traditional preschool program to a more child centered program,
developed enrichment and extended day programs for working parents and
increased alumni involvement in the school.

Appleman School is located in a suburban area where it must compete
against several other quality independent private schools and religious affiliated private schools. This school also has to contend with several public school
districts that are highly noted for academic excellence and that have more
financial resources than Appleman has. The average cost per student for public schools in the same vicinity is approximately $8,400 while the tuition at
Appleman is $6,575. The special education students in the public school dis-
trict are served through special school districts, so local districts do not financially
support their special need students. The tuition includes lunch/supplies, books
and field trips, and some working parents may pay an additional $1,200 for
extended day care/enrichment programs. The after school enrichment program is quite sophisticated, and many children of non-working parents also
participate. Only recently was there a summer camp started at the school. The
intent of the summer school program was not only for working parents but to
develop an all year program that could provide additional enrichment to the
school. Appleman School mirrors its public school counterparts in minority
and income distribution. Due to the high caliber of both public and private

schools in this part of the metropolitan area, the school is sensitive to its rivals and fiercely competitive with its marketing and student recruitment.

Appleman School serves preschool through the sixth grade, and there are approximately 208 students attending the school. There are two teachers per classroom with approximately twenty-two to twenty-seven students per grade. There is a hierarchy among the faculty with lead and assistant teachers. The more experienced teacher is considered the lead while the assistant teacher serves as an aid. The school is presently examining the relationship of these positions in the hope of moving toward a team teaching approach.

In some classroom situations there is little or no hierarchy as the teachers move to equalize their teaching load. In some cases the lead teacher prepares the language arts lessons which include reading, spelling, and writing while the assistant teacher may be responsible for preparing math and may provide additional teaching in the language arts area. The relationship between the lead and assistant teacher can differ from classroom to classroom. There are no set procedures in the faculty manual regarding the roles of the lead and assistant teacher. There have been mismatches between lead and assistant teachers which have resulted in room changes. However, this seldom occurs and overall there is a solid relationship between these two parties.

The specials as they are called include social studies, science, music, French, art and physical education. The preschool and kindergarten classes attend the physical education, music, and French classes, and grades 1 through 3 attend art, French, physical education, and music. For grades preschool through third, social studies and science are taught within the classroom by the lead and assistant teachers with the resource assistance of the social studies and science teachers. There are cross discipline exercises with classroom readings and the science and social studies projects. The upper grades of 3 through 6 attend all the special classes in forty-five minute periods. Some specials, like science and social studies, were every day, and other specials such as art, music, and foreign language were every other day.

The administrative structure of Appleman School consists of the principal, director of studies, development director and the business manager. Each plays a specific role in the administration of the school. The principal or head is responsible for overseeing the school and is accountable for executing board policies. The principal evaluates teachers and staff, shares responsibility for fundraising activities, attends parent meetings throughout the year, hears parent complaints and provides input to board members. She is also charged with overseeing the cafeteria manager and the two school secretaries. The principal is accountable to the board and is evaluated yearly on goals and objectives she and the executive committee establish.

The director of studies is responsible for curriculum, testing, student learning problems, professional development for the teachers and the after school Enrichment/Extended Day Program. The development director is responsible for public relations for the school, identifying financial resources either in the form of donors or grants, communicating within the school, and working with past alumni. The development director also works closely with the parent organization to provide technical support for publicity and fundraising ideas. The business manager oversees the financial health of the school. She works with the principal to establish the budget, serves as the primary purchasing agent, tracks tuition payments and oversees the physical plant and financial assistance. All of these positions are accountable to the principal.

The board of trustees for Appleman School is composed of past parents, current parents, alums, students and community representatives. The responsibility of the board is to oversee the financial well being of the school, develop policies and ensure that policies are implemented. Approximately 60 percent of the board members are current parents. Board members are selected based on the nominating committee's recommendation for their level of expertise. They do not represent a constituency of parents. Two members from the Parents' Club elected by the parents as chairperson and president of the Parents' Club also sit on the board for a one year term. They give reports about parent activities, and they lead annual giving campaign, a major gift giving campaign to supplement the operating budget. Board meetings are closed although there is no written policy for this. Information about board meetings is shared at parent gatherings and faculty and staff meetings by the principal. Teachers sit on the admissions and education committees to provide their input and leadership for the board.

Board members serve a four year term and are usually asked to chair a committee and serve on two other committees. Board committees include executive, finance, annual giving, admissions, alumni relations, building and grounds, capital campaign, construction, education, development, long range planning, nominating and safety. These committees may be *ad hoc* to meet specific needs of the school. For example, a new *ad hoc* committee called diversity will be assembled for next year to examine diversity issues at school. Chairs of board committees give progress reports at the once-a-month board meetings. Board committees at the beginning of the year develop goals based on the school's long range plan. Agendas for board meetings are completed jointly by the board president and principal. Approximately 20 percent of the board members are women while the rest are male. The board has no minority representation.

The principal has a supportive relationship with the board. She provides insights and clarifies any concerns for the board but sees her role as a passive participant. She wants the board to feel empowered and not like a token or rubber stamp body of policy makers. Board meetings move quickly with relatively little discussion on committee work. The principal attends board committee meetings and assists chairs with goal direction if necessary. The principal also has an advisory board that provides technical support that the board may be unable to offer. The advisory board meets once a year or more often if necessary.

Parents are quite involved in the school with large attendance at conferences, school programs and fundraising activities. Parent club meetings are held three times a year. These meetings have small attendance; the agenda includes updates on parents' fundraising activities, 'state of the school' remarks; questions from parents are submitted to the principal prior to the meeting. Parents are encouraged to assist the school as room parents, and chairs of fundraising activities, with the school auction and in running the school store. Parents are quite visible at the school and are often seen sharing a cup of coffee and visiting with one another or eating lunch with their children.

The school has a high percentage of stay at home moms who assist with school activities. Approximately 30 percent of the female parents work outside the home. School policies do not allow parents to do teacher aid kinds of activities such as reading aloud or checking homework. This policy is to assure the children's privacy at the school and to prevent a parent from talking about another parent's child. Two teachers per grade provide enough professional support to the children so aids are not needed in the classroom. Due to the small community type atmosphere at the school the staff try not to segregate children out for learning or behavioral problems. However, an educational consultant is employed by the school eight hours per week to provide remedial support services to children and targeted teaching strategies to educators.

Communication from the school is a daily occurrence. Once a week an Appleman Roundup (newsletter) is sent home with the children to give to the parents. Information usually includes specific meetings times, holiday parties, vacation dates, school calendar, educational articles, parenting news and advice. Information about specific policy changes, such as tuition and dress code changes, is handled through personal letters from the principal. A student and parent handbook and buzzbook are developed each year for parents. Teachers usually send notes home to parents along with their child's work on Friday. Parents are to sign the letter and return the student's folder at the lower grade level. Parents are encouraged to call teachers whenever necessary. Since there is no bus service to the school, parents have to drive the child to school. This practice invites parents to come in and visit with the teachers.

The children's learning potential at the school ranges from marginal students with mild learning disabilities/attention deficit disorders to high achieving children. Discussions with teachers indicate that most of the children have average ability with a few children above or below the class mean. Individualized instruction is used for those children needing remedial assistance or enrichment. Since the school does not have the resources for children with severe disabilities it typically does not accept these children. The educational consultant is available for parents if additional tutoring is needed; outside referrals are also made.

Admissions testing is used to determine acceptance into the school. Appleman accepts 77 percent of the students who apply to the school. Preschoolers are screened using a battery of early childhood measures. These instruments identify children who may have behavioral or academic problems.

As a result these children are not admitted since the school would be unable to meet their needs. Children in the lower and elementary grades are given an intelligence and achievement test to determine acceptance. If a student's ability falls within the limits of the school the child is accepted. Acceptance into the school can sometimes be subjective since it can also be influenced by the principal's interviews with parents, past alumni status and teacher input. The school uses 2 percent of its budget for scholarship assistance. The amount of assistance ranges from a few hundred dollars to a maximum of 50 percent of tuition. Tuition assistance is kept confidential. No records are kept regarding parent income but rule of thumb indicates that 80 percent of the parents are in the middle to upper income with 20 percent of the parents struggling to pay tuition. Parent interviews indicated a great concern about the increase in tuition and the struggles to be able to afford private schools for their children. Many parents talked of great financial sacrifices but felt it was an investment for the future.

The school is committed to its children and makes every effort to retain the child once he/she has been accepted. Parents are educated throughout the elementary school years about their child's progress. Report cards are given twice a year, and there are conferences including quarter grades in November and April. Each year the children are given standardized tests in reading and general achievement. Results from the tests are shared with parents and board members. The school's test results are in the higher percentiles when compared to public school norms. During the 5th and 6th grade years, parents are guided toward secondary school selection with great care.

Students at Appleman are predominantly White with an 18 percent minority rate. Interviews with parents indicated a great concern that the school was not doing enough to recruit African American children to the school. There is considerable religious diversity at the school resulting in children being exposed to various religious traditions.

The school's mission statement reveals that it provides a strong education with an emphasis on the basics. Standards are high; there is a sense of tradition. This is indicated through a student dress code, structured curriculum and accelerated learning. The school's mission states that 'Appleman provides a strong, well-balanced education in a nurturing school community committed to excellence'. The overall educational program seeks 'to promote a positive self-image and promote the realization of each child's potential, to provide an appropriate balance between formal and informal learning experiences both in and out of the classroom, to engage children in the learning process through experiences that promote analytical and critical thinking, risk taking, investigation, and individual creativity and to work with parents to teach children self-discipline, respect and compassion for others, appreciation for differences among people, strength of character and positive leadership'.

Appleman School's mission is revised and evaluated every five years when the school does a long range plan. The school evaluates its program in conjunction with ISACS. The school does a self study every seven years with an on-site visit from the accrediting association of ISACS. This process involved an overall evaluation of the school from general operations to the educational program.

Bakersfield School

The Bakersfield School, founded in 1962, has been in existence for over thirty years. Initially, a privately owned Montessori School, in 1971 it became a not-for-profit school. The school hired its present principal in 1976. Initially, the new principal was confronted with debt due to back taxes and with other financial constraints. However, by 1978 the school was financially secure and had moved to its present location. In 1982 the school received ISACS accreditation, which is considered the highest standard for independent private schools in the region.

In 1984 the school underwent a name change to reflect its true identity. The rationale behind the name change from the Montessori Academy to its present name was to move from a preschool mentality to a true elementary school program. The intent was to give credibility to the school as an all-day program that met the needs of its growing student body of elementary age children. Also in 1984 the school program was reorganized to include the K-1 students together. This was advocated by parents who wanted their children to have a smoother transition to the elementary program.

Since 1987 the school has undergone many physical changes to compliment its educational program. Recently the 4th–6th grades were moved into a new addition that was designed to give more of a middle school image with the installation of lockers, a wing exclusively for older students, and traditional classrooms. The intent was to make the transition to the secondary programs easier for the children. In 1991 the school purchased a house next door to the school for expansion of its preschool program. The rationale for this was to provide parents with either a half-time or a full-time program depending on the needs of nonworking/working parents.

Bakersfield School is located in a suburb of the metropolitan area and is further west than the Appleman School. It is located approximately twenty miles from the heart of the city. The metropolitan area continues to expand in this direction with residential construction. This school, like Appleman, must compete against other quality independent private schools and religious affiliated private schools. The school is located near two of the more prestigious public schools where the cost per student is approximately $8,400, while the tuition at the school is $5,750. The cost of tuition at Bakersfield School is comparable to other private schools located in the area.

The tuition does not include lunch, and there is an additional fee for school sponsored trips. Since the school does not have cafeteria facilities, students bring their lunches or participate in the catered lunch program. The principal was instrumental in finding a caterer who would supply the school with lunches. Bakersfield School has a 'before and after' school program for working parents. The school charges monthly for this service and many working parents take advantage of it. The intent of this program is to provide the children at the school with a supervised nonstructured environment with an opportunity to complete school homework. There is a 'when-there's-no-school' camp for school holidays and a summer enrichment/tutorial program for when the school is not in session. Bakersfield School mirrors its public school counterpart and is located near one of the wealthier public schools. The economic wealth of the parents at the Bakersfield School is comparable to the income level of parents who use the public schools.

Bakersfield School serves toddler (18 months) through the sixth grade. There are approximately 265 students at the school with a class size ranging from twenty-four to twenty-eight students. There is a toddler and an all day and a half day preschool program that serves as a feeder program into the school. The Montessori method is used as a basis for the school program which allows the child a balance of freedom and structure. The educational program is divided into language arts, mathematics, science and social studies. There are two to three teachers in the classroom depending on size. The teachers are in charge of various subject matters and develop an expertise in a specific academic area.

Teachers have divided the subject matters for each grade level. For example, in the third grade there are three teachers. One teacher focuses on language arts/reading while the other two are responsible for science/social studies and mathematics. This allows teachers to focus on a specialty area and participate in cross discipline activities. Because there is much focus on the Montessori emphasis there is much usage of manipulatives and independent learning. The classrooms are very large to provide for traditional desks, small group areas and learning centers. The school has participated in an inservice program on the Meyers Briggs (a personality test) so the teachers are sensitive to each other's learning and personality style. Teachers have considerable freedom in developing curriculum and work cooperatively in developing the school's program.

The specials include German, music, art, library studies and physical education. The toddler and preschool program integrates music and art. The preschool children attend the physical education classes four days a week and German class twice a week. With the lower elementary (K-1), the students attend physical education daily and attend music and German twice a week. Lower elementary children attend art and library studies once a week for longer periods of time than just the twenty-five minutes. Middle elementary (2nd and 3rd) and upper elementary children (4th, 5th, 6th) spend more time in all the specials with greater integration with the educational program.

The administrative structure of Bakersfield School consists of the principal, assistant principal, development director and the business manager. Each plays a role in the overall administration of the school. The principal's duties include responding to the board's concerns, executing board policies, curriculum, testing and evaluation of staff. The principal is also responsible for attending board committees, working with the parent guild and responding to parents' concerns. Her major role is to ensure that the school's mission permeates the school program. The principal is evaluated yearly based on criteria developed by the board.

The assistant principal and the principal share many responsibilities so it is difficult to factor out the nature of the assistant principal position. Both the principal and the assistant principal deal with discipline issues. The assistant's main duties include overseeing the toddler and preschool program and supervising the Montessori teacher training program located at the school. She also serves as an outlet for parent complaints and teacher concerns if the principal is busy or unavailable. She is second in command if the principal is away from the school. The assistant principal reports to the board about the overall progress of the Montessori training program.

The development director and business manager oversee the finance and public relations of the school. The administrative team of the school is very close with the head giving them much initiative into the running of the school. The administrative staff along with the teachers have input to the board committees and a voice during the board meetings. The administrative team is quite close and most ideas for the school tend to generate from the sharing of ideas that takes place throughout the school day. The administrative team does not work as isolated individuals but as a unified team.

The board of trustees for Bakersfield School is composed of parents and a few members from outside the school. The school is only beginning to examine its alumni and past parents as potential board members. The majority of the board is made up of present parents who have been elected because of a talent they can provide for the school. The board's role is to set the policies for the school, ensure fiscal responsibility, raise funds, promote the school, and appoint the head who delegates the operations of the school. Board meetings are held monthly and the administrative team is required to give school reports. Information at board meetings is shared with faculty and staff, but there seems to be no formal outlet for disseminating board information throughout the school.

Board members, who serve a four year term, are also asked to serve on a board committee. Board committees include diversity, development, executive, school health, finance, education and buildings and grounds. Board committees study complicated issues in depth and provide leadership to the full board. The full board has the final vote based on the input from the committee. *Ad hoc* committees are formed as the need arises to deal with less frequent issues. Chairs of board committees give reports to the board while board members are given the opportunity for input. Approximately 50 percent of the board members are women, and only 5 percent of the board members represent a minority group.

The principal and her staff have a supportive relationship with the board.

Each administrative staff member gives a report to the board about his or her area. The board president in conjunction with the principal develops the agenda items. The board meetings work from the school long range plan with each board committee establishing goals for the year. The principal is very interactive at board meetings and quite vocal about her insights on school issues. The principal attends all board subcommittee meetings, and board members appreciate her input. The principal expends considerable efforts educating board members.

Parents are quite involved at the school. The school has a very sophisticated computer process to identify parent volunteers for school and fundraising activities. The development officer works in conjunction with the Parent Guild for fundraising and school activities. The Parent Guild program does not have group meetings like those at Appleman School but instead identifies school and fundraising activities where parents might assist. These activities include working on book fairs, and teacher appreciation lunches, or serving as classroom helpers, listening parents, lunch helpers, etc.

There are many activities for all parent volunteers at the school. The school boasts a 100 percent participation rate in some form or another. The school has a high percentage of stay-at-home moms who volunteer at the school. However, the increasing number of working moms is a concern for the school since it will create a shortage of labor. The school has an open door policy and encourages parents to volunteer in some capacity. The school believes it is a transparent place for all to see. The school is quite sophisticated in its approach to engaging parents in the school program.

Communication from the school is a daily occurrence. Parents are encouraged to call the teacher at home or to visit the classroom. Once a week the Bakersfield Communique is sent home to parents; it lists what is occurring at the school. In addition, the preschool through the upper elementary send home a weekly newsletter which keeps parents informed about what is happening in their child's classroom. A parent handbook, calendar and buzzbook are given to parents at the beginning of the school year. The handbook is quite detailed with information about academic programs, school governance, business, school operations, student traditions and parent related policies, procedures and routines. The school also has a radio station that parents can receive on their car radios. The school's radio station keeps parents informed about social meetings, fundraising events and school information.

The ability level of the students ranges from low achieving to higher functioning students. The school takes several students with learning disabilities in the belief that the child will benefit from the school's program. A child with Tourett syndrome was retained until the school could no longer meet the needs of this child. The principal is committed to those children with learning and behavior problems and tries all interventions to retain the student. During the parent interviews, several mentioned their concerns that the principal should do more to exercise her right to have problem students leave the school. However, the principal is committed to meeting the needs of all children attending the school. The school has a 90 to 95 percent acceptance rate of students.

The head works with the sixth grade students to make the secondary transition. Parents and students meet with the principal to discuss the various types of secondary school options. Teachers work with parents in defining their child's ability then matching a secondary school with the child's needs. Parent conferences are held in November, February and May. Parents are given a verbal progress report about their child, and each grade section has its own report card format. The students (grades 2nd through 6th) are given standardized testing in verbal and quantitative aptitude, language arts and mathematics. Students' scores are shared with the board and parents in May.

Students at Bakersfield are predominantly white with a 20 percent minority rate. The public schools surrounding this school do not have as high a rate of minority students as the Bakersfield School. There is considerable religious diversity at the school resulting in the children being exposed to many different religions. The school has established a goal of 10 percent of its budget for scholarship assistance. The school uses an independent assessment agency to determine financial need. The amount of assistance varies depending on the financial needs of the parents. Information regarding many of the families who receive financial aid is kept confidential. Many of the middle class families talked about financial sacrifices to afford the tuition at the school.

The school's mission statement reveals that it is committed to providing education to children from diverse backgrounds from 18 months through sixth grade. 'The program is a child centered, parent supported school that promotes joy in learning, positive character development and develop life long learners. The school implements the Montessori philosophy and methodology in the lower levels and combines a more traditional approach at the upper levels. The classroom environment stimulates intellectual, emotional, social, physical and cultural growth and promotes the development of initiative, independence, responsibility, curiosity, cooperation and respect for others.'

Bakersfield School's mission is revised and evaluated every five years when the school undergoes a long range plan. The school is accredited by ISACS (Independent Schools Association of the Central States) and the AMS (American Montessori Society) which serve as regulating agencies for the school.

Crestview School

The Crestview School has been in existence for over six years. The school, founded in 1988, offers a year round elementary program. It was created to serve working parents in the downtown area of the metropolitan region. The school offers working parents a safe, enriching environment that provides children with extended day care, cultural programs and investigative projects. The convenience of the school helps parents manage work and home responsibilities. Working parents can focus on their responsibilities better if their children spend the day in an educational setting rather than in day care or home alone.

The proximity of the school to the workplace allows parents to be physically close to their children. This gives parents the opportunity to be available for lunch, make classroom observations and participate in the school program and governance. The expanded lunch hour and longer school day give parents more time to meet with the faculty to discuss the school program and the child's progress. The joint commute to and from the school lets parents talk with their child about events occurring at the school. Children have free use of the phone at the school and often call parents to report school progress or positive events in their lives.

The founder and principal of the school developed the concept for the school while working at another independent private school. The principal wanted to develop a school that would be responsive to the needs of working parents. She approached many downtown corporations about her school idea and was met with encouragement from the business community. As a result many employees from the various downtown corporations applied to the school. She initially began with ten families resulting in twenty-five students attending the school. As the students progressed, the school added a new grade up to the sixth grade. Some consideration has been directed to expanding the school into the junior high grades. Having a marketing background before moving to education, the principal had some experience in the business arena. As a result, she wanted a school that would develop a partnership between corporations and schools. The principal believes there is a need for schools to be located near the workplace to attract corporations to the downtown urban environment.

The school is located in the heart of the downtown community where it is surrounded by many large corporations. The downtown area serves as a rich and diverse resource with children using the public library, public transportation and city parks. The school has little competition from the city public schools but is in an area where there are many independent, private, religious affiliated and city magnet schools. The school, which recruits children from the city and from the downtown corporations, attracts a unique, diverse student population. The tuition at the school is $5,000–$5,900 for nine months of the year and $6,000–$7,000 for twelve months. Tuition varies if parents pay in a lump sum or in installments. The summer school program can be prorated from a week to the entire summer session. Included in the tuition costs are lunch, afternoon snack and other related services.

The Crestview School is located in an urban area of the city. The school rents space from a downtown local church. The church shares its meeting rooms, cafeteria, gymnasium, theater and other parts of the building with the school. Since the school opened much of the church space has been renovated by the school to create an open classroom atmosphere. Cubicle dividers are used to segregate the students by grade. Teachers use the cubicle areas for large group or individualized attention. There are no desks in the cubicles so students sit in semicircles on the floor. Students complete assignments in the larger center of the open classroom. Students are encouraged to share working space and are given much independence in completing assignments. Because of the small class sizes there are many interage activities among the grades.

Review of the student statistics indicated that a large portion of the children attending the school are 'only' children. Many families in the school have only one child in their family. The school structure, with children of all ages working together, seems to attract only children since many only children feel like they have brothers and sisters and appreciate the family type atmosphere.

As the school undergoes growing pains, it will eventually need to find a larger space. The school has been expanding at a rapid pace for the last two years and is at a critical stage in its growth. The board is developing a five year growth plan to consider other sites for the school. There are concerns about locating space in the downtown area which may affect its present mission and the cost of tuition. Due to the school's location teachers often use a city park located one block from the school for recess and picnics. The school also has a joint program with the downtown YMCA to provide swimming lessons.

Crestview School serves preschool through sixth grade. The school increases its population by 10 percent each year. The school does not use graded classrooms due to the small numbers of students. There are approximately sixty children attending the school with a larger percentage of the children being in the preschool and lower elementary grades. There are four full time teachers at the school along with many local artists who are hired for the arts program. The preschool and kindergarten teachers work cooperatively to implement a whole language reading program. The lower grades use the public library as a source for literature books. The other two teachers work with the upper elementary teaching reading, language arts and math. During the holidays and school breaks, the school does what is called transitions. There is no formal schooling, but enrichment activities occupy the school day. Many times parents come in to help during the transition days.

The school hours are 7.30 a.m. to 6.00 p.m. School officially begins at 8.30 and runs until 5.00. The academics are taught in the morning with the emphasis on reading, language arts, spelling and math. The afternoons are divided between the arts and social sciences. The school hires local artists to teach visual art, drama, music and dance each week. The physical education program is provided by the downtown YMCA which includes swimming lessons and sports. There is a social studies, research and science component that is taught by the three teachers from the lower and upper elementary program. The programs are often integrated and many hands-on enrichment activities are the focus of the curriculum. The school also offers computer and Spanish lessons for the students. The various classes are taught on a rotating schedule to include all grades.

The summer program focuses on the arts, investigative science, computer camp, field trips, and expanded recreation and swimming. Recently a tutoring/remedial program was added to help students improve their math and reading skills. However, the main focus of the summer program is enrichment and hands-on learning. The faculty present a theme that is used to develop the curriculum over the summer. For example, this past summer the school's theme was transportation. The teachers developed a thematic unit across the curriculum. The science program examined how engines worked and research was done on different types of transportation. The final activity of the project gave the children the opportunity to try the city's new metro system. The summer program is open for other children outside the school.

Teachers at Crestview work on a 12 month contract. The school is only closed on specific holidays like Christmas but otherwise the school is open all year round. The teachers work long hours from 8.30 until 5.00. They have a great deal of planning time to develop curriculum and community outreach programs during the day to relieve some of the work load. The school has no set curriculum, and the teachers are given considerable freedom in planning programs. The teachers are given two weeks vacation and have more release time during the school's diversion weeks. The school has only recently realized that the ongoing school year can drain teachers' enthusiasm. The administration is beginning to re-evaluate its 12 month contract with its teachers.

The administrative structure of the school consists of the principal and assistant principal. The principal is responsible for administering the school program while the assistant oversees the curriculum, hires and evaluates teachers, and assesses the children's progress. The administrative staff view their division of labor in terms of 'inner' and 'outer' focuses. The principal is charged with implementing the school's mission and responding to the board. The external tasks such as recruitment, development, finance, physical plant, and public relations maintain the school structure. While the assistant principal manages the internal workings of the educational program. The two work together in responding to parents' concerns. The school has an accountant to assist with financial concerns who is not considered part of the staff.

The eleven board members of Crestview School are mostly composed of people from outside the school. Only three board members represent parents from the school. The rest of the board members come from business corporations, other independent private schools and local universities. The board meetings, held once a month, are closed. The author of the study was not permitted to attend board meetings during the data collection stage. The parents at large and the parents in charge of annual giving were on the board to provide feedback to the parents. However, many parents were often frustrated with their lack of input. Parents at the Crestview School had worked in conjunction with the board president and the principal to attempt to reorganize to provide more parent representation to the board. In discussions about this concern the board president stated that since the school was financially insecure during the first four years, the board was afraid parents would leave the school if they were fully aware. However, now that the school was beginning to pull together financially the board was considering more parent representation.

As the board becomes more sophisticated and more secure, it is beginning to examine its ability to raise funds and develop policies. The board members and the parents are floundering in defining their roles in relation to the school. Although the school is experiencing growing pains, it has become more visible in the downtown community. Since the school has been relatively unknown, the board and the parents are doing much to advance its name within the community. The board of the school was reorganized twice during the early days and has undergone many board committee changes. The board committees include development, finance, executive marketing, nominating and tuition assistance. The board has recently completed a five year growth plan to ensure financial security and a sound location for the school. The board has recently undergone a change in president to provide new direction and leadership for the school. (The former board president was in this position for five years.) As this school continues to grow, it is becoming better known so it attracts many parents located in the city. At present, the school is not as well recognized in the suburban area as the other two schools in the study. This is partly due to its newness and its location.

Parent involvement at the school is very strong despite the fact that many of the parents work. There are many single parents and parents with only one child attending the school. Most of the parents have not been exposed to the independent school model as they come from a public school background. The parent organization is relatively new and often grapples with its role within the school. Typically, in independent private schools the parents' organization serves as a fundraiser to provide the school with additional revenue. However, in this school the parent organization views its role in supporting the school program, providing assistance to the teachers and providing family socials in conjunction with educational projects such as the science fair. The structure of the parent organization is quite sophisticated. It is made up of several subcommittees such as social, publicity, fundraising, resource enrichment and education. These committee chairs meet monthly to give progress reports on their committee projects. The school attempts to raise some money through selling T-shirts and food for school socials.

The parent organization sees its main purpose as assisting the teachers at the school. The teacher and the parent organization work cooperatively to develop joint projects. For example the science teacher approached the parent organization to assist with the science fair. The parent organization developed a social around the science fair event and provided the name of judges, developed the ribbons for the winners and furnished the refreshments. Presently the school is examining the computer program so parents are working in conjunction to assist with ideas, funds and technical support. The role of parent involvement in the school's curriculum is very clear. Parents are only to provide technical support, but they do have the opportunity to make suggestions. Discussions with parents indicated they do not feel comfortable making curriculum decisions, but they like having input and providing technical support to the school.

The communication to parents about various school issues is very unsophisticated. Notes to the parents are placed on a table as parents come in the school door, and notices about parent meetings are posted on the bulletin board. This process worked when the school was small, but now parents and staff are finding problems with miscommunication among the various school groups. For the past two years the school has tried to develop a school/parent newsletter but problems of ownership have occurred. However, the parent organization and the principal are in the process of ironing out the last of the details for the proposed parent communication newsletter.

The ability levels of students at the school are quite varied. Since the principal and the assistant principal have backgrounds in special education, and language and reading development, the school is willing to accept children with severe learning problems. The strength of the school's curriculum is the ability to meet the needs of the students. The small class size, individualized instruction, and the minimal structure provides many of the children with learning problems with successful school experiences. Interviews with the school's parents indicated that they were very impressed with the academic success they had seen with the other children who had learning problems. They also expressed that the school had a unique ability to develop challenging projects that developed higher order thinking and problem solving skills. The school has no entrance exams and has a 100 percent acceptance rate. The school is traditionally different from other schools because of its unique setting, large open classrooms, and minimal structure. Parents visiting the school have to be assured that the children are learning in this unstructured setting. Test scores indicate that students are performing well above grade level, and children with learning problems continue to make great strides.

There is great diversity at the school with a minority rate of over 40 percent. The school curriculum is very multicultural and many of the school's programs for parents and children are geared toward cultural awareness. Parents at the school are very progressive and place their children in the school so they will be exposed to an urban setting. Parents want a protective environment for their children, but also want them to experience the realities of life. During school outings the children are often exposed to homeless individuals and urban concerns, but the school uses these incidents to expose children to differences. Many of the parents at the school live in the city and value diversity. The school has more than 30 percent of its students receiving financial aid.

The school's mission is to meet the needs of working parents and provide academic excellence in a stimulating urban environment. It also views itself as contributing to the revitalization of the downtown area by providing quality education. The school believes it should capitalize on the vast educational opportunities the downtown area has to offer its children. The school wants to provide a balanced educational program that integrates the arts, academics, and athletic experiences. The school is designed to celebrate the love of learning for each child, treasure individuality and diversity. The school affords parents with a unique program that is close to work, open year round, flexible in curriculum, conveniently located, available for extended hours, and family oriented.

The school has gained experience in managing finances, clarifying mission, and recruiting of students as it matures. However, the commitment to working with families has always been the focus for the school. The school is a safe haven for single parents who have developed a network of support for themselves. As the school continues to grow there are concerns that the family type atmosphere will disappear. Many families have become very dependent on the school to assist them with raising their children. The school has just undergone its first long range plan which will be implemented in the 1993–4 school year. The school is facing many financial and physical plant concerns. The school is accredited by ISACS and has recently undergone an evaluation of its program.

Reflections and Limitations

Although an entire year was spent in these institutions, I often worried if this book could truly communicate the interconnectedness between privatization and the development of a communal existence. These institutions shared their power in the governance structure, and a degree of mutuality resulted in each school. The schools existed because they established a sense of ownership that led to a collective responsibility to maintain the school's traditions yet continually evaluate what the school's mission represents to recruit new students. Parents chose these schools and invested in their values, beliefs and commitments. The teachers, with considerable autonomy in curriculum decisions, worked collaboratively to educate students on the basis of its mission. Teachers responded to the school's mission through their instructional practices and their commitment to remain current in their professional development. Parents had a voice in the governance structure of the school through the board and parent organizations. Parents believed the school's commitment to them went beyond mere retention and representation, but an obligation to focus on mission adherence.

In many ways I felt a part of each school structure even though my intent was to retain some distance from the participants. It was very difficult not to be pulled in by the kindness and caring of these school communities. At times I had to ask myself whether these schools were trying to win favor through their supportiveness of this study, or if they habitually demonstrated caring ways to those who came in contact with the school. However, given the amount of time spent in each setting, I discovered that the schools' interactions with all their participants was always warm and caring because of the community each school generated. Each school promoted collegiality among its participants that was internalized through the school's traditions. Many times the three principals would ask who were the other participating schools within the project. My same response was that the schools were to be kept confidential for obvious reasons. But it was this fierce spirit of believing in their educational mission that bound these schools as a community. My interviews with parents always ended with them asking me if I thought their school was the better site for the study. Much to my surprise parents were always trying to convince me that I should like their school the best. This parent promotion of their school was not a prestige or bragging issue. Parents believed that their school was beneficial to the success of their child. They believed they were fortunate to find the right school for their children. These parents obviously cared deeply about their school and sought validation for their choice of schools.

Because the schools had such varied philosophies it was difficult not to let my personal feelings affect my interpretations. For example, since most of my professional schooling was in special education and educational administration, in the early days of the study I found myself leaning toward Appleman School because of my awareness that many special education students would benefit from this structured program while Crestview School was totally unstructured. However, with time and a better understanding of these schools' educational mission, I was able to factor out my preferences and focus on how each school's mission attracted the type of student that would benefit from its program. It was this matching of students' style with parents' desires that established an interactive partnership with the school. Given an opportunity for choice, parents bought into the mission of the school and supported the goals of the program.

Another limitation of the study was the transition from public to private schools. During this study I was also overseeing several student teachers in the better-funded and highly acclaimed public schools. The difference between the public versus private sites was often quite apparent in my daily contact in both settings. The comparisons were always in the forefront of my mind. As I was doing observations in these two contexts, there were many questions that crossed my mind: In the public settings, I asked why those schools could not be more like independent schools in their responsiveness to parents and students. While in the independent school settings I asked why all children couldn't have access to the same type of community that prevailed in these independent schools. While I hadn't intended to assess the relative merits of private versus public schools, I found myself constantly confronted with this dilemma.

Advocates of privatization believe that independent schools become more efficient and innovative leading to better achievement for students. Autonomous schools focus on the needs of students resulting in greater client responsiveness. However, most importantly, these schools created a voluntary community where value was placed on shared responsibility for educating socially responsible children. If we are to learn anything from these settings, it is that these market driven schools were more than just autonomous places with a specific mission; instead, they were environments where educators listened to what students and parents wanted and sought to inform and involve them through their mission. The schools were not market driven but mission driven where the focus was on what the school represents to the participants.

Chapter 2

The Organizational Structure for Privatization

Organizational Culture and a Sense of Community

The argument for the privatization of public schools is based on the premise that such institutions must be allowed to work as cohesive units, united behind the school's mission and to its participants. Market-driven schools are given more authority in defining their mission and empower their participants to be responsible in keeping the school accountable. In addition, privatization means that schools must run like a business that entails planning, setting specific goals and objectives, measuring performance, linking costs to results and evaluating the school's intent. Privatization creates an environment where there is a strong organizational culture based on collaborative decision-making. The intent of this chapter is to examine the nature of privatization and its effect on each school's organizational structure. Independent schools are arranged to create a participatory management that allows school participants to have a voice in defining the school's goals. Each school's market driven responsiveness leads to greater accountability, and a commitment to remain innovative and accountable.

Deal (1985) maintains that businesses much like schools must articulate a softer, people oriented, symbolic strategy for enhancing special internal qualities. A privatized context is dependent on a cohesive structure — a shared set of values that motivates and shapes the behavior inside the school and inspires commitment and loyalty from its constituencies. Deal believes that corporate practices offer lessons for schools as they seek to create a culture. 'Culture' in organizations, or 'the way we do things around here', implies a consistent pattern of thought and behavior and a collection of artifacts that symbolize and give meaning to the workplace. Meaning for the participants is derived from the shared values and beliefs, heroes and heroines, and an informal network of cultural players.

Deal (1985) and others (Clark, 1983; Sarason, 1971; Swidler, 1979; Waller, 1932) believe that a strong organizational culture is based on the following: shared values and a consensus of practice; leadership that embodies the values of the organization; widely shared beliefs reflected in tradition, workers who emulate the organizational values and are collaborative; rituals of acculturation and cultural renewal; ritual to celebrate past history; a balance among innovation, tradition, autonomy and authority; and widespread participation in cultural rituals. This organizational context establishes the dichotomy of profit and community. In successful companies there is a tradition of heroes and heroines representing the past as well as innovative practices that allow individuals within the organization opportunity to contribute and belong. There are distinctive rituals of collaborative management and personal exchange that provide individuals with opportunities to feel their input is valued.

Each independent school in this study has a strong culture rooted in a consensus of practice and widely shared beliefs articulated through the mission. These schools have established traditions, cultural rituals, and a balance of authority. Each school created an organizational culture that led to a unique affiliation among its school participants. There is an interconnectedness that turns the school membership into a voluntary community. An interactive relationship develops among past parents and students and current members that maintains continuity. These schools are dynamic institutions that continually assess the quality of their students in relationship to their school's mission. Each school values its traditions yet retains a balance between innovations and mission adherence.

The strong organizational culture in independent schools produces a community where all participants have emotional ties to one another. Newmann (1990) believes that creating small communities of parents, teachers, and administrators over an extended period of time with daily contacts establishes a communal relationship that extends beyond the boundaries of the school. These contacts establish trust and bond the school participants. The extended forms of communication allow for a sharing of personal backgrounds, knowledge of students' strengths and weaknesses, and responsiveness to parents and students, all of which create a school community. This community, a responsive interactive school, integrates the values, aspirations and desires of its participants.

Raywid (1993) believes that the success of alternative schools relates to the sense of community that evolves when all participants seem to share a number of qualities. One of the qualities that is apparent in these contexts is respect, reflected in a willingness to hear the voice of the participants and to sustain an authentic courtesy in exchanges even when all agree to disagree. Giving all participants a voice ensures an equal distribution of power. Authentic courtesy provides an atmosphere of compromise where solutions are encouraged or supported. Caring, while different from respect, also involves response to the participants. Respect means giving, (in a passive fashion), the opportunity to be heard, but caring involves reaching by being supportive, appreciative, concerned and proactive. Noddings (1984) uses the term 'engagement' as a dimension of caring. In schools that care there are mechanisms or practices which create a community of nurturing participants.

Another quality of school community is inclusiveness (Raywid, 1993). Schools that build community are not made up of subgroups with different agendas. Schools with a high degree of community make continual attempts to draw participants into the discussions and all attempts are made to hear everyone's perspective. Coherence of purpose and participatory management emerges in the group's structure and representation. The element of trust (Raywid, 1993) in the participants allows them to disclose their needs among the community members. By establishing trust, school personnel can begin to build a team. Team building among the constituents ensures a level of commitment to and investment in the educational goals of the school. Finally, empowering individuals in a participatory manner establishes decision-making practices involving more than just voting representation and assuring individuals of the opportunity to affect school policy-making (Raywid, 1993).

Each of the schools in this study reflects a strong organizational culture and embodies a community of participants. These schools cultivate a social order based on norms, values and traditions rather than on formal rules and regulations. Establishing community in these schools was a time-consuming process that demanded great patience on the part of school personnel. The desire for participatory management required these schools to establish outlets for dialogue among all participants. These organizational structures, founded on collaborative decision-making, create an interdependence among participants. The independent schools' culture — 'the way we do things around here' — is manifested verbally and behaviorally. Community in these settings is enhanced by each school's strong culture. The mission statements creates shared values that lead to a strong organizational culture. Because of the dependency of mission adherence, there were established traditions that many participants used to establish each school's culture.

Each school has a board structure that consists of parents, past parents and alumni. The board's role is to establish policies that enhance the school mission. Parents know their role in supporting the school. Teachers, board members and parents established a collaborative environment where all opinions are heard and respected. Each school sought out its traditions through fundraising, school programs and alumni activities. The board structure established a strong organization through its mission to establish a consistent pattern of thought. Board members contributed to the school's intent through their level of expertise so board members felt their input was valued.

Another dimension that maintains the culture and community of these schools is their interactions with past graduates. Each school values the input of these individuals as a way to validate their mission and to evaluate the quality of their educational program. Each school cultivates its graduates to retain the students' connection to the school. For each school, the graduation ceremony was a reflection of what the school represented. Students gave speeches of how their school's mission will make them good students and citizens.

The public relations directors at Appleman and Bakersfield keep databases on students' activities over an extended period of time to retain a pool of past alumni who will always have a connection with the school. Class reunions are important to maintaining the traditions at Appleman School. As independent schools mature over time a pool of past alumni becomes an important source for recruiting. With each school in the study there was a deliberate focus on the lives of former students. Because Appleman School is the oldest school, the marketing of its traditions are more noticeable in its approach to students and parents. Bakersfield is only just beginning to tap this valuable resource of recruits. Crestview, while quite new, maintains its relation with past parents to continue the propagation of its school agenda. Each school uses sophisticated marketing strategies based on the school's strong cultural identity to recruit and to maintain its community.

Cultural Linkages in the Educational Mission of the School

Bureaucratic linkages are formalized mechanisms that establish a bureaucratic authority where there is a hierarchically arranged system. The principal establishes a system of subordinates where the goals and interests of teachers are often ignored. This hierarchical system based on power rather than expertise often leads to arbitrary mandates assigned for implementation to appropriate individuals (Firestone and Wilson, 1994; Sergiovanni, 1994a). Bureaucratic linkages result in establishing and defining tasks while cultural linkages lead to thoughtful collaboration which fosters emotional linkages to the school. Participants who are culturally linked to the school share common values, beliefs and commitments and become interdependent (Firestone and Wilson, 1994).

Caldwell and Spinks (1992) believe it is the schools' values and beliefs that create cultural linkages in self-managed schools. Self-managed schools have the capacity for problem solving, connectedness and continuity that leads to a curriculum that reflects in their philosophy of education. Each of the schools in this study uses its mission to develop a consensus that is reflected in the educational program. The cultural linkages in each setting involve the continual examination of what the school means, what the children represent, and how the mission is reflected throughout the school. The guiding force in these independent schools is adherence to the mission and the ability to collaborate in developing long range plans for their schools. The mission is used to determine allocation of fiscal resources, school and facilities improvement. Similarly, curriculum, parent organization activities and board agendas revolve around the school mission and the five year long range plan. Each school's marketing themes and public relations brochures reflect the educational goals as a recruitment tool.

The common themes apparent in the mission statement of all three schools were 'quality' related to the basics, spiritual development through promoting personal values and preparation of children to become lifelong learners. While the commitment to mission remains constant, limitations in resources have forced these three schools to develop the capacity to set and reset priorities. This ongoing evaluation of the school mission and long range plan gives each school the opportunity to make improvements based on new educational trends. The mission becomes the focus for creating cultural linkages among the participants.

The Appleman School mission statement reflected:

> a traditional organizational culture that emphasizes a strong well-balanced foundation in the basic subjects as well as providing development in the fine arts, physical education, foreign language, science and social studies. Students are encouraged in analytical and critical thinking, individual creativity and a love of learning. The faculty with interdepartmental cooperation, uses a variety of approaches with the sequential curriculum to accommodate individual learning styles to overcome weaknesses and to build on strengths. The development of a positive self-image and the realization of the child's potential intellectually, physically, aesthetically, socially and emotionally are objectives. The school is small enough to provide a joyful, personal and supportive climate with each staff member taking responsibility for a safe, orderly environment. To enhance the climate, there are constructive relationships between the school, the families and the students. Appleman fosters the personal qualities of self-discipline, respect for others and strength of character. An Appleman graduate should be motivated, responsible, academically prepared for the secondary school level, capable of dealing effectively with his environment and a productive member of society.

This philosophy of education at Appleman established the type of school program that all participants are committed to following in educating the children at the school. The school is well known for its rigorous program of preparing children for the secondary schools. Participants at the school believe in a holistic program, but the primary focus is rigorous academics and teaching children to become independent.

At Bakersfield School the educational mission reflects a child-centered approach through a Montessori program. Their mission is stated as follows:

> Bakersfield is committed to providing excellent education for children from diverse backgrounds, 18 months through sixth grade. This child-centered, parent-supported school promotes joy in learning and positive character development. It strives to prepare each student to become a lifelong learner and to meet with confidence the challenges of successful levels of education. Bakersfield School's curriculum implements the Montessori philosophy and methodology in the lower levels and combines these with more traditional approaches in the upper levels. The classroom environment stimulates intellectual, emotional, social, physical and cultural growth. In addition to a strong academic program, the school promotes the development of initiative, independence, responsibility, curiosity, cooperation and respect for others.

The educational program is tied to a specific teaching methodology, but it integrates elements of personal autonomy and values.

At Crestview School the educational focus involves integrating support for working parents with a strong liberal arts education for its students. The school newly founded only six years ago has minimal experience in developing a philosophy as sophisticated as that of the other two schools. This school is challenged to define an educational mission reflected in an independent organizational structure that suits working parents. Their mission statement was designed particularly for the children of working parents. The Crestview's mission reflected:

> The school is dedicated to promoting family values along with academic excellence in a stimulating urban family environment. Crestview School affords a unique closeness to school for working families through a year-round program, flexible curriculum and convenient location; celebrates the love of learning for each child, treasuring individuality and diversity, combines innovative design with traditional values for joyful, active and secure learning; offers a comprehensive curriculum of fundamental skills in all major subject areas; integrates academic artistic and athletic experiences; capitalizes on the vast educational opportunities of a downtown location; and contributes to the revitalization of downtown by improving the quality of life in the metropolitan area.

The mission statements of the three independent schools although different in nature have many similarities. All schools see their primary focus as academic, in preparing children for the demands of a secondary curriculum and in promoting individuality, self-esteem and respect for diversity. This philosophy focuses on the 'whole child' rather than just the academic curriculum best suited for preparing students for a secondary curriculum. All three schools share this philosophical base and seek to integrate it throughout the curriculum and the school community. By establishing educational goals each school is then able to become self-governed. The mission statement permeates all aspects of the school community allowing each school to be autonomous, fiscally responsible and accountable. The board structure uses the mission to define how the school will be administered. Consensus building among school participants leads to a high degree of mutuality where compromise and joint action become part of the cultural linkage among the school participants. These self-governed schools each created an environment where all are encouraged to participate in defining the school's mission. There is a strong organizational culture that leads to a consistent pattern of thought. And a commitment for improvement and adherence to the schools' traditions.

The mission of each independent school is the mechanism that establishes a cultural linkage to the school community. The mission fosters a communal school organization that establishes emotional ties to the school. Each school continually seeks validation of its intent through its relations with parents and faculty members. The 'whole child' approach, established in the mission, places demands on faculty and parents to establish personal and professional inter-actions that extend the objective of schooling beyond academics. The cultural linkages of an independent school requires a continual examination of its pur-pose and its success in educating the 'whole child'. The cultural linkages of an independent school's community rely on a clear mission statement, a long range plan to implement it, budgeting for efficiency and policies that have been derived from a collaborative process. These schools believe they have the capability to be autonomous in order to maintain the educational program that their parents have chosen for their children.

Focus on Mission Adherence

Independent schools thrive on a collaborative decision-making to define the school's mission. Each school has a governing board that consists of parents, past parents, alumni and other school participants. This board is responsible for defining and insuring that the school implements the mission and is fiscally responsible and accountable. School personnel provide information to its board members and parents so they can have input in the school's decisions. School leaders trust, in the ability of parents and faculty to make the appropriate decisions for students. School leaders believe all school participants can con-tribute to the school's mission by assisting the school with its educational goals. There is an effect of synergy where individuals work as a cohesive unit and where everyone believes that the group can achieve more good than individuals working separately. The tangible product of this collaboration is a general investment in the school mission and in 'the way things are done around here'. Because independent schools are more autonomous, all con-stituencies feel more accountable.

Each school's mission is integrated throughout the curriculum and its suc-cess is measured by the quality of the graduates or the school's test results. The focus on graduates as a means for measuring the school's success in implementing its mission was apparent during meetings and discussions with school personnel. For example, Appleman's graduate surveys from second-ary school teachers indicated that their students needed to develop critical thinking skills. Since Appleman's philosophical intent is to educate children to achieve higher order thinking skills, the curriculum coordinator and a fellow teacher developed a strategic process to assess the children's critical thinking at the elementary level to determine what curriculum changes were needed. They determined ways to assess their students' skill in critical thinking. They established a pre- and post-test using a standardized measure and student portfolios. Thus, student outcomes were used to reinforce the Appleman's mission. Similarly, Bakersfield School works with secondary schools to ensure that their mission is reflected in the graduates. This school contacts parents whose children have graduated to insure this school is preparing its students to be lifelong learners. Although Crestview had few graduates, it places an emphasis on being accountable for their test scores to ensure the children's learning. Many parents who had children with severe learning problems noted the teachers' commitment to insure the children's scores improved over time. All three independent private schools seek validation of their mission through accountability mechanisms such as test scores, parent conferences and secondary school placements to insure the school is accountable for implementing its mission.

Process of Mission Evaluation

Accountability and responsiveness play an important role in the ongoing efforts for improvement through the evaluation of the educational mission. The school mission at each independent school is re-examined every five years by all school participants. Review of the mission is tied to the development of a five year plan the school uses to establish its goals. When the school reviews its mission, it also develops a long range plan. This plan becomes the blueprint for each school to focus on its needs and to make improvements. The plan, in conjunction with the mission, becomes the focus that ties the participants toward a collective responsibility for educating its students.

The long range plan and mission statement are so entwined that the long range plan is the instrument used to update the school's mission. One cannot factor in changes in the mission without considering how they will affect the long range plan. Each school varies in their processes for long range planning. However, planning and goal setting are crucial to maintaining the school's niche within the community. These institutions continually examine their image in the marketplace and then move the school in innovative ways to define their educational program. The long range planning committee consists of many school constituencies who worked collaboratively in defining the school for the future. During this observation period, only Appleman and Crestview schools were undergoing a review of their long range plan and educational mission. Bakersfield had reviewed its plan the year before and was in the process of implementing its goals to expand its program for more students to attend the school.

Evaluation of Bakersfield School's Mission

Bakersfield School brought in an expert who persuaded the long range planning committee composed of parents, teachers, and community members to examine their mission from a global and national perspective in planning the school's future. Moving from the international to the local level, the long range planning committee brainstormed the future of the school in order to see the school twenty-five years from now without worrying about financial constraints. The Bakersfield long range planning committee developed a series of goals to ensure that the school would increase its program to allow for more students to attend its school.

The Bakersfield School's plan to increase its program surfaced when the school was considering major capital improvements to increase its size. However, a builder approached the board participants about building a school in the metropolitan area further west so more parents would have greater access to choice. He argued that the metropolitan area was moving outward from the city leaving new residential areas with few options for private schooling. With an independent school in this area, the builder could promote more residential building. The Bakersfield five year plan considered ways to expand the school but had not considered opening a sister school. By opening another school, it could provide more options for families and secure better use of its resources. The board and school personnel held several meetings to address the worries that many Bakersfield parents and teachers had opening a new school versus increasing the number of students resulting in many problems of how to interpret the long range plan. Many were concerned about the loss of personnel and the division of school resources between the two sites. The board and the parents agreed to disagree about their options and to address the concerns of their school community. After many meetings and much heated debate the school felt it could establish another school campus which would also enhance the school's mission. The school community exhibited trust in the board's decision that the school could expand but would still maintain its original intent. Both faculty and parents placed great emphasis on the mission statement and long range plan to maintain the organizational culture of the school. The mission and goals of the school became the blueprint for school change. The mission for this school created the vision for the school to expand so it could provide more opportunities for its children. Upon my return to the school a year later, the school not only had a satellite campus but decided to expand its program to the secondary level. The school plans to open a middle/high school program so both schools could become feeder schools.

Evaluation of Appleman School's Mission

Appleman School used a sophisticated process of collaborative decision-making to review its educational mission through their long range planning process. At Appleman School, planning began with an examination of the educational mission statement. The first phase of reviewing long range planning and the mission statement at Appleman involved the board of trustees. The school mission and five year plan were approved by this governing body which is responsible for overseeing the administration of the school's policies. The board appointed an *ad hoc* long range board committee that focused on the future needs of the school to assist the school in developing the long range plans. This *ad hoc* committee met regularly to determine the questions to be asked to the focus groups and the participants for these groups. General questions for the focus groups included: What are the essentials of a mission statement? How might the mission change in the next five years? How does the philosophy statement which is in place differ from the realities of Appleman School and its graduates today? What elements of Appleman graduates' needs are not being completely addressed today? What innovations, if any, do you think are important for the next five years?

Specific questions were later developed for the various school groups:

Alumnae What part of the curriculum do you remember being the strongest when you left Appleman?

Current parents What about the curriculum attracted you to Appleman?

Past parents When your children left Appleman, in what areas of the curriculum were they best prepared?

Faculty What innovations in the curriculum should we be looking to in the future?

Based on the information from the various school groups, committees were formed in the following areas: program, organization, students, faculty, parents, administration, governance, finance, facility changes, marketing and alumni development. These committees then met to review the previous five year plan and update the new plan to meet the needs and wishes of the school community.

The connection between the faculty and the mission was made apparent at one particular faculty meeting that was spent reviewing the mission statement and defining the way the curriculum and the students were interconnected for the future of the school. This faculty spent considerable time reviewing the language of the mission's intent and considering how a new philosophy would be reflected in their classrooms. The teachers discussed the needs of students in relation to the school's future agenda. The faculty raised the following questions: How does the school reflect the mission statement? What is Appleman about and how is its essence reflected if the mission does not focus on the whole child? How is the idea of accountability to be incorporated in the new mission? How does the new emphasis on social responsibility mesh with the old mission to teach factual knowledge? My observations of this focus group approach indicated that the faculty was committed to the school's mission and interested in how the mission reflected what the graduates should be. The faculty felt a sense of autonomy in interpreting the mission that allowed them input into the school's intent. Teachers felt accountable for implementing the mission throughout the school curriculum and accepted responsibility for its quality.

Appleman's current mission statement differs considerably from a previous statement of philosophy. The new mission statement at Appleman reflects a need for educating children through a diversity perspective and includes computer technology. The mission statement will also reflect the mentoring role the school will play when more of its female parents return to the workforce. The long range plan from 1989 was upgraded to include planning about issues of diversity, developing an all-year-round program in conjunction with a summer camp program, creating more awareness in the areas of alumni development and moving the school to a higher level of technology. The long range plan for 1994 reveals that within the next five years the school will review all eight of its curriculum areas. The plan from 1989 noted that the school would only contain 200 students with twenty to twenty-eight students per class while the 1994 plan increased the enrollment to 220 and increased the class sizes to twenty-two to thirty. The student:teacher ratio in 1989 was 1 to 15 while the 1994 goal remains the same. The difference in the ratio from 1989 to 1994 was affected in the preschool program where it was reduced to l to 11 for the next five years. There are also more demands to include additional time for a learning specialist to assist students who may have learning problems in the rigorous academic environment.

The continual theme throughout Appleman's 1989 and 1994 long range plans and school mission is the importance of excellence in the academic program and the need for accountability of its graduates. The school established an organizational culture based on a traditional curriculum that prepares its graduates for the demands of the secondary schools. The coherence of the mission leads to a sense of 'how we do things here' as a way to unify the school. All school participants are in consensus about the goals of the school and the process to achieve those goals. There is a cultural linkage through the accountability mechanisms that used present and past parents, faculty and alumni as resources for improvements in the school program. The school examined its mission to establish a cultural content that reflects the desires of its participants, allows for innovation to meet future needs and encourages participants to be committed to what the school represents. A collaborative decision-making process allows participants to have a voice ensuring the school's accountability and traditions. Throughout the school's history there has always been widespread participation in reviewing its mission. During the school's planning there was a continual concern for balancing the desire to maintain the school's traditions with a need for innovation to attract students.

Evaluation of Crestview School's Mission

During this study, Crestview School was only beginning its second five year plan and did not have the tradition of long range planning like Appleman or Bakersfield. The long range planning was not as inclusive as either Appleman's or Bakersfield's. Most of the long range planning was completed at the board level with very few school parents and teachers involved in the process. The board consists of individuals with a degree of expertise but limited connection to the school. (Board meetings at Crestview are closed to outsiders and parents so the researcher was unable to attend meetings through the observational period. Information about board issues was gained from board documentation and discussions with the principal and a few board parents.) Crestview's original long range plan focused more on recruitment, marketing and fundraising as a way for the school to begin its operation. As the school increased in size during its original plan, the next phase for the school was to locate a larger facility. Because the school had doubled its student population, its first priority was finding a building downtown that could reflect the school's curriculum and integrate the artistic and athletic perspective. The school was also grappling with how to market its educational program so working parents would consider their school.

Due to the limited resources, board members played dual roles by providing information about facility planning, marketing and fundraising to establish the school within the metropolitan area. The school struggled with finding its identity and marketing that image. However, as the school continued to grow it began a more sophisticated process of needs assessment. The school initially began at a church site but has expanded to where it needs a new location.

The school, housed in an old church downtown, lacks any resemblance to a traditional school. Crestview's long range plan from 1988 focused on developing mission adherence and increasing student numbers. Since the problems of 1994 were similar to those of 1988, there was little difference between the two long range plans and the mission statement for the next five years for Crestview School. The new plan focuses more on retaining a marketing consultant, improving the site where the school was currently located and contacting business corporations for their support to renew the downtown area. There was little change in the educational mission with the focus on academic excellence and integration of the arts within an urban setting. The long range plan also includes far more parent involvement within the governance structure. The cultural linkage to Crestview School is built on its entrepreneurial spirit in starting a school that assists working parents. The purpose of the school is to connect downtown corporations with the school's community so parents can become more involved in their children's learning. The school provides parents with resources to support their busy schedules and relieve their daily stresses.

Independent private schools use the long range plan as a way to instill cultural linkages in the school participants, creating a strong organizational culture and school community. The organizational structure of these institutions was purposely established to create a community of participants. Students and parents are treated with respect and made to feel like functioning members, not occupants who have no choice. There is a strong affiliation to the school developed through activities that enlist the support of former parents and alumni. A carefully nurtured sense of responsibility encourages everyone to give support to the school. The attempt by independent schools to build and sustain a community of participants is reflected in their mission, organizational structure and collaborative planning of mission. The schools in the study developed a center of values, traditions, sentiments and beliefs that provide the necessary conditions for creating a collective sense of 'we'. The schools' commitment to its traditions and its ability to mold the long range plan to its mission creates a sense of community. Each school established cultural linkages through the examination of its purpose. Through retaining close ties among the school participants and maintaining a strong identity, these schools create an environment dedicated to developing academically well rounded students. The focus is mission and doing that well. Mission adherence is then used to market the school to recruit and retain students.

Governance Structure and the Board of Trustees

The privatized school's governance structure is not a top–down delineation of rules and regulations, but a bottom–up system of contribution where parents, graduates and teachers interact with each other to define what school participants want the school to be. Independent schools are governed by a board of trustees responsible for overseeing the financial well being of the school and establishing policies that promote the educational mission of the school. Boards are comprised of parents, former parents, alumni and community members with an affiliation to the school who define the direction of the school. Independent schools use a board structure to develop a collaborative model of school management that involves parents and teachers in the decision-making process. The board structure at each school is responsible for goal setting its long range planning, policy making, curriculum revisions, financial and budgetary resources and the implementation and evaluation of the school program.

A particular organizational hierarchy is common to all three independent schools in the study. For each, the board establishes school policies and sets the direction of the school. Because many parents and school personnel serve as board members, the bureaucratic authority is limited. Instead, parents and school personnel share power (see Figure 2.1). The board of trustees is usually composed of school participants who report to the president of the board. Board members are selected for expertise who can contribute to the board's goals. Board members are assigned to board committees and respected for their contribution to the school. Board committees are structured to report to the board to ensure that the school focuses its educational mission, examines its resources for school needs, establishes goals for future development and institutes policies to administer the school (see Figure 2.2). Various board committees have goals and objectives that determined their purpose in reporting to the board. Each school has different board committees that are needed to meet each school's needs. The principal reports to the board president and board committees about the school and its policies and also is responsible for overseeing the faculty and the administrative staff. Board members are

```
                        ┌─────────────────────┐
                        │  Board of Trustees  │
                        └─────────────────────┘

                             Composed of

Parents    Former Parents   Alums   Students   Community Participants   School Staff

                    President  ←   Board   ←  President of
                     of the      Committees     Parent
                      Board                   Organization



                                   Principal



   School          Administrative           Faculty
  Personnel            Staff
                  Business Manager
 Maintenance         Curriculum
                    Director and
   School          Development/
  Cafeteria        Public Relations
```

Figure 2.1: An Independent School's Organizational Chart

Appleman	**Bakersfield**	**Crestview**
Executive	Diversity	Finance
Finance	Development	Marketing
Annual Giving	Executive	Nominating
Admissions	School Health	Executive
Alumni Relations	Building and Grounds	Tuition Assistance
Building and Grounds	Finance	Development
Diversity — *Ad Hoc*	Education	
Technology — *Ad Hoc*	Nominating	
Education		
Development/Endowment		
Nominating		
Safety		

Figure 2.2: Board Committees

identified by a board nominating committee that selects candidates for collaborative skills that contribute collectively to sustaining the mission of the school. For example, in a school undergoing a capital campaign, the board nominating committees would review its present and former school members to identify an individual to assist the school with their renovations.

In interviews, parents and faculty noted that the board governance gave them an opportunity to provide input. They felt that their opinions were valued. School staff and parents noted that while the board was the ultimate authority, it was not autocratic. Instead, the board was seen as collaborative, and willing to listen to parents' concerns. Thus, the linkage between the board, principal, faculty and parents creates a framework of collaboration which allows the board process to meet the school's needs by overseeing the implementation of the long range plan.

Board members are selected to meet particular needs rather than to represent constituencies of parents like public school board members who are voted by the local community. Each year when a board position is open, the board nominating committee assesses its needs to determine which individuals connected with the school might provide the expertise to assist the board in implementing its school policies or long range plan. Board nominating committees search the present and past parent pool and alumni before considering going outside the school membership. The intent of the board structure is to engage participants into the school governance through the board structure. As noted in the school summaries, each school tries to retain a percentage of parents serving on the board. Both Appleman and Bakersfield have the highest percentage of current parents on the board. Crestview plans to increase its parent representation when the school becomes financially stable.

Board Structure

At the three schools the board organizational structure is quite similar to the figure presented earlier. The differences lie in board committees and the level of expertise of school participants needed for board positions. Appleman, Crestview and Bakersfield all have executive, nominating, finance and development committees, but other committees vary according to each school's mission. These schools see the financial, nominating and executive committees as the main pillars for administering their school program. These three board committees are concerned with school finances, evaluating the role of the principal, finding additional funding through private giving, developing policies for board approval and identifying people to serve on the board. The other board committees were developed in relation to the school's long range planning or its mission. Each school's committees evolved over time, reflecting the school's age, tradition and need. The long range plan determines the type of committees that are needed to implement the goals of the school. For example, Appleman was reviewing its long range plan to address concerns about technology at the school. An *ad hoc* technology board committee was established to examine the role of computers in the classrooms for the next several years. The intent of the technology committee was to identify the school's needs for additional financial resources and to keep board members informed about the school's progress in improving technology.

Analysis of the various committees at the three schools reflects educational issues at those schools (see Figure 2.2). Appleman, the oldest school in the study, has more board committees that specifically address a certain area, such as alumni relations and development/endowment. These committees are responsible for developing a strong alumni base as a way to provide an additional pool of recruits and to tap into past parents and alumni for private giving. The school has a tradition of serving 'the city's foremost families' and markets its programs as a rigorous education with emphasis on the basics for families who have a sense of tradition (Tucci, 1992). Although Bakersfield is beginning to tap into its alumni pool, its board committees represent greater emphasis on school health and diversity. This school has been active in encouraging minorities to attend the school and has developed a scholarship to provide financial support for lower income families to facilitate economic diversity. The longer the school had been in existence, it appears, the more likely it is to emphasize the traditions and mission as a way to bond alums to the school.

Crestview School, in its early days, is struggling to define itself through the board structure. Its board structure focused more on its image and financial well being, serving as a conduit to the business community to promote the school's mission to serve working parents. Board members who also served on many corporate boards do have some difficulty understanding the academic issues and tuition concerns. The board works collectively to serve the image of the school, but it also struggles to define its relationship with working parents.

Both Bakersfield and Appleman have education committees containing parents, faculty and administrative staff. These committees have input into the educational program and keep the board informed of curriculum changes, test scores and professional development activities of the faculty and staff. At Appleman the education committee plays an important role in defining curriculum; the board has final approval on curriculum decisions. When the school was undergoing a change in its foreign language program, several board members were unhappy that the school was planning to eliminate Latin from the curriculum and focus its foreign language curriculum on French. However, after much discussion and two board meetings, the board approved the curriculum committee's decision. According to the principal at Appleman, challenges to curriculum are rare because the board believes that the principal should run the school, but occasionally the board does question certain curriculum decisions. The education committee's role is to communicate with the board about education issues, but its control in defining the overall program is limited. The education committee serves the purpose of ensuring that the school mission is apparent throughout its curriculum. In some ways the education committee serves as a courtesy to Appleman's parents by allowing them some control over the school's curriculum. In allowing parents a form of representation and respecting their input, the school establishes a partnership where they too contribute to the school and are responsible for educating students.

At Bakersfield the education committee contains more parents than Appleman's education committee, but it has less influence on curriculum matters. This committee meets only three times a year and is more informal in its agenda than the education committee at Appleman. At Bakersfield much discussion focused on topics such as sex education as a curricular issue and community resources available to families to be presented at the monthly breakfast meetings with parents. Bakersfield education committee also addressed serious multicultural concerns through the curriculum. This joint action of board members, parents and teachers allows these individuals to address sensitive concerns collectively in order to educate students about adult issues. Minutes from a board meeting from the education committee reported about the important role the families and school played in defining the school calendar. While the education committee obviously serves as a mechanism for reporting curriculum issues, the parents are kept at bay in defining the instructional program at the school. Parents participate in the curriculum through the board process that allows them appropriate access to assessing the school's program. The education committee at Bakersfield supports the school's curriculum through parent participation in the mission. However, at Appleman the education committee serves as a mechanism to hold the school accountable for its educational goals through the long range plan. Both schools use the education committee as a way to provide parents an outlet for their involvement in the school curriculum.

At Crestview there is no education committee because the principal believes that curriculum concerns are the school's and not the board's responsibility. The principal noted that many of her parents had little or no experience with independent schools so they did not understand how the process of the board worked. The principal was adamant that the board's role is to set policy for the school while the school's curriculum is defined by the faculty in relation to the mission. The faculty has the right to establish their instructional program based on their interpretation of the school's mission. The parents' organization at Crestview is similar to the board education committees at either Appleman or Bakersfield. Crestview's parent organization provides support for the teachers' interests while the parent organizations at Bakersfield and Appleman are more socially oriented. For example, a Crestview teacher doing a science project with his students involved the parents' organization to assist him with the school's science fair. According to the principal and school participants, this use of the parent organization is a better means for empowering parents in the educational mission than through their membership on a board committee.

Crestview's board of trustees has the fewest number of parents from the school, and it does not allow elected officers from the parent organization to serve as board members as the other schools do. Crestview's board president views her role as connecting the school to the business community. Most of the board members at Crestview are from the community because of the need to connect with downtown corporations and to provide a level of expertise in marketing and fundraising. Many of the school's parents were unable to bring that level of expertise to the board. In the early days when Crestview struggled with its funding and with marketing its educational mission, the school wanted to control the amount of information that was given to parents. If parents had heard that the school might close because of a loss of revenue, they might leave to find another school for their child. Limiting parent representation on the board reduced rumors that would occur about the school's ability to remain open. However, as the school achieves a level of financial stability it is re-examining its board process to encourage greater parent participation in the governance of the school.

Board Structure Accountability

Each board committee is held accountable through a goal setting process tied to the long range plan. At the beginning of each school year, individual board committees meet to determine their objectives for the year and establish a timeline for completing their goals. Board committees vary in relation to their timelines for completing their goals and are influenced by the importance of the committee. Chairs of board committees develop goals and dates of completion that are given to the board president and principal.

The finance and executive committees meet regularly to address policy and financial issues or other serious concerns that occur at the school. These committees are the most influential in defining policies and addressing school budget issues. The budget is tied to the long range plan which often affects the school's financial decisions. For example, one goal of the long range plans at Appleman and Bakersfield was to increase the faculty and administrators' salaries to a specific percentage level by the end of the five year plan. This meant that when the finance board committee met to complete the budget for the following year they would need to consider the percentage of increases for staff salaries for the following year. Bakersfield School established in their long range plan that they wanted to consider a policy that would allow sabbaticals for their faculty. The executive committee will address that concern through discussions with teachers and the administrative staff. The long range plan is the driving force that keeps the mission in sight and keeps the board working in a collaborative manner. Those committees that appear to have minimal relationship to the plan do not carry the weight or prestige of the executive and financial committees. The crux of board meetings revolve around the financial issues and executive concerns. The board seldom play a role in administering the school program. That responsibility was overseen by the principal who reported to the board about the school's educational program.

Board Membership and Responsibilities

Each school's principal attends all board meetings, but each principal's administrative team only attends those meetings that are relevant to their areas.

So the curriculum director attends the education committee and the budget director would assist the finance committee. Faculty either volunteer for committees who are appointed by the principal or another board member. In certain cases parents who were not board members are asked to serve on specific board committees but are not considered board members. If a parent expresses a specific preference for a committee then usually the school grants the request. A parent can be as active as he or she wants in respect to board committees or parent organization activities. Parents often express guilt about turning down a request to serve on committees, because they value and feel honored to have the opportunity to give their input.

Typical board terms at the three sites last approximately four years for two consecutive intervals. However, independent schools have the flexibility to establish their own board policies. Each independent school can establish its term limits to reflect the wishes of each board. At the three schools, board meetings are held once a month for several hours. Each board committee updates its committee work, then other board members hold discussions depending on the nature of the issue. Board committee reports are informational so other board members who serve on other committees are kept current. Board meetings provide opportunities for all members to examine all aspects of various board committees and contribute to the decision-making. Board members with specific knowledge of finance or law, for example, often served as the head of the more important committees, like the finance or executive committee. Board meetings show respect to parents and teachers as board members examine how all decisions will affect these two groups. The boards remain close to teachers and parents in order to promote adherence to the mission and show their commitment to preparing quality students. Although there are no written policies, board meetings are closed to outsiders and school participants who are not specifically board members. The principal determines whether it is appropriate if other administrators or faculty wish to attend board meetings. Each principal established her own policies to determine whether their staff should attend board meetings. There are no formal mechanisms for board information to be given to parents except through parent meetings or informal contacts with the principal. However, because many of the parents are board members, board information is usually exchanged with other parents during social encounters. The principal takes responsibility for conveying sensitive information so all parents hear the same things. The schools are attentive to their communication to staff and parents to prevent any misunderstanding about board decisions.

Each school has specific policies that determine the process board nominating committees use for selecting board members. Board members are selected for their experience in working with the school and their commitment to education; an educational perspective that is compatible with the philosophy of the school; previous volunteer experience with the parents' club or other volunteer work; interest in children; and demonstrated ability to work collectively with others. In addition to having a collaborative personality, board members also provide a level of expertise that can meet the board's needs. Individuals with financial, legal or educational expertise are most often selected. Other areas of expertise, also viewed as important, are advertising, fundraising, insurance and school construction. Some consideration is directed to selecting board members who have substantial financial resources or have access to individuals who can contribute to the school. But, for the most part, independent schools in this study focus their selection of board members on the level of expertise rather than the potential for financial support. A parent who was a former board president at one of the sites indicated her understanding of what a board member represents:

> Board membership is not based on money but wisdom, work and wit. It is comforting to know that the school will never select a board member because they might donate to the school. The selection of trustees is fair and represents the school. One year a board member came to represent the parents and she would give all the gripes of the school. It took a while to make her see what her role was on the board.

These independent schools also have a policy regarding the number of school participants and parents who may be identified as board members. School policies determine the percentage of present parents who are allowed to serve on the board. Present participants are selected in relation to their work with previous school activities and their ability to balance their immediate and personal concerns with the long term perspective of the school. For example, at Appleman School the cost of immediate asbestos removal was weighed against the costs of removing it at a later date. Parents who were board members had to make a difficult decision whether to vote on the removal now (which would reflect in the tuition costs) or pass the responsibility on to a future board. Parents often have to put aside their differences to vote for what is best for the school even if it means more money for tuition. Board members are respectful of parents in making school decisions, often discussing how decisions will affect parents and how parents will react to the board's decision-making.

The rule of thumb for independent schools is that no less than 25 percent and no more than 60 percent of board membership should be composed of individuals whose children do not attend the school. The schools also seek to achieve representation of various constituencies on board committees. For example, the education committee at Bakersfield and Appleman consists of two faculty members and two members from the board. The policies regarding the balance of constituencies are clearly established to provide direction to the board for selection and representation. Each independent school is autonomous in establishing its own board and membership policies.

The principal and veteran board members place considerable importance on educating new board members to serve on various board committees. The education is particularly important for parent members. Because these boards must balance parents' concerns with the mission of the school, there are political implications for current parents on the board that alums and past parents need not consider. Parent board members have to contend with calls from other parents about board policies, and concerns about teachers and administrative issues, but they cannot lose sight of the school's goals and mission. Board parents have to balance their immediate desires with the future needs of the school. Board membership is also very time consuming including various board committee meetings, attendance at school functions and monthly board meetings. When board members take calls at home regarding issues at the school, they must be circumspect in their reactions. Board members are educated about the school's mission and its long range plan and their role in serving on board committees. Within each school, board membership provides cultural linkage to the school's operation and administration, unites school staff and parents and establishes the organizational culture.

Each school has a different process for educating new board members. Bakersfield schedules two evening meetings where new board members, in conjunction with the board president and administrative staff, are given a history of the school and its mission. There is an explanation of their role as board members and serving on board committees and of the role of the principal and board members in defining policies for the school. New board members receive a board policy manual, a list of suggested readings and the financial handbook. Appleman School has less formal meetings with new board members, but they are given similar information from the National Association of Independent Schools. Both Appleman and Bakersfield board members attend a city-wide board of trustees' workshop which provides a more formal orientation about board membership. This orientation gives examples of the way a board member might handle a political situation and assists the board members in distinguishing a board issue from school curriculum matter. Crestview School does little in the way of educating board members since most of their board members come from other independent private schools or corporate boards.

The ideal board member is well-prepared for board meetings and attends all school functions. Board members are encouraged to visit the school and take an interest in what is occurring in the classroom. This practice allows the members to become familiar with the school culture and gives them a sense of their school's mission. Board members are required to keep board information about financial school matters confidential. Board members work in a collaborative atmosphere to create a governing body that provides leadership and direction to parents and school personnel. Board members make long range decisions to ensure the perpetration of the school's mission for a future generation of children. Board members address mission, planning, and involve themselves in a decision-making process rather than a forum for discussing school issues. A board member with a child in the school is expected to look beyond the present to the long term good of the school. Caldwell and Spinks

(1992) believe that a culture of self-management is dependent on the ability of participants to 'see the larger picture' and appreciate the elements of a school's culture that are shaped by forces of society as a whole and incorporate the need to manage continuing change.

The role of the board and the role of the principal must be very well defined to allow for effective interaction between the two governing bodies. The board in conjunction with the principal establishes the policies of the school, and the principal operates the school to achieve the desires of the board. Although the board and principal have separate responsibilities, they act as partners in defining the operation of the school. The board structure allows the self-governed school to scan the external environment for new trends while allowing the principal the opportunity to administer the school's mission through its daily operation. Collaborative school management relies upon clear roles for decision-making and established lines of accountability for both parties (see Figure 2.3). The board expects the principal to be account-able to all board members not just specific board members; to promote the mission of the school through the educational program; to interpret the needs of the school and guide the board in making decisions; to keep the board informed about the concerns from various school participants; to develop a budget in conjunction with the finance committee; to keep the board current on innovative educational trends; and to recruit and retain the best personnel for operation of the school.

The principal in turn expects the board to counsel and advise the prin-cipal and provide a level of expertise and a sense of the school community; delegate authority to the principal in order to manage the school program and refrain from handling administrative issues; support the principal in all deci-sions and actions that are consistent with the philosophy of the school; hold the principal accountable for managing the school and evaluate the work of the principal. The critical element of good interaction between the board and principal is the board's obligation to support the leadership of the principal. This means that the board supports the principal's decisions and refers any parent complaints to the principal. These referrals establish lines of commun-ication for the school and uphold the authority delegated to the principal. Par-ents, board members, and other school participants are well educated about the process of school complaints; they understand that the board is not a forum for handling a parent's gripe with the school or principal.

Theoretically, these roles are clear to the board and principal, but in practice difficult power struggles can raise between the two entities. How-ever, the collaborative decision-making process built into the organizational structure, allows the board and the principal to agree to disagree on occasion. The interaction between the principals and boards of trustees at the three schools was characterized by trust and respect so that sensitive issues could be addressed in board committees to preclude any surprises at board meetings. If necessary, *ad hoc* board committees convene to study sensitive issues or to provide a fresh perspective when new policies might be controversial. These

Policy Administration

- establish and approve mission statement
- ensure long range planning
- establish policies

Resource Management

- approve program and budget
- insure financial solvency (fundraising)
- maintain physical plant

Program Development

- approve program plan
- approve program and budget
- evaluate school performance

Personnel

- appoint head
- evaluate head annually
- approve salary scale and benefits
- approve personnel policies

Public/Community Relations

- help identify constituencies
- promote public image with constituencies

Board Development and Continuity

- recruit board members
- orient board members
- evaluate board performance
- organize board to carry out its duties
- insure continuity of board leadership

Figure 2.3: General Areas of Board Responsibility

ad hoc board committees find common grounds and give board members and the principal an opportunity to reach a consensus on school policies. Several sensitive issues at the three schools, such as diversity, satellite campuses, and financial concerns, were handled through *ad hoc* committees. These committees planned strategies and developed policies that addressed each school's concerns. By being proactive through the board structure in handling future problems each school's board can diffuse parents' concerns and support the principal's decision and school mission.

The board president plays a mediating role between the principal and the board, provides leadership for the board and guides the board in fulfilling its responsibilities. In each setting the board president provides support to the principal. The board president and principal appear to have an interactive relationship that involves mentoring, listening and supporting. All three principals rely heavily on their board presidents to support their administrative duties. When parent complaints become overwhelming principals often call their president for guidance and support. At other times the board president approaches the principal about an unhappy parent at the school.

The board president and board members have a sense of ownership of the school and feel responsible for the quality of its leadership. A positive relationship between the board president and principal is necessary for the board to remain committed. They trust each other to make sound decisions because the selection process focuses on the expertise needed to ensure the school's mission. This sense of responsibility among board members leads to collegiality and interdependence. The respect that develops among members produces a give and take mentality at board meetings.

The relationship between the principal and board is often affected by the mission of the school, the board's conception of the principal (years of experience, intent to remain at the school, or role as founding principal or a newcomer to the school), and commitment to the school mission. All of these variables influence the relationship between the board members and principal. Both the principals at Crestview and Bakersfield have an historical tie to the school because of their years of experience and roles as founders. Both principals have an easier time getting the board to work towards a common vision based on the school's present and past history. The principal at Appleman often struggles with her board to move the school more in line with the needs of the parents and to redefine the school's future in the areas of technology, recruitment and diversity. Because of the autonomous nature of each school setting, principals must understand board members, the school's mission and its traditions when implementing school changes. These principals must create a collaborative atmosphere so consensus building can move the school into the future. Each principal struggles to keep the vision of the school in line with the needs of board and school members. Getting the board to understand the future needs in relation to the school's mission requires that principals establish a collegial environment for enhancing views. The five year plan helps the principal and the board work collaboratively. As the school moves in the direction of the five year plan, the principal assumes the role of the leader who implements board directives.

Board meetings provide examples of the way the board and the principal define their roles in relation to the school's goals. For instance, the principal at Appleman made the decision to revise the dress code and informed the board of her rationale for the change and the objections that a few parents might raise. According to the principal, the school's dress code needed to be updated because parents had not always conformed to Appleman's standards of dress. Redefining the policy, she believed, would provide more conformity in the school. The principal at Appleman believed her role was to ensure that the dress code was reflected in the mission. There were traditions governing how students should conduct themselves, and the dress code represented the image of the school. However, many parents were unhappy about this decision, placing the Appleman principal in a difficult situation. The Appleman principal informed me that one of her board members had talked to her regarding her decision. She noted:

> The man who is going to be the chairman for the parents' committee called and asked me to go to lunch which I thought was nice. So we are both going together on the leadership of the school and I told him he will get calls from parents and told him to listen carefully and let me know if he hears things two or three times. It's important to listen to parents and find out where they are coming from and what they want for their children as well as how I can respond to their needs. But also to see if we can make modifications.

Ultimately, the principal in this instance received the board's support. At the Appleman School, the principal administers the school program and the board members support her decisions.

At Crestview School the principal had problems when parents did not understand the role of the board and its interaction with the school. Parents confused the board's role in defining policy and the principal's role in overseeing the program. In addition, parents wanted more representation on the board and felt the president of the parent organization should be included on the board. However, the principal did not feel the board needed additional parent representation. The board supported her decision to limit the number of parents for board membership. The board president at Crestview noted:

> We went through a really bad time with some parents who were very resistant to the board. The principal set down some rules about what she wanted *vis à vis* the parents, and when they confronted her about this she would implicate the board and parents would say who is this board. The parents knew no one on the board, and at first, the principal was reluctant to have parents on the board; she did not want them to know the financial situation of the school. She was very protective of the board, and she kept referring to them in terms of decisions and what not. So it took a while to overcome the fall out, and the principal has learned how to work with a board. She has really grown a lot, and I said we have got to do some examination and get this board organized.

The Bakersfield principal faced similar issues in dealing with her board. Because of her strong leadership and personality, her board often gives her considerable freedom in defining the direction of the school's goals. Her board trusts her decision-making and knows her judgment is sound. The Bakersfield principal has been there almost thirty years and is credited with developing the school's reputation for academic excellence. The board often defers to her wishes leaving her with greater freedom and flexibility than her counterparts. The Bakersfield principal has such credibility that she often had no trouble garnering board support for the school's vision.

Board Evaluation of the Principal

The board of trustees at each independent school plays a role in evaluating the principal. All three schools have different procedures for evaluating their principals as established by the school's bylaws. Board evaluation of the principal clarifies the decision-making process and serves as a way to set goals for the upcoming school year. The form of evaluation varies from a rating scale at Bakersfield to assessment of the principal's goals and her success in attaining them at Appleman. Crestview uses an open-ended question process, and board members write letters either in support or not of their principal. Because a percentage of parents are represented on the board, they too have an opportunity for input. Through evaluation, the principal is held accountable for implementing the school's mission, the quality of student outcomes and recruitment and retention of students.

At Bakersfield the entire board completes a rating form that examines all elements of the principal's skills and abilities. The information is compiled by the executive board committee and shared with other board members. At Appleman the executive board committee reviews the goals and accomplishments of the head to determine if she met her goals. The executive committee gives a report to the board (without the presence of the principal) about their findings, and a board discussion ensues. Crestview uses a similar evaluation process. The principals in this study have an excellent rapport with their board and school participants. The principals are truly respected and valued not only by the board but also by the school's parents and teachers. The principals also are evaluated on the recruitment procedures and the number of students they are able to attract. Principals are also scrutinized with respect to retention. They must do exit interviews to discover why parents decide to leave the school. Principals provide updates to the board regarding numbers and retention. Many parents, in their interviews, cited the principal's ability to respond to their needs and her ability to implement the school's mission as the reason they selected and remained at the school. Many parents believe that their principal is essential in defining the mission of their school.

The Interactive Role Between Parents, Board Members, and the Principal

The board committee structure serves a specific purpose in administering the educational program of an independent school. The board provides an approach to school management which focuses on the mission of the school and the implementation of the long range plan. This organizational structure facilitates collaboration in decision-making and involves as many participants as possible in shaping the school's program. Each board committee set goals and are accountable for their completion. These schools used goal setting through board committees to examine their curriculum and future needs and to allocate resources. The interaction between board members and school members is collaborative in establishing common goals that all agreed to pursue. The board structure balances planning for the future with responding to the present needs of the school.

The interaction among board members, the principal and other school participants creates a community of constituents who promote and preserve the mission of the school. Power becomes diffused when all participants move in the same direction and agree on the process for implementing the vision. Discussions with board presidents and principals indicated a synergy of individuals working as a collective whole rather than as individual parts (see Figure 2.4). The culture of self-governance is created through the interaction of the board and principal. Interestingly enough, when asked whose vision had been implemented, principals responded that the board was responsible, while the board presidents felt the principal had created the vision for the school's future.

Conversations with board presidents and principals about their school's future produced interesting comments on the role of the principal. At Appleman School the board president spoke glowingly of his principal:

> The principal is an excellent administrator and a wonderful business person. It is a school and a business. Public schools have been operated as schools and not as a business. If you do not operate it [the school] as a good business then you cannot operate it as a good school in this competitive age. The principal's strength is definitely business, administration and leadership. The principal has a clear vision for the school and she marshals the school. A great deal of the school's vision is due to the principal, but she has attracted people who have the same vision for the school as she has. There is no conflict here. Part of the principal's vision is to be responsible to the clientele who send their children there. It is consistent with parents' vision and there has been no conflict. The principal and parents are involved in the long range plan.

Clearly, the board president saw the principal as the source of the vision. However, the principal at Appleman saw the board as the goal setters. She noted:

> The board does not give itself enough credit. All of the school improvements being made was their vision. They stood behind unbelievable dollars and generosity and that was an enormous risk. When I think of the time and money and the trust they had, it was incredible to me. I think it's a long range plan of the board that I cling to. I think that's the gathering of committees in relation to their timelines and the importance of the committees. Chairs of board committees develop

The Board Expects Its Head Will:

- promote the mission and philosophy of the school
- serve as chief operations executive of the school
- serve as professional advisor to the board
- recommend appropriate policies for consideration by the board
- implement effectively all policies adopted and decisions made by the board
- inform the board fully and accurately regarding the program and operation of the school
- interpret the needs of the school and present professional recommendations on problems and issues to be considered by the board
- develop a budget — in conjunction with the finance committee — and keep the board current on financial matters
- recruit the best possible personnel; develop a competent faculty and staff and supervise them
- assist the board in staying aware of the attitudes of the various school constituencies — parents, students, faculty, alumni
- support the board and president in carrying out their roles
- model behavior of high ethical standards and integrity

The Head May Expect the Board to:

- Counsel and advise, giving the benefit of judgment, expertise and familiarity with the community
- consult with the head on matters the board is considering
- delegate authority for all management functions to the head
- refrain from handling administrative details
- make all employees responsible to the head
- provide support to the head and staff in carrying out their professional duties
- support the head in all decisions and actions consistent with policies of the board and standards and philosophy of the school
- hold the head accountable for the management of the school
- evaluate the work of the head

The Board and Head May Expect the President to:

- provide leadership to the board in its activities
- guide the board in fulfilling its responsibilities
- chair board meetings effectively, assuring adequate discussion of all issues, but keeping the meeting moving
- use the board's time effectively
- advise, counsel and support the head
- coordinate committee chairs
- represent the board in certain school or school related activities
- working with the nominating committee, develop selected board members to assume future leadership roles on the board
- enhance the school's image in the community

Figure 2.4: The Roles and Expectations for Board Members and the Principal

goals and visions. The most important is knowing you can trust your board president.

At Bakersfield School the interaction between the board president and principal is similar. The board president stated:

The principal is the person who has the vision and problems with high energy. Clearly the principal is the visionary. The board is responsible to set the policies and to carry out the mission. The goals were set for the board for the next five years. The principal did not set those goals for the long range plan but now it's the principal's role to make sure the goals are carried out and monitored. The board sets the goals but the principal does a great job of trying to implement the goals.

In response to the board president the principal at Bakersfield noted that:

I have an incredible love and a strong sense of responsibility and I've had such good people working with me. It takes all different people to make it such a good place; no one can do it on their own. A person can play all of the instruments in an orchestra, but no one can play them all at the same time. I know how to do most of it but I can't do it all. So we need really good people. You have to be the pacer and close enough to everyone not to lose everyone.

Because Crestview's board president is from outside the school, she does not have children attending the school like the other board presidents. She envisions the school as a way to serve the downtown corporations. She noted:

I think I have brought a business person's perspective to the school. The principal was very committed to the school arts program to see the school emphasize reading, writing and arithmetic. Corporations are looking more at family issues as well, so we now sell the school as quality education as well as family friendly, as an asset to downtown, adding to the diversity of downtown and that it has a very good arts program as well.

The principal and board president at Crestview have a mentoring relationship due to the newness of the school. Both of these individuals struggle to define their roles. This struggle in conjunction with parents' desires results in growing pains for all constituents. The principal noted her relationship with the board as evolving along with the mission of the school. She noted:

Crestview attracts high energy trustees, and they want to do things; they are very creative people. There is another independent secondary school in the community whose principal thinks you should always be in charge of your board, but that is not the case at our school. I am thankful to be able to say that I am a member of my board. We are an independent school by definition and accredited by NAIS and the structure is there. The content of our place is very different and I'm not so sure that for us and our clients that those guidelines are appropriate because the issues they were written for are very different for the Crestview School.

Each of the three schools has an interactive relationship with their board that fosters a collective vision based on shared values and goals. Most of the boards' time is spent designing a long range plan that supports the school's mission which ensures its implementation. Board members along with the principals continually return to the mission and the long range plan in their discussions of vision and goals. In these communal settings, leadership is not defined as exercising power over others but as empowering people to accomplish shared goals. The open exercise of wit and will, principle and passion, time and talent, and purpose and power allow these varied participants to accomplish a set of goals. The board structure of independent schools resembles the school advisory councils found under site-based management. But the board model at the independent schools allows for opportunities to participate that are well beyond advisory. This model gives present and past school participants a voice in the decision-making process. These participants work collectively to establish a mission that serves the school and defines its program. Facilitative power is the key to achieving significant change in schools (Goldman, Dunlap, and Conley, 1993). Participants in these independent schools are free to choose their vision and the ways and means of implementing their goals for schooling their children.

Developing Community through the Parent Organization

Privatized settings much like these independent schools offer many opportunities for parents to participate in decision-making. The schools also provide activities that allow parents and teachers to interact around the school's goals. Because of the nature of privatization, these schools find ways to give parents a voice in the school governance. They encourage participation in many areas of the school, such as representation as board members, fundraising and teacher appreciation activities through the parent organization. A partnership grows between the school and the parents' organization which supports the mission of the school and meets the needs of parents. All three schools in the study have parent organizations that support the school mission by providing fundraising activities and social events. These parent organizations function as a part of the school community, providing support for the board's mission for the school.

At the three independent schools, the parent organizations serve two functions. First, they provide social events that bond newer parents into the school community, thus creating a network among the parents, teachers and administrators. The parent organization also establishes cultural linkage through school functions and activities. School traditions, like teacher appreciation dinners, school auctions, parents' night and cookie exchange, provide opportunities for families to gather in the school setting and for parents and teachers to interact. Secondly, this organization is responsible for fundraising activities in the form of annual parent giving as well as auctions and other money-making social events.

Although each of these schools has a parent organization, these associations differ in how they assist their school. Each school's board of trustees and the parents themselves view the role of the parent association differently. In fact, parent representation from the parent organization is often misunderstood. Questions continually arise regarding the group's role in fundraising and its responsibility for social events; should it be responsible for one function or the other? Although defining its role is challenging, the parent organization is able to carve out its niche within each school and to serve as a place for parents to interact and support each other. The parent organization allows parents to be as involved as they want. Thus, this group provides an important context for supporting the school's goals, not only though fundraising but also through social events and networking among the parents.

At the Appleman and Bakersfield schools the parent organization president represents the social/parent perspective to the board of trustees. The parent organization keeps board members informed about school social events and fundraising activities. The president of the parent organization updates the board, and, in fact, attends the board meetings to report on the ongoing events of the parent organization. Allocated time on the agenda prevents the parent organization from being a key player in the decision-making process. The parent organization president plays a minimal role in the board's decision-making process. This president usually serves a one year term and reports to the board on the amounts of fundraising monies and annual giving contributed yearly in addition to tuition. Annual giving is discretionary, and parents can choose the amount they wish to donate. The school uses this additional capital for budgets or endowment, and each school develops annual campaigns differently.

At Appleman and Bakersfield the parent in charge of annual giving collects the donations and reports on the percentage of parents who contribute. Because Crestview does not have a representative from the parent organization serving on their board, the board identifies another parent representative from the school who assists the board with their annual giving. This outside parent representative is responsible for reporting to the board about Crestview's annual giving campaign. The parent organization at Crestview is fairly new and only beginning to determine how it is to support parents and the board's agenda. The role of Crestview's parent organization and annual giving is often unclear to parents, the principal and board members alike.

Both Appleman's and Bakersfield's parent organizations, established for many decades, have a tradition of events and fundraising activities that have become rituals, including the beginning of the year parent meetings with new families to assimilate them into the school and to solicit their support in school fundraising activities. These parent organizations also identify room mothers to assist with the schools' parties and field trips. The parent organization at Appleman also runs the school store as a way to bring money into the organization.

Parent Organization Meetings

Parent organization meetings are held at different times throughout the school year at Crestview and Appleman. Bakersfield does not have established parent meetings during the school year; they use school socials as a way to connect and inform their parents. Bakersfield has a sophisticated computerized parent volunteer program that identifies parents for projects based on their interests in various types of volunteer activities. These parents usually work in conjunction with the principal and her staff to form small cohesive groups for specific projects like the school auction, grandparents' day and teacher appreciation activities. (All parent volunteer projects are identified in the Parent's Handbook that assists the parents in selecting an activity. The school boasts a 100 percent participation rate according to records kept in their computer database.) Parent officers at Bakersfield hold meetings to update volunteers about the various school projects. While no formal parent meetings are held at Bakersfield, there are many informal social activities.

Appleman and Crestview, however, hold traditional evening meetings with parents several times throughout the year. The principal at Appleman meets with parents three times a year to keep them informed about school issues (tuition, summer program new school policies) and board information (long range planning, board nominations, ISACS accreditation, curriculum). Crestview uses parents' organizational meetings not only to inform parents about board/school issues but also to provide social events such as a supper for the working parents in conjunction with a traditional Halloween party. Crestview sells sodas and slices of pizza at several parent meetings to raise funds for their parent organization. Appleman's and Crestview's parent attendance at these events is high, and there is much discussion among the parents, teachers, and the principals about the school's concerns and practices. Parent meetings provide a forum for parents and an opportunity for principals to educate and respond to parents' issues.

Fundraising Activities

The fundraising activities of the parent organization play an important role in the financial stability of the school. Parent organization money is used to fund school goals, teachers' wish lists, scholarship or endowment or to supplement the general operating budget. A past parent organization president at Appleman made this comment:

> I kinda get the feeling that the board is more attentive to the parents' organization during an auction year. They are much more solicitous, not sure if that is the right word, to the parents' organization.

Two of the major fundraising activities that occur at these schools are the school auction and parent annual giving. The auction is held yearly at Bakersfield, while at Appleman and Crestview it takes place every other year. (The parent organization at Crestview did not administer the auction; it was run through the development board committee with the support of the parents' organization.) The auction places donated items up for bid by school members. In addition to raising money, these auctions are huge social events for all parents to attend and contribute to the school. The parent organization is very creative in its attempts to find donated items, develop new money making devices, and create a lavish environment for the evening of the auction. In most cases the auction is housed at the school, and all are involved in the preparation for the event. The board, principal and faculty donate items for the auction as a way to support the school financially. Comments from parents indicate they enjoyed the event as they made money for the school. Money from the parent organization auction ranged from $25,000 to $60,000 or more depending on the donated items and the size of the school. Both working and stay-at-home moms play a pivotal role in the success of the auction. While the fathers were not necessarily involved in the minute details, they were responsible for donating items and participating in the auction.

Annual Giving

Annual parent giving represents additional money, beyond tuition payments, that parents donate to their school. Annual giving funds are used differently at each school, but for the most part, the money is used to keep tuition low, provide scholarship funds, and make school improvements. Parents are well-educated about the important role that annual giving plays in the school's financial stability. Parents are informed during their admissions' tour about this additional financial support. The board's role in implementing the annual giving process is clearly defined at Bakersfield and Appleman. Parents are contacted early in the fall regarding their donations. The representatives for annual giving give regular updates to the board about the dollar amounts and percentages of parent representation. In the early days Crestview's parents were unclear about the important role of annual giving and the way these additional funds were used to reduce the cost of tuition and to make school improvements. The board and parent organization at Crestview have had to reeducate parents about the importance of annual giving.

Each annual giving campaign specifies a monetary goal that each school feels it needs to raise to achieve its financial well being. Each school tries to achieve 100 percent parent and board participation. Annual parent giving is usually administered by the parent organization in conjunction with a specific board committee. The board committees and the parent organization are accountable for establishing financial goals and defining their parent percentages. During the year of the study, Bakersfield passed their financial goal with a 70 percent participation rate. Because Appleman received a grant from a local corporation, it far surpassed its goal and achieved a 96 percent parent percentage. Crestview met its financial goals but only achieved a 50 percent parent participation rate. The amount of annual giving at the schools ranged from $6,000 to $110,000 depending on the wealth of their parents and corporate sponsors.

In interviews regarding annual giving, parents noted that they give what they can and do not feel an additional pressure to give more. The campaign takes place at the beginning of the year, and parents can donate money in one lump sum or over a period of a year. A parent noted:

> They encourage you to give whatever you can give. People (on the annual giving committee) realize that parents who have several children attending the school do not have the extra money so they leave them alone. The committee seems to know who has the money and go to them rather than the middle and lower class families.

Another parent noted:

> The board president and principal share the same view that they are not apologizing for the cost of tuition. Tuition for what parents are getting is the product. The school teaches joy of learning, independence, motivated thinkers so the tuition is worth the investment. The school should pay the faculty which drives up the cost of tuition but annual giving supports this school and all parents know that.

A minority parent made the following statement about annual giving:

> I do not feel guilty, but I was probably one of the lowest donors, but I still received a nice letter from the board. So it all counts.

Parents are positive about annual giving because it supports the school and helps defray the cost of tuition.

Defining the Role of the Parent Organization

The role of the parent organization is more than fundraising. It offers the opportunity for parents to meet to discuss school and family issues. Parents use their relationship with other parents at the school to solve problems, share resources, and develop social interactions (Swick, 1988). The parent organization becomes the place to discuss concerns with other parents. In fact, it often serves as a forum for parents to air their complaints with the school. When parents enter the school they are informed about the formal process for handling complaints. If a parent has a concern they usually begin with the teacher. If the issue is not resolved, then they meet with the principal. Parents are encouraged not to complain to board members because the board's role involves policy not school issues. However, my observations and interviews indicated that the parent organization in these schools became a place for parents to vent their frustrations. The process worked like this: Parents participating in school volunteer projects talked to other parents to test their theory of a possible problem. Through conversation, parents gained support for their causes. If a parent discovered that others shared the problem, then a discussion ensued about a potential solution. If the problem did not get resolved then usually a call to the president of the parent organization followed. The past president of the parent organization at Appleman and the president at Crestview noted that the parent organization became a forum for complaints. These two noted:

> This year has been a quiet year but past years the president [of the parent organization] was bombarded with complaints and phone calls. Like the weather wasn't so bad so there should have been school.

and:

> When a parent complains to me I tell them the best thing is to talk to the teacher. She complained to the principal and in the end that parent should have contacted the teacher about their concerns. The school is very responsive.

In a healthy way, however, the parent organization becomes an avenue for parents to meet with other parents, to visit about school issues and to address their child rearing concerns. The parent organization, a community of support, provides opportunities to focus on the school's goals. This group seeks to engage all the families in the life of the school. In spite of these efforts, discussions with parents indicated that the role of the parent organization was unclear. At times it provided social events and raised funds, but at other times it seemed a place for parents socially to interact with other parents. The more parents were involved with the parents' organization, the better their understanding of its financial role. However, most parents viewed their parent organization as an opportunity to share and meet other parents. Most discussions with parents revealed they were unclear about the parent organization. They often wanted to know its purpose and its connection to the schools. Some parents noted:

> The parent organization is there to support the parents and to be a liaison between the school and parents. The main objective is to be there and assist the board;

> The parent group is the intermediary between parents' concerns and facilities. Concerns lead to school improvement and a change in policies; a representative voice for us and a go between. All the grades are involved;

From my perspective the organization is not so much financial but is a link to the school through a wish list for the teachers and a great way to get parents involved;

The parent organization is a control mechanism for working mothers. Mothers are around all day in the school if anything weird is going on, then everybody would know;

It serves many purposes but is a bridge to the school. The parent organization is fairly new and not well formed;

I see people venting all the time but with the type of contact here it is bound to happen. If tuition goes up, they gripe but they are going to pay it;

Crestview is made up of single parents and working parents so the role is to create an environment and events with the opportunity to be a support group and a social group.

It is clear the parent organization plays a crucial role in the independent school's mission. Although the Crestview parent organization is newly established and, as such, is grappling with its identity and purpose, there is still a sense of commitment to this organization. At Appleman and Bakersfield the parent organizations are more established through long-term traditions that are held every year. These two schools use the parent organization to anchor the school by raising funds to support the long range plan. The parent organization allows parents to be autonomous in deciding how to be involved and at what level. Parents are empowered when the school gives them the flexibility of determining how parent organization funds will be distributed.

Conclusion

The survival of the independent private school depends upon the creation of cultural linkages where participants are given opportunities to contribute to the school. The school creates a community through the parent organization and board governance structure where parents are given shared power in defining policies and the use of resources. Parents understand what the school is about and they support its mission. Each school has a strong organizational culture based on its traditions and rituals that parents and students anticipate as they go through each grade. There is mutual respect among its participants, which allows for differences and facilitates compromise through open and honest discussions.

Being privatized enhances the school's capacity to be responsive. The schools are able to retain parents by creating an allegiance to mission and by responding to their needs. There is a balance between traditions and progress that allows the school to focus on its goals and future needs. The school's mission is continually evaluated through a collaborative process that involves studying the future needs of students in the areas of curriculum, technology, facility and market forces. The development of the long range plan is a collaborative process that involves input from all the constituencies. The planning process of a privatized school requires its participants to shape their vision by re-examining their traditions and reflecting on their future needs. The mission — not the market — drives the school toward self-improvement.

The organizational structure of the board of trustees allows more individuals to exercise power in the administration of the school. Collaborative involvement by all school participants gives these individuals a voice in the school. An element of trust is created due to the equal distribution of power in the school's governance. Each school in the study is committed to including a certain percentage of parents within its board structure. Board members, selected for their expertise rather than their political power, are well educated about the board committee process, their roles in defining the school's mission, and establishing the long range goals.

Independent schools define their mission by responding to the voice of their constituencies. School participants are held accountable for their ability to educate students and implement their mission. Competition within the metropolitan area requires these schools to define their mission base as a way to attract and retain parents. Quality of mission is the focus and not on what other schools are doing. Parents identify with the educational mission and entrust the school to teach their child. If parents are unhappy with the school, they have the opportunity to voice their concerns or leave. To maintain a strong affiliation with parents, each school establishes many ways parents can become involved in the school program and governance. Parents are also held accountable by their participation on board committees and school activities. This shared responsibility leads to joint ownership and a commitment to student learning.

The culture of privatized schools establishes a community that is rooted in tradition and balanced with innovation and accountability. Independent schools are more like communities than organizations. Members of these communities are interconnected and committed to the school mission. There is a bonding that relies on the interdependence of all the school participants. Privatized schools are communities of individuals who share the same educational goals for their children and work collaboratively toward that vision. In contrast, public schools that are centralized are created by others who may not have the same intentions as those who receive the service. Moreover, they provide no mechanisms for voice, as they are controlled by a bureaucratic hierarchy. Bureaucratic linkages, as opposed to cultural linkages, establish a hierarchy where constituents' desires and mandated policies have no commonality. Independent schools, on the other hand, are communities, culturally linked by shared norms, similar needs and purposes and a natural interdependence. The organizational structure of independent schools allows for collaboration, open dialogue and accountability. To retain their participants, these privatized schools have to create an organizational structure that empowers constituencies with a significant role in defining the schools' educational goals.

Chapter 3

The Leadership and Management of Independent School Principals

Realities of Leading a Privatized Setting

The collaborative decision-making model found in independent schools provides an integrated process for policy-making, planning, resource allocation and evaluation of curriculum and educational goals. Because the board members, parents, and principals share power, all constituencies feel a sense of ownership which leads to accountability of student outcomes. School participants work toward the same mission and goals because they have a vested interest in maintaining the school community. A sense of belonging, continuity of traditions and an inner connectedness provides meaning to the participants. Creating school ownership is dependent on the leadership and management of the private school principal. The administrative style needed in these settings requires the principals to balance their authority and autonomy so that participants are empowered in the governance structure. The role of the principal is to establish an environment where school participants are partners in pursuing common goals and share the responsibility for educating its students.

The intent of this chapter is to examine the type of leadership and management needed to administer self-governed schools. The context of privatization requires a leadership style characterized by responsiveness and empowerment for participants. A principal in an independent school needs to have the capacity to hear the many voices in the school and lead the school community to realize a common vision. This context requires a participatory management style, and an ability to work collectively to manage the affairs of the school focusing on learning, teaching and the educational goals. The principal must listen to each constituency and articulate each group's perspective in the decision-making process. In addition, the principal has to educate the participants about policy issues and future trends that may impact the school and their mission. Principals must create a coalition for change and politically negotiate all the school's participants' needs.

Because parents can remove their children from an independent school at any time, principals, accountable for retention, must be responsive to their needs. A difficulty comes with keeping the wishes of parents in the forefront, yet still maintaining the vision of the educational program. Principals also have to distinguish when a group of parents has a legitimate grievance and when a few disgruntled parents are merely unhappy. Principals spend considerable time and energy educating parents about the process for voicing their concerns. Often parents, who view themselves as initiators of change, approach a principal about some idea or school innovation that might be integrated into the school mission. Parents and principals engage in an interactive dialogue that leads to compromise for the good of the school. Principals must maintain a collaborative environment by listening and responding to parents in order to establish a parent's ownership to the school.

The leadership and management style necessary in a context of collaboration requires an ability to compromise, discern future needs, and retain a sense of the school mission. The principal's leadership qualities must build a communal environment so that the school continues its mission and redefines itself through the long range planning. As new participants join the school community, a new sense of goal consensus emerges. Leading the ever-evolving community of a self-governed privatized school requires that the principal rely on the ability of community members to assist in shaping the school program. To translate the wishes of school participants into administrative actions, the principal must listen and lead with consensus in mind. The principal must involve the participants and harness their energy to build and maintain morale. Such leadership creates a strong institutional culture by empowering individuals to participate in the decision-making process and equipping them with the necessary knowledge and skills to support the governance structure.

The job of an independent school principal produces considerable strain. To retain parents, they must be responsive to complaints while maintaining control of the school program. They must balance the desire to collaborate and work toward consensus with the need to assert authority in order to maintain a coherent program. Creating consensus among school participants without appearing to favor a specific group requires openness and diplomacy. The struggle to acknowledge everyone's opinion, yet maintain a common vision for the school can produce stress. Principals need coping skills that foster the capacity for problem solving. Although these principals are grateful for their support systems, which involve parents, board members, faculty, and staff, listening to everyone's complaints and leading the various constituencies to a common vision is a constant challenge. Sergiovanni (1990a) believes that 'value-added leadership' indicates that principals are less concerned with controlling what people do, when they do it, and how, and are more concerned with controlling what they accomplish. Managing the vision for all school participants in independent schools requires a leadership style where the 'playing fields are leveled' and all have a voice. Facilitating everyone's needs while maintaining a certain degree of authority can produce stress for an independent school principal.

The principalship in independent schools involves many organizational dimensions besides administering the school program. Independent school leaders function as a combination of public school principal and district administrator. The principal bears the responsibility for fundraising and development, fiscal management of the school budget, alumni development, selection of faculty and school staff, student admissions' tours and recruitment. These principals use support staff to assist them with fundraising, marketing and curriculum development. The principals must maintain amicable relationships with parents and staff in order to maintain the collaborative environment of the school. Working to create a school environment that fosters ownership can be both frustrating and fulfilling for principals who must schedule the time it takes to ensure participatory decision-making. Principals create opportunities for teachers to work collaboratively so the school mission becomes a reality in the school culture. Principals act as advocates for both parents and teachers to ensure that there is a high degree of accountability.

Leadership for Self-governed Schools

Caldwell and Spinks (1992) believe that leaders in self-governed schools, like independent schools, must have a cultural, strategic, educational, and responsive leadership style if the school is to improve. Ideally, the leaders at these independent schools create a cultural leadership based on the school's mission and its long range planning. The principals build a 'value laden' organization that leads to the ability of collective problem solving and accountability. These principals use long range planning sessions that allows them to determine the school's future needs. Opportunities to improve an independent school comes from the long range plan, but the ability to implement these initiatives depends on the leadership of the principal to direct the school towards completion of its goals.

Because the leaders of these independent schools are accountable for the quality of their graduates, they must continually evaluate their school's program. This means they need to trust and empower their teachers to make good decisions about the educational program. In addition, these principals must develop performance indicators that assess the type of graduate shaped by the school's educational program. Independent school principals have to be responsive to parents, balancing their agendas with those of the teachers, listening with respect and compromising when necessary. The leadership of independent schools requires a style that creates a collective 'we' and a tradition of 'the way things are done around here'. Being autonomous in administering the school's program would have prevented them from developing communal support for the school goals.

Bolman and Deal (1994) believe that we need to change the way we prepare leaders for schools, shifting emphasis from management to leadership. Management implies controlling through budget, planning, and performance appraisal. Leaders for the future must be able to set the right direction, establish vision and strategies, get people aligned and commitment, and inspire people to action to overcome obstacles. These principals demonstrate their ability to lead schools from past practices to new paradigms for the future. They are facilitators who promote open, frank, and frequent communication with school participants. These educational leaders are flexible thinkers, responsive practitioners, and risk takers, able to translate their ideals for the school into practices that all participants understand and accept.

Leadership Needed for an Independent School

The independent school principals in this study have many commonalities in years of experience, eclectic backgrounds and personal lives. All were females with independent school experience, and none was trained in typical educational administration programs. The Crestview and Bakersfield principals were considered founders of their schools. The Bakersfield principal had been with her school the longest, while the Crestview principal had only started the school seven years ago. The Appleman principal, although not a founder, was known for her ability to lead the school forward. Both the Appleman and Bakersfield principals were older with grown children and similar experiences. The Crestview principal, on the other hand, was younger and inexperienced in dealing with school issues.

The principals at Appleman and Bakersfield are married women, approaching their early 50s, who had raised their families. The principal at Crestview School, in her late 30s and divorced, is a single parent who recently adopted an African American child. The Crestview principal had worked as a teacher in another independent school before beginning the Crestview School. Mrs Bates was the admissions director at Appleman before she was asked to become the principal seven years ago. Previous to Mrs Bates' appointment as principal of Appleman, there were problems with too much parent involvement and a lack of coherence to the mission. She earned the board's respect for her ability 'to turn the school around' during her early years as principal. Dr Brimming had been with the Bakersfield School almost since its beginning when the school expanded its service from a preschool program to a full elementary school. During her tenure of nineteen years, the school increased in size and developed a satellite campus in another area of the county.

All three principals have college degrees in areas other than education. Dr Brimming has a doctorate in counseling which she considers essential to creating a collaborative environment. Her previous work experience includes university teaching. Her connection to Bakersfield School came through her children's enrollment at the school and her involvement in their Montessori program. Dr Brimming was asked to be the principal when the original founder left. With a degree in marketing, Mrs Bates was a retailer for a business firm before her marriage. She returned to the workplace as Appleman's admission director after her children were in high school. Ms Clue's undergraduate degree is in speech pathology, and she has a masters in business administration. Employed at another independent school, she noted that the school was not responsive to the needs of working parents. She founded the Crestview School to develop a community where working parents could find additional support and resources. But she lacked experience particularly with respect to promoting and leading the school community.

Leadership and management are not always mutually exclusive. Bolman and Deal (1994) believe that good leadership involves the ability to draw consensus among the participants and become a consultant in the process. Leadership is seen as synonymous with making major changes to the present system that will guide the institution to systematic changes. The public schools have focused on management rather than leadership which enacts rules and procedural changes. Management, an authority structure, ensures the system functions well; thus a well-managed school is one that does not tinker with the present system. Bolman and Deal (1994) believe that the bureaucratic structure of public schools must be reduced because it is resistant to change. The focus for educators today is to re-examine the leadership in order to make substantive changes in schools. Leadership is contextual, and administrators must have a deep understanding of the cultures in which schools are embedded. Administrators who are good leaders understand politics; they are political negotiators, who build the right coalitions and reach upward to the forces that have more power. Leadership involves more than implementing one's vision; the principal must reflect on the various competitive points of view and orchestrating all parties toward the harmony of a common vision.

The principals of these independent schools are well regarded by school participants for their ability to lead. Mrs Bates is recognized for creating a cohesive board and redefining the direction of Appleman School. Dr Brimming successfully led her school through many capital campaigns that made Bakersfield into a highly acclaimed academically rigorous program. Ms Clue is noted for creating a school that meets the needs of working parents. In each school setting the principal is able to implement a common vision and create a consensus of purpose. Each principal understands what the school means to its participants and how her leadership serves to create cultural linkages for the school community.

In addition, these independent school principals bring a feminist perspective to their leadership which seems ideally suited to their environments. Shakeshaft's (1987) analysis of women school administrators revealed that in their language characteristics, women were more concerned with listening, using more emotional and detailed speech than their male counterparts. Women were perceived as being more democratic and participatory than men. Less committed to formal hierarchy than men, women build coalitions in order to reach their desired goals and evaluate their decisions more often than men. Women in this study truly value the input of their school participants and seek validation of their decision-making. Valli's (1992) analysis of feminist pedagogy indicates a women's approach with the goal of creating a more balanced world view. A feminist values' approach means a leadership style that creates dialogue among school participants bonded as a reflective community.

Because of their feminist perspectives, the principals in these independent schools were collaborative rather than autonomous in administering their school programs. These women principals take a gentler approach in working with families. Parents noted that the principals were wonderful in their ability to engage them in the school setting. Somehow the principal at each site is able to enlist the support of parents through her own personal influence. It is unclear whether the principal's gender or her leadership style creates this sense of community. However, observations of the principals' interactions with board members, students, faculty, and parents affirm many of Shakeshaft's (1987) tenets about the female educational administrator. These women are very caring, and engaging individuals, who listen to the parents' needs, and seek validation for their decisions through a collaborative process.

Mrs Bates' Leadership Style

Mrs Bates began her duties at Appleman as the school secretary assisting the school admissions director. She had returned to the workforce after raising two children and had reached a point in her life where she noted:

> I volunteered throughout the community. I then reached a point in my life where I had to do something. I got lucky being able to come out here and then two years later the principal got ill and I was asked to be the permanent principal.

She believes her mission for the school is to

> always strive for excellence, always work with the individuals in the school and motivate the students to work hard towards excellence. I think the key is a standard of excellence for everyone involved in the school and strong academics.

She is noted for turning the school around when it was unclear about its mission. Teachers and parents who had known Mrs Bates in the early days believe that she was able to clarify the school's intent and moved the school toward the twenty-first century. Her leadership accomplishments include:

- increasing the teachers' salaries;
- initiating a capital campaign to increase the size of the school and improve the science program;
- appointing a task force to implement new technology into the classroom;
- implementing a child centered preschool program;
- developing an after school enrichment school program and parents' extended day care for working parents;

- increasing the endowment to provide for more economic diversity at the school;
- developing a summer camp program in a nearby setting to provide summer enrichment programs;
- developing a stronger network for identifying alumni;
- appointing an *ad hoc* committee to examine the recruitment of minority children into the school; and
- creating opportunities for the school's growth through the summer camp exchange program and through reorganizing the school program.

She felt the school needed these changes to expand its marketing and attract students. Accomplishing her vision, yet maintaining the school's mission and traditions posed a challenge to her leadership. While implementing her agenda involved risk, Mrs Bates created growth potential for the school.

Under her leadership, the school re-evaluated its mission, becoming more student oriented while maintaining its academic excellence. She identified a pool of students for the school focusing on economic diversity, minority recruitment and former alumni. She has also educated the board to recognize that the traditional nuclear family is changing so new programs were added to meet the needs of working parents. For example, the preschool program was also reorganized to focus on a more child-centered program. Appleman's preschool program was a traditional teacher-directed program that many parents felt was not responsive to newer views of child development. Although Mrs Bates valued the tradition of the nuclear family, she knew that the school needed to be more responsive to the needs of its working parents. She was able to balance Appleman's traditional view of the family with the new agenda. The school used its extended day program as a way to attract new parents to the school while retaining its traditional roots. Thus the school was marketed as a traditional school that is responsive to the needs of working parents in order to recruit new families to its program. In addition to building connections with new parents, Mrs Bates was the first to make connections with past graduates.

Mrs Bates provides leadership to her teachers by encouraging academic freedom and by providing significant funds for their professional development and curriculum needs. She commented that for the school to remain current she needs to support the faculty. She believed:

> I never want to leave the faculty abandoned. I think discipline is not just the responsibility of the faculty but all of us. My personal challenge is finding a balance of parents who want a more rigid school and those that want a more child-centered program. I want a place where the students can make relationships. I do think security can come through that. And if they feel they have adult advocates they can trust, I think we have done something special for them.

She uses a goal-evaluation process to evaluate teachers and provides support in helping them achieve their goals. She believes that to remain competitive with the other schools she cannot afford to employ average or even good teachers; they must be excellent. The school uses a very sophisticated screening process to find teachers. She is responsible for reducing the hierarchy between the lead and assistant teacher, producing a more collaborative classroom setting and, as a result, more cross disciplinary activities. She encourages teachers to do more than worksheets but wants the teachers to experiment with a variety of instructional practices. She supports teachers' requests for professional development and provides many journals for teachers to read.

During her tenure at the school she has only requested that two families leave the school because the school was not appropriate for their children. Her philosophy is to work through the problems with the family and compromise when possible. When parents make complaints she looked for commonalities before she discusses the parents' issue with the teacher. However, she noted that:

> If the parent is a complainer then I chalk it up to a parent pushing their own agenda and lifestyle. This parent is not willing to support the school. Teachers cannot be all things for all people, but it is the responsibility of the school to help the child have the experience of the whole quilt.

Mrs Bates is responsible for the daily operation of the school program. She feels the stress of being held accountable by all the school participants. But she believes parents' observations can be helpful in maintaining the quality of the educational program. The board holds her accountable for both the test scores and the acceptance rates of Appleman students into secondary schools and colleges. She views her commitment to the school as one of her strongest leadership qualities. She believes that 'the school is always striving to be better and that's exciting and not threatening'. The school's continued mission to examine the quality of its former seventh graders in the areas of math and science is important to her for enhancing the school's accountability and reputation. She has worked over the years to 'soften' the board's reliance on standardized measures of student performance, but she uses the test scores herself to reflect the wonderful job the teachers are doing. Initially the transition from the school's traditional teacher-directed curriculum to the more child-centered preschool program worried her because she feared it might affect the students' test scores as they progressed in school. However, the school's achievement has remained high long after the early childhood program was implemented. She, along with the curriculum director, is committed to examining the quality of students through their interaction with the secondary schools. The curriculum director, with the support of the principal, sends letters to the secondary school teachers requesting their input for ways to improve the elementary program. As a result, the school revised its math program and reorganized its curriculum to provide more opportunities for critical thinking activities.

Although it takes much of her time Mrs Bates favors doing the admissions recruitment because she is committed to becoming acquainted with the families. She did approximately 100 admissions' tours that lasted over an hour each and several open house programs during weekends. While she had seen peaks and valleys with board members, over time the board has become more professionally educated about the nature of schooling. She likes the board to think they are autonomous and seldom interrupts or clarifies points made during board committee reports. She is quite passive, less vocal, and very respectful of board members, using the board meetings as forums to share her ideas for school change. Her good rapport with board members results in their support for her leadership and management style. She encourages board members to attend school activities and to observe in the classrooms. Board meetings are closed to her staff members, but she is beginning to realize the importance of their input when key issues are addressed. She is more autonomous in making school decisions knowing she keeps board members informed about school policies. Although collaborative with some of her staff, she appears to maintain some distance from others; she often noted the loneliness of being the principal at Appleman. Her tendency to work with her staff on a one to one basis within an isolated context results in some difficulties. Staff often show concern that Mrs Bates spreads herself too thin, involving herself in every decision and not giving her staff enough autonomy.

However, Mrs Bates has a wonderful way with people. She has very sophisticated interpersonal listening skills, makes supportive comments to the school community, affirms the ideas of others, uses politically correct language and responds in a very personal way. Her strengths come from her ability to listen and react with both savvy and sensitivity. Appreciative of the school's seventy-five years of history, she is both traditional and visionary. When she came to Appleman, the school was going through a difficult transition, grappling with its niche in the marketplace. Under Mrs Bates' leadership, the school has maintained its tradition of academic excellence but softened its image to be more child-centered. Because of the school's sense of tradition, she has had to move slowly to implement new programs and make facility changes. She has united parents from the past and present in the task of re-evaluating the school's mission, gradually broadening the image of the Appleman family to include working parents as well as the traditional nuclear family. Without creating political chaos, she reorganized the school to respond to the challenge of assisting working parents. Politically savvy, Mrs Bates often internalizes many of her worries about new school changes. She is continually conscious of the broader context of the school and the impact of her decision-making on the entire school. Respectful toward staff, she listens to their input but at times is swayed by the need to put families first rather than to support her staff. She greatly values her school participants but feels the need to have the last word in decisions.

Dr Brimming's Leadership Style

Dr Brimming, who has been with the Bakersfield school for over twenty-four years, was asked to serve as principal because of her involvement with her children's education during their school years. She originally taught in the public schools for two years at the elementary level but made the decision to become a certified counselor to serve the needs of her students. When she completed her masters in elementary counseling, the university asked her to administer the elementary counseling program. After completing her coursework in counseling, she returned to the area where she finished the research for her dissertation. She became involved with Bakersfield, serving initially as a part-time principal and eventually as the full-time director. All three of her children have attended the school, which she believes 'has had a lot to do with my children's incredible start in their own careers'. She does not believe the school's mission has changed much over the last twenty years. She stated:

> The first time we wrote a mission was in 1983 and it was very inter-
> esting. All of the teachers, parents and board wrote what they thought
> the mission was. The words were the same: responsibility, respect, the
> diversity, the Montessori. It was all there. The board has supported
> me on some things. In 1983 we were still poor. I brought the idea
> of hiring a consultant to look at long range planning. It was in that
> process that we wrote the mission statement that has been written
> only twice, it's usually one or two words. The overall mission is very
> much the same. The only thing that has changed is the upper element-
> ary. It used to be pure Montessori; if kids wanted to make model
> planes they can. There were no lessons or assignments like multipli-
> cation tables. Part of me wondered if that were OK. The students were
> having some problems in the seventh grade. Now the educational
> program is Montessori through first grade, transition in second and
> third and more departmentalized in the upper grades. This way they
> are ready for seventh grade.

She found that her vision for the school came from the long range planning sessions and her interaction with the local community. She had been
approached from various individuals within the community to expand the
school's size and program. First the school's next door neighbors approached
her about purchasing their home for additional school space. Next, a real
estate planner initiated a plan for the school to open a satellite campus in a
new housing development. In its long range planning, Bakersfield attempted
to envision itself in twenty-five years, considering what the school might look
like, what it could be, and what pool of students might be recruited. Both Dr
Brimming and Mrs Bates were offered opportunities to expand the school's
size and program through their contacts within the community. During Dr

Brimming's many years as principal, the school increased the number of faculty staff members from nine to forty-nine, earned accreditation with the National Association of Independent Schools, reached financial stability, developed the school as a strong entity in the community, reorganized the board structure for the school's needs, and implemented major structural changes to increase the student population. The school recently renovated a home nearby to provide more preschool opportunities and undertook a major plan to expand the school's organizational structure to include a secondary program. The school implemented after-school hours, summer enrichment and 'when there's no school camp programs in its response to working parents. Bakersfield School has planned a major construction phase to develop a high school program for its students within the next five years. Dr Brimming believes that it is important to see where you are going to modify the program to meet new situations and the different needs of a changing community.

Dr Brimming has a high level of energy and a strong personality, yet she is solely dependent on the board and staff for her support in the independent school environment. She has worked to develop a cooperative relationship since she 'did not like coming down hard'. She values consensus and finds that implementing controversial school issues is easier through collaboration and consensus. She does not like being perceived as the 'bad guy' and, over the years, has learned better ways to empower her school participants. For example, her desire to decentralize her authority shows in the development of the school schedule. In the past, every time she made the school's master schedule, Dr Brimming would hear complaints. She decided to meet with the parents, teachers, and administrative staff to compromise on times and dates. After a six hour meeting, the schedule was approved by all the participants. Now the school has a schedule committee open to all participants who want input. Although parents are supportive of Dr Brimming, there has been some controversy over her philosophy of discipline. At one point, a few parents left the school when several children with severe discipline problems were not asked to leave. Dr Brimming was committed to the educational program and believed all children would benefit from its curriculum. While the decision to continue working with the problem children involved risk, she does not regret taking it. In her many years at the school she has only dismissed one child. She suspends children if it is necessary but she encourages her teachers to use role playing and journaling to address their discipline concerns. She believes the 'hands on' Montessori approach is useful in preventing discipline problems.

Teachers do not necessarily view Dr Brimming as their 'boss' but rather as an equal partner in the school program. She noted:

> We have smart teachers with access to their own things. I pretty much give them whatever they need. They go to workshops and classes and make additions or develop new curriculum when necessary. I am against a written set curriculum. The curriculum is left up to the teachers. We look for weaknesses and needs on the standardized

tests. The testing indicates our focus and we address it immediately. Some teachers here may not realize how much autonomy they have. At the other public schools the curriculum is restricted, and I do not want them feeling restricted.

Dr Brimming supports a teaming approach in working with her teachers. She encourages them to pursue professional goals that keep them current. She encourages teachers to work collaboratively when considering any curriculum revisions.

The board at Bakersfield seems less dependent on test scores and second-ary school placements than Appleman's board. The parents have a great deal of faith in Dr Brimming's knowledge of testing and value her opinions about curriculum issues. Dr Brimming's parents share their children's successes with her and recognize that Bakersfield School prepares their children for schooling at the secondary level. Dr Brimming describes her feelings toward parents and students as follows:

Our kids are really neat kids; they are well prepared students, good leaders, and followers. I'm not one to lay too much emphasis on testing. A lot of what we do is by observation. If you look at the reports they write, books they read, and math, you can tell how they are doing. It's not happening by osmosis or magic; its good teaching. The parents also trust and know we have a lot of experience and respect that. We can handle a lot of kids and be successful, that doesn't happen at the other schools.

She does not place value on screening toddlers or preschool children for their acceptance into the school and believes any child can benefit from the pro-gram. The school does test elementary students and asks students for a writing sample to assess for areas of remediation. Dr Brimming could not think of a time during her years at Bakersfield when teachers have not accepted a child at the school.

Each year Dr Brimming sends a personal letter to the parents letting them know what is going on in her life. For example, she had cancer surgery about three years ago and she gave them a health update along with information on the importance of mammograms. She feels that being open with parents creates an atmosphere of sharing and finds great strength in her counseling background. She recognizes difficulty in balancing parents' complaints with a desire to be true to the mission of the school. She noted:

I have to respect their opinion but let them know sometimes they have to make a choice. For some families this is not the place for them. For the family that wanted a science text book, I told them we love them but this is not the place for them. Things like that show we don't sell out. We take suggestions from parents but know we can't do everything. I do appreciate their point of view. Also, there are issues like expelling those two students; I had to make a judgment call and knew I couldn't expel them. It wasn't selling out. I think we have been very true to the mission.

Although she seldom receives parent complaints, she feels committed to responding to parents' needs. For example because the school does not have a cafeteria, the children have to bring their lunches and many parents often expressed the need for some solution to this problem. In response, she recently added a lunch program for the school, taking the initiative to locate a caterer who could provide the luncheon service for the students. The principal finds that parents are invaluable in finding solutions to school issues.

Dr Brimming appears more collaborative in her decision-making than Mrs Bates. There are no clear boundaries of duties, but various staff members are responsible for finances and publications. She makes final decisions but not before she has talked with her staff. Her very cohesive staff regularly have lunch at the same time to exchange ideas. She does not consider her job to be lonely because she has support from her administrative team and other independent school principals. Her family also plays a pivotal role in supporting the long hours of her work schedule. She has had little staff turnover and views the faculty as her family. She remains in contact with former employees who have left the school as well as with many of the families. While the staff greatly respect the principal, at times they are overwhelmed by her high energy. She is viewed by the school community as hard working and driven, but she is respected for her vision and leadership.

Dr Brimming has a very strong personality that many parents feel makes her an advocate for the school. Unlike Mrs Bates, she is very vocal at board meetings and believes that all administrative staff should provide reports to the board. The board president at Bakersfield feels that Dr Brimming's leadership style is an asset to the school because she is a good communicator who gives everyone a chance to be heard. He noticed that Dr Brimming has an uncanny ability to know when to push her agenda and how to engage board members in her way of thinking. He feels a person does not stay in power for as long as Dr Brimming has without knowing the various types of personalities at the school. Dr Brimming believes strongly in the Meyers Briggs type indicator test in defining the personalities of her staff. This testing helps her understand how to cultivate the strengths and weaknesses of her teachers and the other administrative members. Dr Brimming maintains the very strong religious belief that God is in charge of her school without being a religious fanatic. She believes that things happen for a reason like the opportunity presented by a neighbor to buy his house or the invitation to open a satellite campus. Given such an opportunity, she has the initiative and vision to lead the board in a new direction for the school. She is a risk taker who leaves herself open for criticism. As the board president noted she does not want one family unhappy with the school. Dr Brimming's leadership took the school from a mom-and-pop preschool program to a sophisticated elementary program that has increased its visibility within the private school community as a competitive and academically rigorous school.

Ms Clue's Leadership Style

Ms Clue is the founding principal at Crestview School. She had worked previously as an assistant director in another independent school as a liaison between the home and school. In this job she discovered that a third of the families were either working or single moms. She encountered many women who came crying to her about the conflicting demands of working and being a mother. These working parents often felt distant from the school site because they were unable to attend school programs and school conferences. She did some market research to determine if a school had been developed specifically for working families. In doing her research, she discovered there was no such school for working families so she approached several business corporations to identify sources for funding in order to develop her school. After receiving financial support from several corporations, she then had difficulty locating a place for the school in the downtown metropolitan area. Eventually, she met with the staff from a local downtown church which was undergoing a transition to a smaller group of parishioners. She developed a partnership with the church resulting in shared rental space and renovated the building into an open school. The school opened in 1987 with twenty-four students, which has grown to sixty students within the last six years.

According to Ms Clue's vision for the school, Crestview was to support working parents through the school community. She had to consider child care for the future rather than just focus on a latch key program. The mission evolved as a concern for contemporary children and the time they spent waiting for their parents to come home from work. She sees a great need for urban schools to be more responsive to working parents by providing enrichment activities once the school day is completed. Crestview School provides swimming, dance, music, computer activities, and competitive sports through the YMCA as enrichment once the academics are over. The school program is designed intentionally to keep students engaged all day. When parents leave the school at the end of the day, they have family time that is not interrupted by taking their children to a soccer game or music lesson. Ms Clue found that in reaching out to working parents, she is dealing with people who were not educated about private schools. In fact, many of the school's parents had little understanding of the board committee structure that is essential to these schools. Parents often misunderstand the intent of annual giving and parent representation on the board. However, as the school gains in sophistication the families are beginning to understand their role in the school's governance. The parent organization is redefining itself to play a greater role in assisting the school financially and educationally. Interviews with parents indicate that they perceive a family atmosphere at the school and a support system for them.

She sees her role as taking care of the external concerns such as the board's needs and financial planning while the assistant director is responsible for internal issues such as the curriculum and teacher hiring. (At Appleman and Bakersfield the principals play a major role in both the internal and external concerns.) This focus on external issues allows Ms Clue the opportunity to interact with the business community to obtain financial support for the school. Ms Clue took some risks in initiating a school in the downtown site. Over time, she saw herself grow by having a better understanding of her own abilities and limitations. She has limited experience in working with corporations and is developing her leadership skills in working with her board. The board president noted Ms Clue's progress.

> She has really grown a lot. Last year was a hard year in trying to move ahead with the strategic plan. Ms Clue does not have the staff to help her and she also has a confusion of roles in the school. The school is undergoing renovations to provide her with more privacy. That separation alone is really important to how the school functions.

The board president and the principal have a mentoring relationship that began when the school started. Over time, as the principal gained more confidence, she views her role as externally driven, finding sources of funds to maintain the school. The school is at a critical point in its ability to achieve a sense of status within the private school community. She is also striving to find financial support from downtown corporations.

Under Ms Clue's leadership the school has increased its student population and implemented its mission for working parents. She believes the school needs to remain innovative by hiring youthful teachers with little or no public school experience, then shape them into creative teachers without the taint of the public school bureaucracy. She noted:

> The assistant director and I have an understanding that ownership is an action and I allow our young staff to find their own way, which lends itself to their ownership of the school.

She noted that her young inexperienced teachers are overwhelmed by their choices and autonomy, but they are able to look beyond the traditional ways of public schools. She believes that teachers need to be empowered for several reasons:

> Part of our reason is our belief (the assistant director and the principal) in the profession of education and how the traditional model is very gender restrictive, women, all at one level, and then a male principal leading the flock of sheep. That culture is not comfortable or healthy for us here at Crestview. I think children absorb most of their

socialization and leadership skills from observing models as opposed to their being told. And we really want the children at Crestview to understand that they have to take care of the world.

Ms Clue explained that many of her students came from public schools where they were both behaviorally and academically lost in their school. The school's year-round program proved a luxury because they have more opportunity to be involved in the children's daily lives. The school uses an open classroom setting and the curriculum is very nontraditional. Students have great freedoms and opportunities for self discovery. The principal believes that empowering children prepares them for some really hard choices. She noted: 'Power is feeling strong enough to make judicious decisions about your life.' Although the students do well academically at the school according to the school's standardized testing, the principal and assistant principal realize that they need to do more than just talk about the students' successes. They use a screening assessment for incoming students because they want to ensure that the nontraditional school program will benefit all of its students. They will take students with learning problems if the student can benefit from the educational program. Many parents note that several students who had severe learning problems when they entered the school have improved tremendously because of the school's commitment for all children to learn.

Although Ms Clue defined the school under the independent school label, she finds that the accreditation process used by the NAIS is stifling. She is not sure that the independent school guidelines are appropriate for their program. She noted:

> American education is very old fashioned and very staid. Independent schools under NAIS do not study my client, they study the typical client and that does not necessarily apply here.

Ms Clue is not the traditional principal as found at Appleman and Bakersfield. She is a risk taker willing to reinvent schooling on her own terms. Because of her youth and inexperience Ms Clue has to invent and reinvent herself as she gains experience. In fact she is not afraid to appear vulnerable to her board and seeks their guidance. To further her goals, she developed a supportive network of associates who had similar views about education which she used to shape the vision for the school. Through her cavalier ways, she was able to win over those not in agreement with her philosophy of education. Ms Clue can think and react on her feet to master the forces of change and shape the school to her evolving vision. With the school in a critical stage of its brief history, there is growing need for Ms Clue's personal courage in focusing on the needs of working parents and their children. Initially she struggled to establish her leadership, but over time she gained a tremendous amount of respect from her colleagues and board members. She shows more vision in establishing the business and school partnership than the principals in the other two schools. She feels she is dealing with issues now that will confront all independent schools in the future. She believes she is breaking new ground in connecting the school with the workplace.

The principals at all three schools can be classified by their leadership style as risk takers: they show confidence in their decision-making and an ability to develop a collaborative environment where all school participants have a voice. These leaders have a sense of the schools' cultural context that affects how they make decisions. Policy-making and long range planning are grounded in the schools' missions and their traditions. Principals have to be ever sensitive to combining innovation and collaboration with tradition and authority in leading their school. These principals demonstrate political savvy in corralling competitive factions with conflicting solutions in solving school concerns. Their commitment to a collaborative environment requires these principals to face their constituencies head on and accept their criticism. While they can not afford to compromise the school's mission, they must balance the wishes of some parents with the needs of the entire school community. Through responsiveness and active listening, principals lead their school through major changes in order to compete against other independent schools.

Management in the Independent School

These principals are not only leaders but managers whose goal oriented behavior means the implementation of important school improvements. Marsh (1990) believes that school management should involve planning, organizing for implementation, and exercising control. Principals should manage their vision in ways that support the implementation of new reforms. To achieve their visions they must build coalitions, align all parties by supporting professional development opportunities and monitor program goals. In addition, these good managers know how to allocate resources by enabling school participants to set priorities. Marsh (1990) also believes that good managers realize that school improvement goals usually involve conflict, peer struggles, and political manipulations. Good managers create an open climate where participants can discuss their concerns, examine their decisions, and, in the ideal, reach a consensus that transcends politics.

Goldman *et al.* (1993) believe that facilitative empowerment is an important alternate to authoritative power. By exercising facilitative power, good managers can create favorable conditions for subordinates to enhance their individual or collective performances. Facilitative power, manifested through the collaboration of school participants, is effective when managers promote communication and cooperation among school participants whose performance goals become interdependent with the school's mission. Goldman *et al.* (1993) believe that good managers use facilitative power to accommodate change. According to Sergiovanni (1994a), principals are best able to implement school improvement goals when they understand their school community and the bonds that create a sense of belonging and a common identity. He believes that moral and professional authority in a good manager bind together school participants who share values and commitments.

Management Behavior of Principals in Privatized Settings

Goal Setting

All three of the principals in this study are good managers, who use goal-setting to hold themselves and others accountable. Each principal focuses participants on a common vision, to be realized through the long range plan. Open to suggestions, these principals create environments where they listen and work to build cooperative relationships among the teachers, parents and board members. The privatized setting requires that principals act as managers who are responsive to all options in order to meet school goals. One way principals implement school goals is through an educational program which holds teachers accountable for their instructional practices and professional development. Teachers at the three sites are required to establish goals in relation to the school's mission. Each year these principals meet with their teachers to help them formulate these goals in relation to the school's curriculum. Goals focus on professional development rather than performance improvement. The principals place high priority on their teachers' professional development providing special funds for the purpose. By funding inservices and conferences, principals encourage their teachers to keep abreast of innovative school practices. Appleman teachers each receive over $400 in professional monies for conferences, workshops, and membership in professional organizations. In their goal setting process, teachers formulate plans to use these funds to remain innovative in their teaching and to meet the needs of the school. At Appleman, for example, when the addition of new technology produced a need for trained personnel, teachers used their professional development money to attend computer classes and other professional meetings. Similarly, when Bakersfield and Crestview schools focused on the areas of multiculturism and science, teachers invested their professional funds to learn innovative ways to teach science and ensure a more diverse curriculum. Thus, professional development supports curriculum goals which are tied to the educational mission and long range plan. The glue that holds these various goals together is the principal, an effective manager who brings resources together to implement school goals.

The goal-setting process proved useful when Bakersfield School was approached about becoming a satellite campus. Many school participants did not want the school to expand its program because they had not seen such expansion as a long range goal. Taken by surprise, teachers raised concerns about being transferred and about spreading resources too thin. Similarly, many parents worried that the satellite campus would affect the quality of the school. Parents were also concerned that the school would reassign certain teachers or that the principal would be split in her loyalties. While several board members voiced concerns, the decision to examine the satellite option passed by a fairly large margin. Ultimately, although the board was concerned about the financial constraints, it decided to pursue the joint partnership. Dr Brimming, board members, parents, faculty, and staff were involved throughout the decision making process.

During the goal-setting process, Dr Brimming and the board were willing to listen to all the problems that might occur, but after weighing all its options the school could not afford to pass up this opportunity for expansion. Once Dr Brimming had the school's support she envisioned a way to unite everyone to make the 'school's dream' a reality. The new satellite campus opened after one year of deliberating and weighing the school's options. Discussions with the school participants indicated they recognized that the school would have been 'stupid' to miss this chance. According to the principal, 'they had nothing to lose' once everyone knew the school's game plan. The decision was made to retain the school community as it was, but to hire new teachers and an admissions director (a parent whose child had graduated from the school, and who was knowledgeable about the school's program but not particularly loyal to the 'old' Bakersfield School), to recruit students for the satellite campus. The school participants were quite happy with the way the school was expanding into the secondary area. The principal was cited for her ability to stay on top of the stories and rumors by providing constant feedback and soothing the worries of constituents. She was respected for her ability to achieve the school's goals without abandoning any one school group.

One year later, upon my return to the campus, Bakersfield had worked through most of its constituencies' concerns and had agreed to expand the school from its elementary program to the secondary level and open the other satellite campus. The school had reprioritized its goals to meet the needs of the satellite campus. The goal-setting process was a way to bring the participants into agreement. It also helped to establish a process for making school improvement changes.

Both Crestview and Appleman schools have similar goal setting concerns. Appleman School is exploring its options to expand with a summer program in conjunction with one of its competitors. Through goal setting and developing board consensus, the school has increased its program to support its mission to provide more opportunities for enrichment. Crestview School has rallied its participants to the goal of finding a larger setting for the school. The goal setting process ensures that everyone has a voice in the school program. The management of goal-setting by principals is important in managing the school's vision.

Joint Problem Solving through the Board Structure and with Other Participants

The independent principals are good managers who are able to identify and solve problems through their board process. Each school faces issues particular to the setting, and their autonomy forces these schools to create a process of problem solving unique to their needs. When a problem occurred the principal turned to the board for support. None of the three principals worried that her image would be tarnished if she were perceived as not knowing the answer. The principals held themselves responsible for researching a solution to the school's problem and sharing the information with their boards or school participants in order for the groups to make the appropriate decision. The board holds the principal accountable for keeping them informed about all potential solutions for solving school problems.

In addition to using the board members, the principals used other developed networks, such as parents, advisory members, and other independent private school principals. For some school problems, the principals may contact their support system of other independent principals to tap into the process that someone else may have used. Both the Appleman and Bakersfield principals belong to the same cohort of friends who were also independent school principals so there is much exchange of solutions. Also, parents become a resource for solutions. Principals often seek another parent's expertise to gain knowledge about a school issue. Parents reported to me that it was typical for their principal to call parents to ask them about some area of their expertise. Board members and their knowledge base also serve as a source for solutions. Brainstorming sessions often took place at the executive board meetings to find the appropriate decisions to share with the entire board. The board structure also became an opportunity for principals to work collectively in solving problems. Autonomous at the local level, these principals in privatized settings reached out to their constituents to assist them with school problems.

The board's involvement in the problem solving process was noted by the Crestview principal as she worked to locate a home for their school. The school struggled to identify a permanent structure for the school because of concerns that new parents' might not choose Crestview due to the aesthetics of the school facility. Ms Clue's responsibility was to 'pound the pavement' searching for school sites within the downtown area. After many long hours of discussion, board members and school participants decided to renovate the present structure and to begin an endowment fund to build a new school for the future. Mrs Bates had similar construction woes with the asbestos concerns and building renovations at Appleman. Board members and the principal grappled with the responsibility for 'doing the right thing' in removing the asbestos from the school. The board weighed the costs of completely removing the asbestos against the cheaper alternative of covering it. After much discussion the board made the financial commitment to remove the asbestos because it would, in the end, relieve parents' concerns and eliminate future costs. Bakersfield also used the board committees in problem solving as the school examined the alternatives when it decided to increase its program with a satellite campus.

A board's ability to collectively solve problems depends upon the information presented to them. The three principals believe that as good managers their role is to collect and distribute information to keep the board informed. These principals could not afford to be unprepared in presenting a full range of alternatives. Meetings are characterized by a high level of cooperation as members weigh the pros and cons of each decision in relation to the school mission. Broadening the participation in the problem solving process creates a total school system of accountability. Board members along with the principal are viewed as the consensus builders capable of solving problems at the school. The reality of autonomy forces these schools to make careful decisions about how goal setting and long range planning affect the school's mission and parent retention.

Although those involved in the problem solving never complain to their board president, they must feel considerable pressure at times in presenting the board's decisions to parents (their friends in most cases) and teachers. Decisions to increase tuition to raise teachers' salaries, for example, involve some complex dynamics among various parties involved. The stress of facing other parents with the decisions the board made must have weighed heavily on its participants. But the interdependence of the school participants in the problem-solving process fosters greater accountability. Parents noted that they feel the board respects their needs, and in turn, they trust the board to make policies that support the mission, to use resources efficiently, and to listen to their input. In these privatized settings, the principal is not an autonomous problem solver but a resource for collecting information and sharing it with participants so the school can make decisions collectively.

Empowering School Participants

Another management skill that independent school principals bring to the job is their ability to empower the school community. The school's organizational structure creates an environment of mutual dialogue. Parents, teachers, and staff members are connected to the school through choice that ensures an ethos of collaboration and responsiveness. The board structure forces the school to be autonomous and to reach consensus. According to Reitzug's (1994) research, a principal's ability to empower constituencies by supporting, facilitating, and providing resources creates an environment where school participants, given greater autonomy, are encouraged to take risks in their decisions. A principal's empowering behavior establishes a high degree of trust and encourages school members to confirm their commitment to the school.

The three principals in the study provide a supportive environment that allows teachers greater control and autonomy. Principals encourage their teachers to develop their own curriculum and to choose their own professional development activities. Observations in faculty and staff meetings indicate that principals share school information with their staff so they too can have input in the decision-making process. The principals show confidence in teachers' ability to define curriculum and instructional practices that reflect the school's mission. At Bakersfield teachers from the various subject areas like math, language arts, and reading meet on a monthly basis to discuss what each is doing in the classroom. The principal seldom attends these meetings on the premise that the teachers will keep her informed about their progress and decisions. Thus, an element of trust was established between the teachers and principals. Principals were responsible for assuring that the parent organization provided special lunches, dinners, and holiday gifts to demonstrate the parents' appreciation for their teachers. Many teachers cite parental trust and gratitude as the reason for their high degree of job satisfaction and commitment. They also feel that the school responds to their needs and trusts them to implement its mission. Participation in the power structure enhances the teachers' professionalism and their commitment to the principal and the school community.

Like teachers, parents are empowered not only through participation in the board structure, but also through volunteer activities, and open visitation. The principal engages families into the school by encouraging them to participate as volunteers in the classroom and to serve in fundraising activities. All three schools have social events that allow the parents to interact with faculty and other families. Parents are given considerable autonomy in talking with teachers, calling them to discuss problems, and visiting in the school. Social events connect parents to the teachers. Both Crestview and Bakersfield have specific activities for families to assist the staff with their teaching. By being responsive, these principals create a family-like atmosphere that supports parents and teachers. Crestview School has a high percentage of working and single parents who feel a tremendous connection to the school and to other families through school activities. Serving on social committees contributes greatly to the self esteem of many of the female parents. Many 'stay-at-home' mothers develop a high degree of confidence and self-esteem through their fundraising activities. Parents at Appleman and Bakersfield speak glowingly of the opportunities created by the principal that allow them to develop skills they never knew they had. Many of the female participants feel they have grown over the years due to their exchanges with other women in their fundraising activities, leadership roles on board committees, and their interactions in talking with their children's teachers.

All three principals facilitate the interaction between the teachers and parents. Empowering both teachers and parents creates opportunities for parents to become actively involved in their child's learning. Parents are supported in their interactions with teachers and motivated by the principal to become involved at the school. Teachers are encouraged to remain in continual contact with parents by keeping them updated about their child's progress. This interaction between the families and the school creates an environment in which all school participants become involved in the students' learning. Parents keep the school accountable by ensuring that the teachers communicate about the progress of their child. Principals continually interact with teachers about students' progress in order to communicate with the school's families. The common thread running through each of the schools is empowering the participants to meet the learning needs of students. The parents and faculty used their power to express tremendous care for the children and their education.

Creating a Sense of Community

The principals also use their management skills to create a sense of community. One might well ask whether this sense of community evolved from the school's responsive organizational structure or from the board's organization which fosters participatory management, or from the leadership style of the principal. The three schools in the study definitely show a sense of community and a family orientation characterized by caring. However, it is difficult to tell whether this climate is due to the principal's management or the nature of privatization, which requires a higher degree of responsiveness to the community. Sergiovanni (1994b) believes that community evolves as a school defines its own life and practice of schooling. Community building requires a considerable amount of searching and reflection as the school participants struggle with who they are and how they decide to interact with each other. It is my belief that the principal provides the glue that binds the community into what it hopes to become. Its potential for success depends upon the organizational structure and the degree of investment in the mission shown by the families and staff. However, it is the principals who spend many long hours in putting the pieces of the whole school community together and creating a responsive environment. Their management purposefully ensures a collaborative atmosphere, and the sense of community becomes the unconscious outcome.

The three principals in their privatized settings are managers, responsive to their constituents and responsible for their decisions. Board and parents alike hold the principal accountable for retention and for the acceptance of students in secondary programs. The school's organizational structure and commitment to its mission create an environment for facilitative empowerment. The interactive environment between the school and the principals leads to goal directed behavior to implement the school's long range plan. To facilitate this planning, principals listen to participants and seek out sources of information to inform participants in the decision-making process. Principals in privatized settings support participants by giving them voice, honoring their needs, finding sources of support and being responsive to their needs. A leadership style characterized by moral authority creates an environment of self-management. Unlike a typical bureaucracy, the school is not dependent on its principal to motivate, lead, supervise or ensure compliance. Instead, privatized setting needs a principal who can create an environment of autonomy for its participants, develop shared values and commitments, promote a level of collegiality and develop a sense of synergy through a collective 'we' (Sergiovanni, 1994a).

Administrative Structure of Privatized Settings

The administrative team that supports the leadership and management of independent principals usually consists of the business director, curriculum specialist and public relation/development director. This type of administrative structure supports the principal in the delivery of services to the school. The size of each school determines the administrative staff. The administrative structure has minimal hierarchy with reports from specific areas going directly to the principal. The administrative staff of independent schools is generally supportive rather than competitive. Each staff member views his or her role as important but interdependent with the others. The public relations person, for example, cannot successfully promote the school if she is unaware of the school's curriculum. The business manager's ability to collect tuition and determine budget issues is hindered if she is unaware of the amount of annual giving. Likewise, the business manager cannot make recommendations for professional development funds without input from the curriculum specialist. At the center of this interdependence is the principal who pulls the administrative staff together logistically, creating coherence in the school's educational goals in view of the mission. The administrative team plays a pivotal role in supporting the principal. The financial, curriculum, and public relations professionals free the principal to focus on the larger issues of the school and to spend more time with the schools' families.

Each principal at the three schools views attracting and retaining students and families as her responsibility. The administrative team supports this recruitment role with testing, public relations materials, and financial aid. In some independent schools a specific admissions person is hired to do just the recruiting. However, the three principals in this study believe strongly in doing their own admissions tours and recruitment. The principals' argue that their involvement ensures that accurate information is given to parents, and allows them to become more acquainted with their school's families. However, my observations lead me to believe that the principal's admissions tour involves more than just educating the families about the school. Admission meetings begin the interactive process between the school and the families. Principals use this meeting time with perspective families to learn more about the parents' skills and their potential for contributing to the school's goals. Principals establish the expectations for the families, educate the families about the roles of the board and parents' club and empower families to make educational choices for their children. But the principals would be hindered in their ability to attract and retain families if they did not have the assistance of a curriculum director to keep the academic program in line with the mission, the business director to maintain tuition records and to oversee finances, and a public relations director to present the school to the community.

Crestview School

The administrative team plays a critical role in assisting the principal with the administration of the Crestview School. Since the school has few students, it requires little administrative hierarchy. The business and public relations functions are handled by an outside accountant and a marketing firm. The principal and assistant principal both have participatory management styles, empowering their staff to be autonomous in curriculum decisions and encouraging teachers to pursue their own professional goals. As mentioned earlier the principal is responsible for external issues while the assistant director manages the curriculum, testing and teacher evaluations. The assistant principal ensures that the school's curriculum is implemented and the instructional practices support the school's mission. The assistant principal uses goal setting for evaluating teachers and encourages the staff to take risks in engaging families into the educational program. To support the focus on the arts the assistant director hires local artists for the school program. Teachers are encouraged to be innovative in creating cross discipline and cross age activities and in initiating contacts with downtown corporations to enhance the public image of the school. It is not unusual for Crestview teachers to give workshops for the various downtown corporations in some area of expertise they have developed. Taking advantage of the school's location at the local church, teachers initiated an adopt-a-grandparent program with the church's older parishioners. Teachers have proven resourceful in finding projects to advance the school's mission of being involved in the downtown community. Each teacher informs other staff about her goals and the projects she is pursuing. Because of the small number of faculty, meetings are informal and congenial, reflecting a high level of collegial support and no authority structure of 'boss'. The assistant director noted:

> They write goals in the areas of professionalism, curriculum personal. Many of the teachers have special units they are working on. Its their own special interest. One teacher wanted to write an article about her architectural project for a social studies journal. Each teacher besides teaching their grade level comes up with an area of interest, maybe an expertise. They develop goals, objectives activities as they go along.

The assistant director takes pride in the school's preschool program which was started after the school opened. She appreciated the opportunity to design a program that she believes 'helped children'. She used the example of changing the time of recess to show how the Crestview environment fosters autonomy:

The thing that has been so wonderful for me is that I have worked in so many different schools, public, private, all different and I would see things done and say that is so dumb. This is a silly example but why do people always have recess after lunch. Children don't eat because they are so intent on getting outside. I have always said why not have recess first then eat lunch and that's what we do. And it's so nice to have someone listen to me and do it that way. I think that's the most rewarding thing.

The assistant principal and the principal have a very supportive relationship and are close friends. Many of their roles often overlap, but each supports the other and their decisions. The principal spoke in glowing terms about her assistant's ability to work with many of the families.

Appleman and Bakersfield Schools

At Appleman and Bakersfield Schools, the administrative teams are similar in nature, but the principals differ in their ways of working with the teams, which consists of a business manager, curriculum director/assistant principal and public relations/development director. Considerably larger than Crestview, these schools need far more administrative members. The principal at Appleman uses a one-on-one approach in working with her team while the Bakersfield principal takes a team approach in creating an interdependence among her administrative staff. The Bakersfield principal is very close to her team and they often discuss their work during their lunch hour together. Dr Brimming creates a collaborative atmosphere and encourages her staff to interact with the board members and school participants. Interviews with the Bakersfield administrative team indicated that they feel their ideas were valued and that the board and principal support them. While the principal's staff often feels challenged to keep up with her high energy level, they derive great satisfaction from working with her. The Bakersfield staff is committed to the school and views its parent involvement and its ability to carry out its mission as its most positive features. These individuals feel needed and appreciated by the school and the principal.

At Appleman, Mrs Bates allows her staff autonomy in their work, but she wants constant interaction with them to keep her apprised of their work. Through more formal interactions, Mrs Bates exerts more control over her staff's decisions while Dr Brimming provides more autonomy to her staff in pursuing their job responsibilities. Mrs Bates also prefers that her staff not attend board meetings to allow board members greater authority in decisions. Dr Brimming, on the other hand, wants her staff to attend board meetings as a way of promoting interaction and ensuring the integrity of the mission. Because Dr Brimming has been at her school for many years, the tradition of interaction between board and staff is firmly entrenched. Mrs Bates, on the other hand, honors the wishes of her board in retaining the tradition of closed meetings. Thus, although the administrative structures are similar in nature, the opportunities for collaboration vary.

Team Members

The Role of the Business Director

The business directors at both schools have regular contact with the board to report the school's budget. Both budget directors are quite involved in keeping board members advised about financial planning and long range budget planning. The business director reports to the board about the financial status and money market accounts. The operating budget in an independent school is a detailed financial plan that outlines projected revenue, expenditures and transferred funds for the next school year. The business manager works closely with the principal in defining the budget. However, the executive and finance board committees play a significant role in the examination of the school's revenues. Parents who are accountants are often asked to serve on the board's finance committee to provide their expertise on financial issues. Budget directors at the three schools have either a finance or accounting degree. These school financiers also have the responsibility for developing the financial planning cycle which involves as many participants as possible in the budgeting process, developing budgets for both operating expenses and capital acquisitions, and defining the budget in connection with the long range plan. As 'not for profit' organizations, the schools use the budget to ensure efficient use of resources.

Each school handles its funds differently with budget areas such as annual giving, fundraising monies and endowment. The development of the budget is linked to the long range plan which usually defines the salaries for teachers and staff. Both business directors at Appleman and Bakersfield develop the budget with input from the board and staff. Both work with their principals in figuring out the annual budget that eventually is tightened by the finance board committee. The board shows its greatest concern with the rationale for expenses and the affect they have on tuition. The school budget relies heavily on tuition, annual giving, interest from endowment and other private giving. Money raised by the parent club is used for smaller school improvements like computers and library shelves. Annual giving money comprises 50 percent of the budget in some cases. Business directors are responsible for collecting tuition and funding scholarships for families. To ensure confidentiality, the school uses a formula designed by the NAIS to identify families who need assistance. The NAIS people calculate the need and then the business directors subtract that amount from the tuition. The receipt of financial is kept confidential, and only the business director knows who receives these funds.

The two business directors expressed concerns about families becoming delinquent in paying their tuition. The schools have policies in place about late tuition fees and past balances. Families experiencing financial difficulties are encouraged to talk with the business director to find solutions for their tuition problems. Although the schools know their participants very well they often know less than one might think about levels of income and savings. Both the principals and business directors are concerned about 'squeezing out the middle class' at their schools. In interviews parents noted their struggles to afford private education for their children and the idea of sacrifice permeated many of the financial discussions at the school. Aitken (1993) noted in his research that if independent schools are committed to enhanced access, these schools must consider steps to reverse the trend of declining affordability. Private schools must consider lowering tuitions by increasing revenues other than tuition and relying on philanthropic capabilities of the local community, graduates and parents. Of the schools in the study, families at Crestview have the most financial difficulties with the cost of private schooling. According to the business directors at both Bakersfield and Appleman, about 40 percent of their families make great financial sacrifices to attend the school while the other parents had little or no difficulties in paying the tuition amount.

Typically the school's operating budget is divided into several different funds, such as the operating budget, board designated funds (personal property for the school like refrigerators), and the endowment fund. The budget director uses various formulas to anticipate electrical and heating costs, to anticipate other program costs and to make projections for new school additions. There were restrictions on how funds were to be spent and allocated within the budget. The budget director at Appleman is responsible for overseeing the facility of the school while Bakersfield's director works with the principal in maintaining their facility. Budget directors feel great isolation because of their job responsibilities. For example, they need to pressure parents to pay tuition without alienating them, and they struggle to keep tuition at a level that allows the school to progress and, at the same time, maintains economic diversity. However, the support from the board, principal, and other staff members sustains them, and, in addition, both directors feel positive about their role in working with parents.

The Role of the Public Relations Director

The public relations/development director is responsible for promoting the mission of the school through advertisements, recruitment materials, and fundraising activities. Campbell and Crowther (1991) believe that an 'entrepreneurial' school exists when there is a passionate commitment to use all resources and to create new ideas to enhance the quality of the school. Crestview School hired a marketing firm to handle their public relations while Appleman and Bakersfield have their own marketing specialist on staff. Both the public relations personnel at Appleman and Bakersfield had worked in PR jobs before coming to their schools. Both of these women are consumed with their jobs spending many long hours at the school. The public relations person at Bakersfield plays a greater role in development and acquiring funds for the school. She feels she needs to be visible and interact with the community and the school participants to enhance her role as the development director. At Appleman School the public relations person perceives herself as a 'behind the scenes' person in promoting her school. This public relations staff member feels that her role involves empowering school participants to take a greater role in marketing the school and preparing admissions material. The public relations person at Bakersfield attends board meetings to keep them informed about development (funds from annual giving and private donations) and fundraising activities. Both individuals also sit on several board committees and work with the parents' club on fundraising activities. While the Appleman PR director does not attend the board meetings, she works closely with many board members on admissions and development board committee. Each year the PR people meet with the various school participants and some board committees to outline a plan for them to use for the year. Both of the PR directors view development as a cooperative effort. Their roles require them to listen to the desires of the constituencies and then become the 'cheerleader' and enabler in completing the fundraising tasks.

Another dimension of their position involves eliciting financial support from the community. One of the public relations directors noted that she had worked with both old and new donors and often found it more difficult to cultivate 'new money' for the school. Board members at Crestview and the two public relations specialists at Appleman and Bakersfield talked about the problems in encouraging private corporations and foundations to give money to private schools. Many corporations and foundations fear that they will be perceived as elitist if they assist private schools. Independent schools often have to search their alumni population for both donations and connections to persons or companies who might be willing to donate funds to the school. Both PR directors believe that for an individual or corporation to support the school requires belief in the school's cause and some meaningful connection to the school. The public relations personnel at these schools are incredibly creative in locating funds and packaging the school's mission and goals. In some cases the PR director contacts a private donor while in other instances the principal or a board member makes the approach. Cultivating private funds is a collective endeavor as these schools continually search for philanthropic donors who are financially committed to the school and willing to build the endowment. Such fundraising allows the school to reduce the tuition while maintaining economic diversity.

The need to raise funds is a constant reality at Appleman and Bakersfield since these schools reside in a very competitive market where families' incomes are far above the median and public schools spend almost twice as much per pupil as the independent schools charge for tuition. Also, the public schools are perceived as high quality even by the wealthier constituents.

Because they have to compete against many quality public and private schools, these independent schools work very hard in recruiting families including minorities whose numbers exceed those in the public schools participating in a court ordered desegregation program.

The PR director at Appleman is beginning to tap the alums as a source for revenue and recruits. She is responsible for locating people and putting together a mailing list of alums. Even though the school had been in existence for seventy-five years, it had never kept records of graduates. However, Mrs Bates introduced a new era with her goal to retain the school's connection to its graduates. Access to alumni donors is critical when the school undertakes a capital campaign. Mrs Bates and the PR director are credited for developing a sophisticated fundraising campaign for the school's renovations and classroom expansion. The PR director is also in the process of defining regular dates for reunions. She believes that celebrating regular reunions keeps the graduates connected to the school and helps maintain its traditions. She believes the school has greater accountability toward its mission because of the constant interaction with past graduates.

The PR director at Bakersfield focuses more on past parents because of the limited pool of alumni. Bakersfield uses a computer system to track its graduates and spends its energies focusing on past parents as sources for funds. Bakersfield also sends a cute package of new baby gifts to parents who have children in the school. Bakersfield School relies largely on 'new money' so most of its development energies are spent encouraging new families to donate funds. They also tap into community money through the school's parents who often give the PR director names of potential donors.

Both schools use marketing tools like shirts, mugs, pencils, folders, and many other items with the school's name and logo on them. These are sold daily at the school's store and during the fundraising activities. All three schools' logos are recognized in the city. The schools even have car stickers that parents display to establish their connections to the school. Logos and other advertising gimmicks promote the schools' organizational culture to the community.

In addition to their development functions, the public relations directors are responsible for creating the school's image and marketing strategy. Advertising creates awareness of the school, projecting a particular image of the educational mission and the long range plan. Both schools have budgets for advertising in local papers to ensure media coverage of the school's events. Most of the marketing on such things as admissions and development is done in collaboration with board committees. Through market research, the schools learn what information families need to choose a school, how closely the communities perception of the school corresponds with its reality, how to increase the number of students enrolled in the school, how to match the school with those families most likely to benefit from the educational goals of the school, what niche they can occupy in the marketplace to maintain a competitive edge, and how to monitor the quality of programs by continual assessment. Typically each school establishes a marketing plan, with an area of focus, that defines a message to convey the school's philosophy. The plan includes time-lines for accomplishing its communication goals and identifies methods of communication such as advertising, publicity, publications, events, and special programs. All three schools value honesty in their publications. To ensure that 'the school does what it says it does', publications go through several boards and parent committees before they are approved. The marketing plan is governed by a strong ethic: Never promise anything you can not deliver, never malign a competitor, and avoid high pressure sales tactics. Independent schools can not afford to be 'slick' in their promotions if they are to retain credibility with the community. The marketing for independent schools focuses on significant issues — their ability to prepare children academically for secondary schools and their unique educational missions.

All three schools are seeking ways to market the school's program to increase their minority student population. Appleman in particular hired several 'minority' experts to examine the school's educational program and publications as perceived by the African American community. All three schools have examined their curriculum in view of diversity. These schools work to ensure that multicultural goals are integrated rather than presented separately in curriculum areas such as history, science literature. Each school examines its publications for political correctness making sure that pictures show students of color in the classroom, in leadership positions, performing in school programs and interacting with teachers. Committed to recruiting children and families of color, each school is working to educate participants about diversity before making long range plans that include increasing the numbers of minorities as a goal. Another independent school within the same area as Appleman and Bakersfield developed a plan to recruit and retain a specific number of students and teachers of color by the year 2000. All three schools are also interested in economic diversity in creating a heterogeneous school population. Are these schools just being politically correct? Are they facing demographic realities as they consider their survival? Or do they genuinely believe in the importance of exposing students to differences? It is very hard to say. In my heart, my observations lead me to believe that there is a commitment to diversity that goes beyond market concerns. While this commitment is not one of the first priorities for moving these schools into the twenty-first century, it is ever present in the minds of board members and school participants.

The Role of the Assistant Principal/Curriculum Director

The duties of the schools' assistant principal/curriculum director usually include the responsibility for curriculum, testing, staff development and after school enrichment. At Bakersfield School, the assistant principal's duties include Montessori training and additional administrative duties. Since some of her duties often overlap with the principal's, her responsibilities are not as specifically defined as those of the Appleman curriculum director. Having been a teacher at the school for several years, the assistant principal at Bakersfield has extensive preparation in Montessori training. She originally came from Korea to enroll in a master's program in the states, met her husband, and remained in the United States. She became involved with the school through her children and has been associated with it for fifteen years. She and Dr Brimming collaborate in working with their teachers, balancing each other in their interactions with the faculty. With a doctorate in counselling, the assistant principal at Appleman has been with the school for four years, beginning her connection through her own children as well. At one point she served as the parents' organization representative on Appleman's board of trustees, so she has a fairly good understanding of how the school's organizational structure works. Her job responsibilities, she noted, seem unclear at times:

> I just do what needs to be done. Most of my time is spent in the area of curriculum and professional development. That takes about half my time and the other things take up the other half.

Both of the assistant principals believe they spend more time with the principal than with any of the other staff members. However, they often work closely with other staff members on various projects to implement the long range plan. Because these two women work with the faculty in the areas of curriculum planning and teaming they develop the collaborative management style that works so well in the independent school.

Appleman School

The assistant principal at Appleman views her relationship with her principal as interdependent since both interact with their faculty on a personal and professional basis. The principal and assistant principal encourage staff members to develop their own goals for professional development but assert control over faculty inservices in the area of classroom practices. At the beginning of each year, the school has a retreat for its faculty to identify the goals for the year and to address faculty concerns. National speakers and experts from local universities educate the staff in areas such as teaming between the lead and assistant teacher, cross disciplinary activities between the grades and the specials, technology and the use of computers in the classroom and teaching through a multicultural perspective. Classroom observations revealed that the faculty makes use of these inservice programs, continuing the conversation that began in the training situation as they seek to implement the cross disciplinary activities. The curriculum director feels the faculty has made great strides in implementing a more developmental process in learning activities and integrating more of the subject areas in their teaching practices. She believes her goal in working with teachers is to encourage them to be more experimental in their classroom teaching and to develop activities that require a higher level of thinking. She wants the teachers to do more than just drill and practice with work sheets. She herself spends much time reading learning theory. She believes that because her vision for the school is 'very radical', it 'should be let out of the bag piece by piece'. She also feels responsible for keeping parents informed about their role in educating their children. The board has responded very favorably to her curriculum changes as long as they do not affect the test scores and the school's secondary acceptance rate.

The assistant principal at Appleman perceives herself as having a good relationship with the teachers. She feels that because she and the staff spend so much time together it is her responsibility to keep a balance in all of their lives. She has instituted several social activities to maintain a cohesive faculty, such as a book group, gray cells and a movie club where faculty share things other than their work. Both she and the principal have early breakfasts with the faculty just to talk and share their lives. The assistant principal is a very good listener when it comes to faculty concerns. She has a great sense of humor and often provides humorous comments during meetings to lift staff morale. She showed her concern for the teachers when the school was under-going a revision of its language arts curriculum. Some teachers had acted quite autonomously in developing their own curriculum, and she wondered how they would respond to a program developed by others. Because the teachers were given considerable academic freedom she worried that the introduction of a whole language approach could create tension with those who teach language arts in more traditional ways. To address her concerns, she created a collaborative atmosphere where teachers shared what they were doing in their classrooms so that any areas missing in the curriculum could be filled in and all teachers had a voice in determining the school's approach to teaching language arts. Personally the assistant principal was also at crossroads in her life. With her children in college and needing less of her time, she spent many long hours at the school. She did express concern about the amount of time and commitment required to create an environment where all the teachers feel empowered and where the school facilitates rather than dominates the faculty's teaching practices.

Bakersfield School

The assistant principal at Bakersfield has been at her job longer so she has a clearer sense of her responsibilities. Other aspects of the setting help define her job. Because of the Montessori approach used at Bakersfield, for example, the curriculum is pretty well established. And since the principal's leadership style allows teachers more autonomy in their classroom, there are fewer oppor-tunities to plan and implement staff development sessions. Instead the assist-ant principal encourages her teachers to attend workshops that they can then share with the rest of the faculty. She encourages the teachers and parents to contribute through the education and other board committees. For example, parents on the education committee wanted the school to examine areas of critical thinking and creativity in the classrooms, so she developed a procedure to assess these areas and provided feedback to parents about ways the school could improve. In her years at the school no conflicts remained unresolved because the staff and faculty always work together. The assistant principal serves as mediator when there are conflicts between teachers and the principal. While the assistant principal recognizes the specific role of each member of the administrative staff, she views the exchange among the faculty and staff as the key to its success. She noted:

> We are all very supportive here where we all get along so well and eat lunch together and don't have official staff meetings. Your most creative time is sitting down and eating lunch together. It's a cohesive environment where we help each other to get things done.

The assistant principal is very involved in her job, she is greatly respected at the school. She has a strong sense of what families want. She also enjoys the interaction among the principal, faculty and other staff members.

Crestview School

Like the assistant principals at Appleman and Bakersfield, the Crestview assistant principal, noted earlier in this chapter, has a collaborative style in managing her teachers. Although her staff is less experienced than the staffs at either Appleman or Bakersfield, she creates an environment where teachers are open about their ability to develop their curriculum and instructional practices. She hopes to encourage her teachers to take increased responsibility in defining their curricular goals and gives considerable time and support to their professional development with the goal of greater autonomy for them. Faculty meetings are often very informal so collegial discussions evolve with ease.

The mission statement and the accountability of the educational program provide the theme that binds the school's curriculum. Like Appleman and Bakersfield, Crestview continually examines the quality of student outcomes and secondary school placements, assessing the school's educational program to ensure their students have the skills to succeed in rigorous secondary schools. Teachers are encouraged to develop ongoing professional development plans of their own choosing. To remain current, the school provides extensive resources to purchase the latest journals and to encourage teachers to attend professional organizational meetings. During several faculty meetings the assistant principal gave articles to the teachers about some issue specifically related to the curriculum or classroom practices. Teachers are encouraged to read journals and attend professional organizational meetings.

Conclusion

The leadership style of independent school principals is reflected in the organizational structure of the schools. Empowering individuals to have a voice in the school program creates a facilitative atmosphere in which the principal encourages individuals to take risks, provides a supportive network, identifies resources to support school participants, and establishes opportunities for greater individual autonomy. Responsive leadership seems a key in attracting and retaining parents. However, the school's commitment to its educational program and its own accountability has proven to be another mechanism for responsiveness. The focus on the mission and long range plan through the board's governance facilitates participatory management. Principals in privatized settings use goal setting with the board and administrative team to build a community. In addition, they depend on the board, staff, and parents to assist them with problem solving and identification of resources. Principals use their leadership to empower the school participants either by providing resources or sharing information. A less collaborative more authoritarian style will not succeed in privatized settings. Because parents choose a particular school, privatized schools must be responsive to the mission and accountable to the parents. If these private schools are to attract and retain parents and remain competitive, their leaders must involve all constituents through participatory management in a responsive climate. When participants have a shared vision and allegiance to the educational mission the school becomes a community of caring people who are committed to educating future generations of children.

Chapter 4

Professional Community in Privatized Schools

The organizational culture in independent private schools is pivotal in developing strategies to encourage collaboration among teachers. It allows teachers to have input into the decision-making process, opportunities for professional development and greater autonomy in curriculum and instructional practices. The principal, through her leadership, plays a major role in shaping the organizational culture by: creating an environment that allows teachers to participate in activities that improve their teaching; establishing a social system supportive of observation and discussion to facilitate student achievement; and providing funds for professional growth that is relevant to teachers' needs. Principals also encourage an interactive relationship between teachers and parents, which creates cultural linkage to the school's mission. Environments that are collegial and supportive benefit students by providing a sense of program coherence and faculty cohesiveness that students detect as meaningful as well as consistent.

The absence of a strong organizational culture undermines teachers' efficacy and their commitment to the school. In bureaucratic settings, teachers internalize constraints on their ability to develop their own curriculum and instructional practices. As a result, they do not derive a sense of self-esteem, status or control. Instead of achieving fulfillment in their teaching, teachers redefine their goals focusing more on social relationships with peers rather than a shared professional commitment. Teachers who lack opportunities to attain work-related goals become disaffected and defect from the profession. Teachers who lack efficacy converse more with their colleagues about poor working conditions and the lack of resources to assist them. Reduced commitment results when teachers disassociate themselves from their work because they believe that any teaching success is dependent upon external causes. Furthermore, professional isolation occurs because teachers act to protect their self-esteem in situations where they may lack expertise. Teachers avoid requests for assistance because they might disclose personal inadequacies (Rosenholtz, 1989).

Teacher commitment and efficacy are necessary functions in restructuring schools. Building professional communities within the school culture is seen as a way to establish collective responsibility for teaching students within schools. Principals must take responsibility for providing teachers with greater autonomy, more leadership roles, and a share in the decision-making process.

Principals shape healthy school cultures which result in improved student achievement and greater teacher efficacy. Yet, due to recent public policy reforms in the area of accountability, most teachers have been disempowered and, as a result, robbed of their concern for their schools. The current political ideology of public schools allows teachers to live their service ideal but removes a sense of professionalism by requiring a state mandated instructional practices and curriculum (Sykes, 1990). Public bureaucracies are restrictive in facilitating a sense of autonomy and a common mission. A hierarchal culture with its bureaucratic mode of supervision and its autocratic rules and procedures, leads to a prescribed and mechanized approach to teaching, leaving the participants with no cultural linkages to the school's ethos and purpose.

Private schools have been noted for their ability to develop professional community through their ability to empower teachers. Teachers in privatized settings are more autonomous in defining curriculum and professional development needs (Bryk, *et al.*, 1993; Chubb and Moe, 1990; Erickson, 1989). Private schools are mostly small, personal, value-laden institutions, the clients of which choose to attend a particular school. The element of choice leads to an equalization of power or a partnership between parents and teachers. Such a setting prevents competition among teachers and fosters a collectivist ethos where like minded individuals work collaboratively for the good of the students. The individualized mission of private schools compels loyalty and dedication from participants (Sykes, 1990). Private school educators are more likely to perceive parents as positive resources for helping them set student expectations for achievement. A private school principal plays a significant role in establishing an organizational culture that equalizes power. Given the evidence that private schools succeed in promoting such a professional community, much can be learned from these settings.

The intent of this chapter is to examine how privatized settings influence teacher commitment and efficacy which establishes a professional community among teachers in these settings. It also examines how these privatized settings, because of their commitment to the students' learning, create ownership for teachers. Teachers from these settings also have opportunities for participatory decision-making in the school governance and in developing their own professional goals. Interviews with twenty-eight teachers from the three sites were collected and analyzed to give a better understanding of teacher efficacy and commitment in these settings and its effect on the professional community in the school. Private schools are well known for creating a community of participants, interconnected through the mission and organizational structure.

Analysis of Teacher Participants

Findings for this chapter come from several sources that include classroom observations, attendance at faculty meetings and interviews with many teachers at each setting. Formal interviews were conducted about midway through the research period after this investigator had attended several faculty meetings and participated in informal discussions with teachers. By the time of the interviews, the researcher understood the school and the role the teachers played in defining its mission. The researcher also knew the teachers, at least to a degree, and developed a level of trust among them. Research questions were developed based on her contacts with faculty, observation of their interactions with colleagues and her attendance at faculty meetings (see Appendix).

Teachers for this project were encouraged to participate in the interviewing process, and the selection process was strictly voluntary. Those teachers who were willing to participate met with the researcher during their planning time or after school. A sheet with scheduled interview times was placed in each faculty room for teachers to sign up for interviews. All the interviews were conducted at the individual schools in either the teachers' rooms or another area of the building. Teachers were given the interview questions prior to their meeting with the researcher. Pleased to participate in the project, they were very reflective in their responses to the questions. Most of the participants were white females (96 percent) while the other respondents included two males (7 percent) and one female minority teacher (3.5 percent). Crestview's teacher participation rate was 100 percent with all of the elementary teachers participating. At Appleman the participation rate of the total number of teachers was 88 percent, with 83 percent at Bakersfield. Most of the participants were classroom teachers while only a small percentage were 'specials' such as art, music or PE teachers.

At Appleman a total of thirteen teachers volunteered to participate in the interviewing process. Seven of the teachers interviewed had up to five years of experience teaching at Appleman and the other six had more than six years of experience at the setting. The average total years of teaching experience at Appleman was 6.0 years. At least nine of the participants had taught in public school settings with a total average of 5.6 years. At least half of the teachers interviewed at Appleman had a masters degree or were working on one. Over 30 percent of the participants were middle aged and had been 'stay-at-home' mothers before returning to the workforce once their children were raised. Most of the participants were state certified and maintained professional connections with their public school counterparts.

At Bakersfield the teachers on average were older and were more experienced than either the Crestview or Appleman teaching staff. A total of eleven teachers volunteered for the project with one of those being male and one African American female. The average years of teaching at Bakersfield was 9.0 years, the highest percentage among the three schools. Only three teachers interviewed had less than five years experience while the other eight had more than six years experience at the school. One teacher participant, with eighteen years of experience, had been with the school almost from its beginning. Four teachers had masters degrees or were working on them. At least seven of the participants taught in the public schools and left those settings due to lack of autonomy and dissatisfaction. Only four of the participants taught in private schools through the school's Montessori program. Like the Appleman teachers, most of the participants were middle aged, but only two of them had returned to the workforce after being home with their children.

At Crestview School all of the participants were younger and less experienced than either Bakersfield or Appleman teachers. However, Crestview's principal specifically sought inexperienced teachers who were not 'tainted' by the public school mentality. The average years of total teaching for the school was 2.75 years. For three of the participants, Crestview was a first job, while the preschool teacher had taught previously in a public school setting. Only one of the teachers had a masters degree, but two of the other participants were working on their graduate degree. All of the participants were under the age of 30 having recently graduated from a teacher education program. All were female except for one male respondent who had been with the school since it was established. The Crestview teachers, on a twelve month contract, were given only two weeks for vacation and school holidays. The school was open all year round, and the teachers' school day was longer with hours ranging from 9.00 in the morning until 6.00 in the evening.

A total of twenty-eight teachers were interviewed for this project. At least 60 percent of the participants had taught in public schools before moving to their private school setting. Those who had previous private school experience had spent most of their time in the Catholic schools with little experience in independent schools. The participants interviewed had an overall average of 5.9 years of teaching in independent schools, but there was a wide distribution of this experience ranging from very veteran teachers at Bakersfield to very inexperienced teachers at Crestview. Approximately half of the total number of participants had a masters degree or were working on them. Discussions with participants indicated many commonalities among the three settings in terms of autonomy in defining curriculum, input into decision-making, collaborative settings to interact with colleagues and freedom in choosing their own professional development. The participants all noted that they felt a great sense of autonomy and commitment but were often overwhelmed with the amount of time required for preparing their classes and responding to parents' concerns. They were also concerned about the seemingly endless school socializing at fundraising activities and parent events. However, given the considerable freedoms they had in their teaching, they felt a great sense of professionalism and dedication to their school. Participants found the teaching profession very rewarding and had no plans to leave their positions. In some instances, teachers spoke with reverence for their school, voicing strong commitment to their students' learning.

Teacher Commitment

Organizational commitment is defined as an individual's identification with, and involvement in, a particular organization. Individuals within their context are committed to the core values, and they work collaboratively and collegially with others who also share in the same beliefs. This interaction between the individual and the organization creates a commitment among its members only if there are the cultural elements of an organizational mission of shared norms, values and beliefs; leadership that is technical and symbolic, and institutional rewards that are worth the commitment (Reyes, 1990). Teacher commitment is critical to organizational effectiveness. In such a setting teachers are willing to exert extra effort to make it educationally sound and to transcend their own individual interests. Teachers who are committed to the organizational mission become involved with the school, care deeply about students and their learning, respond to parents and feel a part of the decision-making process (Reyes, 1990). Commitment serves to motivate teachers to develop as professionals and to cope with the demands involved in meeting students' needs (Firestone and Pennell, 1993).

Teacher involvement in both the strategic organizational decisions (goals of the school) and the operational decisions (curriculum and instructional practices) is important for empowering teachers. Both types of involvement prove necessary in creating a strong commitment to their students' needs. This involvement in decision-making makes teachers more responsive to parents' desires for their children. Employees who are in a position to identify problems and provide valuable suggestions on operational needs are more committed to the organization. Employee involvement in strategic decision-making provides feedback in securing sound organizational practices and retains clients (Conley and Schmidle, 1988).

Teachers, encouraged to participate in improving student learning, bring important information and advice to the attention of administrators. By increasing teacher involvement in the decision-making process in the public schools, much of the problem solving might be completed at the building level rather than through centralized decision making at the district level. Teachers who are encouraged to participate in the decision-making process at the building level tend to be more consensus oriented and to agree on priorities. Allowing teachers more discretion over their curriculum decisions creates an environment for enhancing teacher commitment.

Participation and commitment are linked together on many dimensions. Teachers feel that their ability to provide successful learning experiences for their students should allow them the opportunity to participate in the school's policy making process. This participation enhances the teachers' view of the institution's practices as fair and worthy of trust. To prepare teachers to make decisions about their teaching, the school provides them with the necessary information. Giving teachers more input into the decision-making process improves their commitment to the organization and validates their professionalism (Firestone and Pennell, 1993). Although participation and commitment are interrelated, not all teachers value having involvement in the personnel and administrative decisions. Involvement in the decision-making is also affected by grade level and perception of decision making as inappropriate or excessively burdensome (Bacharach, Bamberger, and Mitchell, 1990; White, 1992).

Teacher Commitment in Independent Schools

Teachers at the three schools have many opportunities to participate in their school's decision-making. Most of the teachers are given considerable freedom in developing their own curriculum and instructional practices. Teachers are independent in selecting their own areas of professional development. They are provided with professional funds to develop expertise in areas that would benefit the school program and keep them abreast of new practices. Through service on the board committees, teachers have a voice in the administrative structure of the school on salary negotiations, mission adherence and long range planning. These privatized settings encouraged autonomy among teachers yet organizationally placed them in team settings. At Appleman two classroom teachers work as team teachers creating an interdependence between these individuals to support each other's instructional decisions. At Bakersfield the teachers each develop a subject area expertise, but work as a team in developing cross disciplinary activities. Crestview School does not necessarily have team teaching by grade level, but teachers work collaboratively doing group activities in the areas of science, library skills, and social studies.

Teacher commitment seems, in part, due to the nature of decentralization which focuses on enhancing the teachers' professionalism and promoting collaborative teaming and autonomy in curriculum decisions. Each school trusts teachers to make curriculum decisions that reflect the school's mission. Teachers are given considerable support for professional development to remain current and innovative in their instructional practices and many freedoms in defining their curriculum as long as it reflects the school's intent. Team teaching allows teachers to connect with their peers in making curriculum decisions. Teachers, in subtle ways, are held accountable for the quality of student outcomes. Although teachers have considerable freedom in selecting curriculum materials, they are required to maintain allegiance to the school's purpose. This requirement, however, is not a problem because teachers feel they have an opportunity in defining the school's mission through long range planning. Teachers revealed that there were many opportunities to voice their opinions and to participate in the governance structure. Because teachers were able to work collectively in selecting new teachers for their team situations, they were able to identify like minded staff with whom they can work collegially. When new teachers were interviewed, these teachers often were asked what their philosophy of teaching was and how that would fit with the school's mission. The turnover in these settings was not high, but periodically there were vacancies due to retirement or maternity leave.

Teachers in these settings were highly committed to their peers and they often collaborated across subject areas to provide breadth and depth in the curriculum. Conversations with parents indicated that they too had great respect for the teachers and appreciated their responsiveness. Principals also affirmed the teachers' sense of professionalism by giving them a high degree of autonomy in defining the curriculum and serving on board committees. These teachers have control over their work setting and feel a sense of empowerment which leads to a high quality of work life. Because they are given genuine opportunities to make decisions, they are committed to the school. This organizational structure fosters a collaborative environment among peers, an affiliation with the school, and a sense of mutual support.

Providing teachers with opportunities for professional development, is also a priority in independent schools. Teachers are encouraged to be active in professional organizations and to attend subject areas to acquire new skills and knowledge. As a result of this ongoing professional development, teachers develop lifetime goals of professionalism and avoid stagnation. Each principal not only provides resources to encourage teachers to develop expertise to share with colleagues but also supports teachers' involvement within the community through conference presentations. As a result of the school's commitment to professional development, teachers feel a connection between their professional goals and those of the school and its mission. Although many of the teachers complained about the time needed to serve the needs of the school, the burden, they feel, is lightened by their professional pride. These committed teachers expressed strong feelings in focusing their goals to help students achieve academically and spiritually at their school. Occasionally, teachers had to be pushed into areas that created many changes for their style of teaching. Change for some teachers often caused them to be stressed by taking on additional responsibilities.

Appleman's Teachers

At Appleman School the teachers who were interviewed cited numerous opportunities to contribute to the school curriculum, to voice their opinions and to work collectively with their peers. Most teachers noted that they felt valued at the school and by the parents. They voiced their respect for their principal and her management style. Some teachers did note that at times the school was too market driven in recruiting students, but they also understand the need to recruit and retain students. About half the teachers expressed concern that the quality of the educational program was compromised at times because the school was being too responsive to parents. However, all of the thirteen teachers spoke highly of the professional atmosphere at the school which gave them personal ownership of the quality of student learning.

Many teachers believe strongly that they have the opportunity to voice their opinions without fear and feel that the administration, at least, reacts to their concerns. When interviewed, several teachers noted that the school supports them by allowing them freedom in the classroom to develop their programs. Teachers noted:

A teacher here is free to discuss what they think and can say whatever they want to say about the curriculum. There are guidelines to follow, but you have great autonomy in enhancing the curriculum. The sky is the limit;

We have the freedom to do more or less what we want to do. Mrs Bates really does empower and trust us to carry out our program and make the changes that we have to make and do what we have to do. In the public school they have to answer to a boss or an authority figure. They get better pay in the public schools, I know that, but we get the freedom to do what we want;

As a teacher, I feel autonomous. I did not feel that way in other schools, but now I am here and I have a sense that bureaucracy can become a trap. If I need to have something it's done really quickly. You don't have to go through triplicate and make an appeal to this committee or that board. There's accountability here and that's the difference;

I am very new. This is my first year of teaching. I am not a shy person, and I feel very safe expressing my opinions and ideas in meetings.

It is the best place that I have ever been in terms of encouraging you to stay current in your field. We get a professional development fund. I can't remember exactly how much we get, but I think that it's between $200 and $250 a year. I am totally free to do whatever I choose. I belong to AEYC, and I usually subscribe to periodicals with that money too. You can go to a convention and your professional development fund can build over a three year period;

Assessment tools are strictly left to us. We have a lot of input into selecting instruments in the early childhood area; I think they are great for professional development. Now if I wanted to work on a masters and wanted to use my money to go towards that, that would be fine. I think it's great to have the opportunity to go to the different workshops;

I think a perk here is unlimited finances. Everyone keeps saying that it's getting worse and it's tightening up but you have a wish list, a professional development budget. All that stuff adds up.

121

Teachers believe they have opportunities to make curriculum decisions and freedom to define their institutional practices. When asked about the impact of this freedom, Appleman teachers all responded that their teaching improved because of the opportunities to define their own curriculum. Similarly, the freedom to define their professional development goals and the availability of funds to pursue them fostered teacher commitment. Appleman School believes it is important for teachers to stay current so it provides resources to expand their knowledge and remain open for change.

Appleman School's classroom structure involves teaching with both teachers having equal status. In the past there was a hierarchy between the lead and assistant teacher. However, with Mrs Bates' leadership, this hierarchy changed, allowing the positions to be equalized. By reducing the hierarchy, the principal and curriculum director have created a more collegial environment with more cross disciplinary and enrichment activities. At least four of the participants expressed great respect for their other team teaching colleague and an appreciation for the professional exchange that occurs between the two of them. Collegial relationships among these teachers resulted in a sense of affiliation and ownership. Teachers were questioned about their feelings on team teaching and their relationship with their peers. Many faculty noted that these relationships were very special to them. Teachers noted:

> It's like something in the air. When I walked into Appleman for the first time it was like a breath of fresh air. The environment that we work in is so nice and of course that has a lot to do with all of the people that you work with every single day. We don't all hang out together but a lot of us get together and do things over the summer. They've got a book club going and a mind game going and a movie club for people who don't have time to read books. I don't know why this place is so great;

> I think Susie and I have the best working relationship of all the teams. We really work as co-teachers as opposed to lead and assistant, although technically I am the lead. So it's easy to come to school and work with her and know that we get along so well and our philosophies jive completely and we do things in the same way;

> For me personally, I can't imagine what it would be like in there by myself all day. I would go nuts. It is nice to have another adult in there. Not only do the kids get the benefit of having another point of view or another question that I may not think of. I also think I learn a lot from watching Jane, and we interact a lot;

> It may just be my own personal stage, where I am more comfortable teaming with someone like a partner than just going at it by myself. The opportunity that you do have a chance to team teach is really nice

here. One of the bonuses and perks is being able to have another adult in the classroom. I can't imagine being stuck in a self-contained classroom all by myself. Not only does it allow you the freedom to step out for a minute and then step back in, but you are not tethered to the children all day or you don't feel that way because you have another adult;

I always thought I wanted my own room and do it as I want to and I realized there is another approach. There is such a sense of personal satisfaction here. Like I said seven years ago there was such a happy feeling. Not that there isn't now, but it used to be even greater — the laughter. You could never be too tense because somebody was going to break the bubble. You had contact during the day;

Personally, I had some difficult times and if it hadn't been for this school and the people in it that were so supportive, I don't think I would have gotten through it. This was my haven. I came here and I felt good because I functioned in the classroom well. I had people who were caring.

Appleman teachers noted that they were highly committed to their school because of the opportunities for input on their own professional development, autonomy in defining their curriculum and team teaching settings in an atmosphere of mutual support and collegiality. The Appleman principal trusts the teachers to develop their own curriculum as long as it reflects the mission of the school. Appleman is committed to providing teachers' funds and resources to remain current and to keep abreast. Because of the many freedoms, these teachers were committed to the school.

Bakersfield's Teachers

At Bakersfield teachers made similar statements about their autonomy in developing the curriculum, their voice in the school governance, their professional opportunities and their participation in board activities. All eleven teachers were very committed to the school and its program. But at least six of them expressed some dissatisfaction about the demands on their time. The planning required for classes, the meetings, and interactions with parents all consumed their time. The demands of the job in terms of time also troubled teachers at Crestview and Appleman, but the teachers at Bakersfield and Crestview were the most vocal about the amount of energy involved in preparation, school meetings and parent interactions.

However, the Bakersfield teachers find compensation for their time in the many opportunities for team teaching at Bakersfield. There are usually three teachers in each classroom, and they divide the subject areas into math, language arts and social studies. The children rotate throughout the day. Each teacher has developed expertise in a subject matter and is given many freedoms in defining her curriculum. Teachers hold subject area meetings then meet regularly with their other peers to keep each other updated on their classroom procedures and professional development activities. Minutes from the meetings are given to the principal to keep her informed about classroom activities and curriculum updates. Some of the teachers of specials (art, music and PE) feel that the children are not adequately exposed to the arts and physical development because the school is so content driven.

Teachers at Bakersfield were also invited to comment on their opportunities and their freedom. Many teachers feel they have many opportunities to be vocal about their curriculum and instructional practices. Teachers noted:

> We are given every opportunity, absolutely every opportunity to have input. It's just that there are so many things that you need to have input on;

> We have a voice in a lot of the areas. Sometimes we have a voice in so many things. For example, with the calendar and schedule, there would be a lot of places where we would be told what the calendar and schedule were going to be. We could do that here, except that if you want it to be the way you want it, then you want to be on the committee. That's true with so many things, like the budget. There's opportunity for everything;

> I think we have quite a lot of opportunities to express ourselves. As far as curriculum is concerned, I would say that I really have the opportunity to do just anything I want to;

> I can't think, right now, of any thing that I have wanted to do or would want to do, that I wouldn't be allowed to try. I think being a creative person it's been good for me because I can do what I want to;

> Like I said, we have the freedom to let go and try something new. There were some freedoms in the public schools, but I feel that here it's probably a little bit easier to do whatever I feel like doing;

> I have the freedom to do new and different things, not that I always do, but if I want to add something it's okay. I have the freedom for my classes.

Much like the Appleman teachers, Bakersfield teachers did note the positive relationships that they have with their colleagues. Many teachers referred to professional development opportunities but focused more specifically on their collaborative relationships with peers. Teachers noted:

The school, I think, has a spiritual foundation. It's not a religious foundation, but a spiritual foundation. It's very well organized, we have autonomy in the classroom to create our own classroom;

I think it's an advantage to team teach if the teams are compatible, which ours happens to be. I think it's small enough that we all feel that we are contributing to the whole;

We have a lot of input. I think that's unique about our school. The other people here on the staff are a definite advantage. They are nice people to be around and are good colleagues. The other teachers are just as involved and supportive of what we are trying to do here;

The other teachers know what they are doing, and we work together. We have a lot of independence in the upper elementary as far as how we want to schedule our day. We just do what we need to do to get things done and to prepare kids for what they need to know. That's what makes it so worthwhile;

I've taught in public education, and I haven't been as happy in public education because there were too many students and not enough time even to say hi to them all and get to know them. I can see there are a lot of benefits here for the teachers. Especially for me because I can pick up from where I left off each year. I know the students' learning styles, and I am able to adapt my lessons to fit their needs;

The faculty are easy to work with and they listen to each other. We have different opinions, and we can state our opinions and come to a compromise sometimes. It's a good group;

Sue and I work together on some things. For example, we get together for the spelling bee and the whole upper elementary does that, the linguistic competition, and the writing workshop procedure. She was a really big help when I first came here and I've seen a lot of grouping together;

We just try to learn new things every year from seminars so that we can keep abreast of where to get information and the resource books we need. We also share ideas. I've been very fortunate with my co-teachers and their ability to be flexible. If you were not flexible, I don't think you'd survive in this environment because you can have all the plans in the world, but when something comes up you have to be willing to drop them and go with the flow.

At least three of the Bakersfield teachers who were interviewed noted their role on the board in establishing school policies. The Bakersfield teachers are more involved with their board than the Appleman teachers since they are often asked to serve on board committees. They serve regularly on the education committee like the Appleman teachers. However, teachers also were asked to serve on other committees as well, such as the finance committee. While Appleman teachers only served on the education committee, Bakersfield teachers participated on several other board committees. Teachers feel honored to serve on the board committees and believe their opinions are valued by the school participants. Teachers noted:

> The honest truth is that I don't care if I sit on the board or not. I know the people on the board and to me they don't act like they have any more power than anyone else at the school;

> I know the current board president and have her child in class. She and I have a fabulous relationship. She's real down to earth, and I haven't seen power as a problem as far as the board members are concerned;

> I've been on the compensation committee for the last two years. I'm coming from a public school so I know how a compensation committee works. It's a rather antagonistic situation in public education. Here, we just basically state our case and they listen to us. Then they make the decisions based on what's financially healthy for the whole school. There's full enrollment here so they're going to compensate us for that. The board compensation committee usually works pretty good. I've been very fortunate because I haven't really disagreed with any of what the board has done so far. So, I don't feel any pressure here;

> I just feel the board really appreciates the teachers and they always try to do their best for us. They always come through with raises, it's been amazing, and the medical benefits, and just trying to make the best package for us to entice us to stay here.

Although teachers are grateful for their autonomy and feel valued by the school, they often cited their concerns about their work load and the demands on their time. In conversation, teachers spoke about the excessive time needed to prepare for classroom teaching. These teachers were more vocal about this issue than the teachers at Appleman. Much older than their counterparts, the Bakersfield teachers had more years of service and they seemed at a stage when the time factor influenced their commitment. Several teachers noted:

> Teaching here is very time consuming because you are defining your curriculum and always looking for new ideas. I go through withdrawal at the end of every summer, and I mourn the end of summer because I know that I'm not going to do anything again until school is out. It's about time deprivation;

I think if you have a team teacher you become very close. I work alone in my area (music teacher), and I don't really have time to talk to the other teachers. I have to make myself go down and talk to other teachers, but I don't always have the time. I am at school quite a bit;

I am constantly taking classes and reading books, and to me this is exciting and gets me pumped up. A lot of people here are dedicated to their job. I have friends who teach in public schools and they can't believe the hours we spend here over and above our regular school day. Being a teacher here is a special commitment;

We have so many meetings and a lot of other times we have to be at school. It does require a lot of your life. Actually, I think we have less commitment as teachers every year. I think we had a lot more things to do on the weekend when I first came here. That's because the parents wanted it. We'd have speech contests on Sunday, but now that's no longer in existence. Just this week we changed our parent night from a weekend to a weekday. Then there's grandparents' day. Every month there was something on the weekend, but now we're gradually getting away from some of that.

Bakersfield proved unique in having a minority teacher, an African American who often noted her loneliness and isolation at her school. She feels that her management style is not as warm and nurturing as the other teachers. The principal often heard parent complaints that she is too 'tough' on the children. However, as she perceived it, her discipline, PE, requires more rigorous management than other subjects. She noted:

It's difficult in that my culture and background is totally different from some of the people here. A lot of times I'm misunderstood not only by teachers, but also by the children because my perspective is totally different. I try to teach from the perspective that there are other people in the world who are just as worthy as my students are. I have to remind myself that these kids don't have to be reared the way that my kids have been reared because there's a lot of fluff and cushion here. They know if they fall down there are a lot of people to pick them up.

She also noted that diversity in the school does not always include an African American perspective even though almost half of the metropolitan area is African American. But she also admitted that the African American children enjoyed every advantage at the school. In the public schools she had seen many unfair practices toward African American children, but they are never mistreated at Bakersfield. She noted, 'I have to say that I don't see any difference in the way they are treated. We have a great group of teachers here and they do a splendid job.' She spoke highly of the principal and the support she was given when parents complained about her discipline techniques. She was

concerned that her tough management style might put pressure on the principal, and she feared getting her boss in trouble. She appreciated the support
when the principal told her not to worry.

Teachers at Bakersfield share feelings of autonomy and collegiality similar
to those at Appleman. Teachers spoke highly of their work with the children
and other teachers in defining their own curriculum. The Bakersfield teachers
are much older and more experienced than the Appleman teachers, and, as a
result, they expressed more concern about the demands on their time. There
was a great sense of professionalism among the teachers in this supportive
atmosphere. Parents, along with colleagues, are supportive to these teachers
and often assist them in the classroom. Many of the teachers noted their relationship with the board and the value that board members place on their
teaching. Many feel their involvement with board committees is strictly voluntary. 'You could be as active as you wanted in participating in board activities.'
Those teachers who are involved with the board feel that they are a valued
part in the chain of authority.

Crestview's Teachers

All of the four teachers at Crestview volunteered to be interviewed for this
study. As noted earlier these teachers are quite young and inexperienced. In
fact, only half of Crestview's teachers have more than four years teaching
experience. However, the principal purposely hired young inexperienced
teachers who were not 'tainted' by teaching in public schools. The principal
also wanted new teachers who were energetic and innovative because of the
time commitment and the school's nontraditional curriculum resulting from its
tie to business corporations and working parents. The teachers at Crestview
teach all year round — even during school holidays and summers when the
school remains open for their working parents. The school has what is called
a transition curriculum which allows students to participate in enrichment
activities provided by parents, teachers or staff members when other students
are not available. During the summer, Crestview teachers work cooperatively
around a theme that is tied to all the curriculum areas. The theme used for
the summer of this research project was transportation. Teachers had students
complete various projects tied to transportation. To assist them with their
theme, they also sought community resources like how to get access to the
new metropolitan rail system, attendance at the Transportation Museum and
other meaningful related transportation issues in the area. Teaching all year
round produces considerable stress. Crestview teachers are concerned about
the time commitment required for developing their curriculum.

All four teachers feel empowered in selecting their area of expertise and
having a say in the school governance. But at least two were disgruntled about
the limited time available for preparation which left them feeling overwhelmed
in finding curriculum materials. Because these teachers were inexperienced in

developing their own curriculum, they were extremely worried about their ability to develop the school's mission. These teachers noted:

> We spend very long days here at the school from 9 to 6 in the evening, and even though there is planning time during the day, there does not seem to be enough time to plan for all the things to do. The curriculum here is very overwhelming, and they hired me with no preconceived notions of how to really establish curriculum;

> There was no job description when I came so there was so much freedom in developing the preschool curriculum. There are very long days here but built into the schedule is planning time. You still go home with an arm load of work, but it is work you want to take home, and it does not mean you have to do it right away. I enjoy working with the kindergarten teacher, and we share many of the activities together so we work in conjunction doing joint projects. The other teachers also supported his role in developing the curriculum and serving on board committees;

All the Crestview teachers who were interviewed were pleased that the school is willing to provide funds for professional development and that the teachers collaborated well with each other. They spoke highly of the supportive atmosphere of the assistant principal who was responsive to their needs. The assistant principal encouraged teachers to attend many professional development sessions to remain innovative, and to select activities that give them creative ideas for the classroom.

Some of the teachers noted problems with the 'arts' emphasis at the school. Specifically, teachers expressed dissatisfaction with the instructional methods of the arts teachers who focus on performance. Because the arts teachers have little or no teaching experience, the Crestview teachers must assist them. But many of the Crestview teachers themselves have limited experience in defining their own curriculum and connecting it with the school's arts emphasis. They often expressed self doubt about their ability to enhance the school's mission in this area, noting a conflict between their academic curriculum and the arts program. Although teachers often feel at odds with the arts perspective, they also believe that their views are being heard. They stated their concerns about this issue:

> There is a balance in the curriculum with the arts and academics, but artists are artists and they do not always show up on time leaving me with little time to do my planning because I then have to watch the students;

> The focus on the arts here helps those children having problems in school excel, but sometimes the arts overshadow the academic curriculum.

These teachers struggle with their lack of experience and the challenge to develop professionally in an environment that demands so much. The staff is evenly divided in their commitment to the school. The longer teachers remain at Crestview or the more they gain in experience, the more they tend to thrive in this autonomous setting. The two teachers who were at Crestview the longest noted the time concerns. However, once they were able to manage their curriculum issues, they really enjoyed their teaching at Crestview. However, those teachers with limited experience in curriculum development feel the stress of having to develop their own program and manage their time. Crestview teachers spoke glowingly of their principal and the parents who value them as professionals.

Teacher Efficacy

Much study has been done in the area of the interactive relationship between personal teaching and organizational efficacy (Dembo and Gibson, 1985; Fuller, Wood, Raport and Dornbusch, 1982). In addition to organizational factors, teachers are also influenced by their belief in their ability to have a positive influence on student learning, their ability to adopt new practices and the accountability process to evaluate their competence. There is also evidence that a teacher's efficacy varies with experience and professional training (Gibson and Brown, 1982). Higher levels of experience and training bring higher degrees of efficacy for many teachers.

In this study teacher efficacy is examined in terms of the organizational context, which is defined by the principals' leadership, the parents' involvement and the teachers' commitment to student achievement. While a teacher's commitment plays a role in his or her ability to affect change in students' learning, the organizational culture establishes the conditions for teachers to achieve efficacy in their professional lives. As indicated earlier, teacher commitment arises from opportunities for input into the school governance and autonomy in making curriculum decisions. A person's efficacy can be enhanced by the principal's leadership, parent involvement, and the teachers' commitment to student learning. Many of the teachers interviewed for this study cited the principal, parents and the school for creating an environment for 'personal teaching efficacy'. The development of a teacher's personal sense of efficacy is tied to the school's organizational health. A teacher's belief in her ability to effect student learning as well as her perception of the school is instrumental in creating teaching efficacy.

The relationship between a teacher's efficacy and the school's organization is reciprocal; climate affects a sense of efficacy and efficacy affects perceptions of climate (Hoy and Woolfolk, 1993). Organizational health in schools is viewed as harmonious when all school constituencies are able to cope with disruptive external forces and direct their energies toward the school's mission. The dimensions of organizational health include: institutional integrity, principal influence, consideration, resource support, morale and academic emphasis (Hoy, Podgurski and Tarter, 1991; Hoy, Tarter and Kottkamp, 1991). In a healthy school the principal, unimpeded by the administrative hierarchy, can manage in an open, friendly manner that shows a genuine concern for the welfare of teachers. There is also a high degree of morale among the faculty members and adequate resources to promote a sense of professionalism. The school also creates an environment where parents are involved and committed to academic excellence.

Newmann, Rutter, and Smith (1989) found that teacher efficacy is affected by the orderly behavior of the students and by a supportive, understanding principal who encouraged them to be innovative and to try various teaching strategies. Particular aspects of school climate and health help teachers to accomplish their goals. However, the literature is unclear regarding the connection between a school's organizational culture and teacher efficacy. While many studies (Dembo and Gibson, 1985) cite the connection, inconsistencies among the various teacher efficacy instruments obscure the link between the two variables. Teacher efficacy is multidimensional, it is influenced by organizational factors and personal commitment to affecting student behavior. A teacher's sense of both personal and teaching efficacy also relates to organizational support for his or her goals for students (Hoy and Woolfolk, 1993).

Wynne (1989) notes that teacher efficacy is enhanced when the principal fosters activities that promote the academic excellence in the pursuit of collective goals. Often the pursuit of a positive culture is accompanied by controversy. However, in the ideal, the principal creates an environment where judicious compromises can be made and teachers can engage in tactful confrontation. The principal also serves as the gatekeeper in deterring unsympathetic teachers from sabotaging new policy directives. Principals play an important role in defining the context of academic excellence by supporting teachers and encouraging them to be innovative in their teaching practices. Principals try to create a collective environment where teachers are compatible in their philosophy of teaching. The end result is a collaborative school where the emphasis is on the students' learning.

Johnson (1989) contends that principals vary substantially in their attitudes toward involving teachers formally and informally in the school organization. Teachers feel less efficacious when the principal fails to be receptive and to take seriously teachers' ideas and suggestions. This approach leaves teachers with no formal or informal means to enact change in the school. Principals who are controlling and exclusionary prevent teachers from having input into the school decision-making process. When the principal is more solicitous and open to teachers' suggestions, teachers feel they can approach the principal with their ideas. Teachers are more willing to participate in new programs if they have had input and feel their opinions are valued by the principal. Teachers, in such a context, establish working relationships with one another that are shaped by similar beliefs and develop a sense of professional equality. Teachers become more efficacious because they are given the right to make independent professional judgments concerning their teaching. Teachers' willingness to participate in school decision-making is influenced primarily by their relationships with their principal (Smylie, 1992).

Another organizational factor that affects teacher efficacy is parent involvement. A major source of low teacher efficacy is their relationship with parents of low achieving students (Ashton, Webb and Doda, 1983). Teachers become frustrated when parents are uninvolved in their child's learning and do not attend school conferences. Due to these frustrations, teachers reduce contacts with parents resulting in lower standards of behavior for their students. The complex interrelationship between the parents, teachers and the principal creates tension and even hostility. Waller (1965) believes that parents and teachers are natural enemies. Both have authority over the child, and sometimes they clash over the child's obedience and affection. A teacher's approval of a child's behavior rarely coincides with the parent's perspective because the parent's view is particular while the teacher's is universal. When a teacher is asked to meet with a parent, the teacher invariably wonders who the principal will side with. Holmes and Wynne (1989) believe a parent's request for meeting a teacher results in misgivings on all sides. Often the principal tries to please both parties instead of mediating. Thus, the principal is perceived by the teacher as undermining the teacher's authority. Harmonious relationships between teachers and parents promote shared goals and encourage parents to become involved in the school.

Teacher Efficacy in Independent Schools

Teachers at the three sites noted positive relationships with their principal and parents. Participants noted that they derive great satisfaction from working with their principal and feel that the parents greatly enhance their ability to teach. Teachers feel the principal is pivotal in providing leadership in the areas of curriculum and student learning problems. If the principal proves unable to assist a teacher, she directs the teacher to additional resources. Principals seek teachers' advice on curriculum decisions and school policies. Each principal at the school supports teachers in working with parents and encourages them to involve their parents into their classroom activities. Teachers value input from parents in helping them make decisions about their students. Participants feel that the school's organizational structure is important in helping them improve their teaching and work cooperatively with parents.

Organizational factors such as parent involvement and principal support can affect a teacher's ability to have a positive influence on their students' learning. A healthy environment where teachers can accomplish their goals is critical to enhancing a teacher's efficacy. In such an environment parents support the orderly behavior of their children and the efforts of the teachers, in establishing an interactive relationship. When parents are too involved, this study shows, there is a potential for problems. A principal in a privatized setting who is overly responsive to parents may affect teachers' efficacy. Although many of the participants in this study find parent involvement very valuable, some concerns arose with the principal's ability to control parents. Teachers believe that principals face a challenge in balancing the two groups that can best be met by educating parents about their role in the school curriculum and instructional practices. Because the principals are involved in marketing and recruiting, they must be solicitous to parents. Yet, they must also remain distant in order to provide teachers more autonomy in the classroom, maintaining the balance is difficult. If self-governed schools are to provide an environment where teachers can focus on student achievement, the principal must educate parents on how to provide support without hindering progress.

Appleman School

Of the thirteen teachers who interviewed for this study, most feel that the school is supportive to their teaching and their ability to enhance student achievement. All of the teachers noted that Appleman's students are highly motivated, and they are rewarded when they see their students doing well academically. Teachers believe students benefit from having them as teachers and take pride in the quality of Appleman's graduates. Although these teachers feel very efficacious in their ability to teach, they are often frustrated with the extent of parent involvement. While they generally feel the principal supports them as teachers, approximately half of the teachers interviewed noted that the principal is often swayed by parents' complaints. During the observation period for this study, the science teacher was asked to leave giving rise to mixed emotions in teachers and parents. While only inexperienced teachers felt threatened by the science teacher's dismissal, the more seasoned teachers questioned the way the issue was handled with respect to the competency of the science teacher. Thus, organizational factors undermined teacher efficacy to a degree, as teachers viewed the Appleman principal as a bit intimidating and, at times, too willing to listen to what parents want.

While all the teachers noted that the school was a wonderful place for them professionally, they expressed concerns about their relationships with parents. Teachers noted that the school environment makes them want to remain throughout their professional careers, and they feel very positively connected with their students. Teachers interviewed at Appleman feel parents value their professional expertise, but, they noted, some parents do not always listen to their suggestions. The teachers almost seem to have a love–hate relationship with parents. On the one hand, they feel the support of parents in teaching. Parents insure their children behave and complete homework tasks. However, teachers resent parents for the amount of freedom they have over the principal and the school's need to continually place parents first.

In interviews, the teachers expressed gratitude for the respect and support parents show. However, when asked about the role of parents at the school, teachers noted that parents often pressure them to make decisions that do not benefit the whole class and ignore their suggestions. These teachers realize that they have to be responsive to parents in a privatized setting. Yet, they sometimes feel a loss of control when parents make demands about their children and the administration seems all too willing to give in to their demands. This often occurred with learning problems when parents felt their child was above average yet the teacher was not supporting this view. It also occurred when teachers were responsible for identifying secondary schools for the 6th graders. Parents often did not agree with these secondary school placements. There were many mixed responses from teachers about the involvement of parents and the way that involvement affects their ability to teach. At least five of the teachers interviewed noted that parent involvement was an important factor in supporting them in the classroom. Teachers noted:

> There is a strong positive parental support for the kids. The school uses the concept of family as a marketing device to attract students. You can really teach at Appleman because of the support of parents. The parents help me with planning field trips, parties, and everything else with the teacher's input.

> Parents here are a valuable resource to the school. It is wonderful to see parents involved in the planning process at the school. Parent involvement is really different here. I'm not saying that parents at public schools did not back you, but I see here that parents are truly concerned.

> It's true they've paid lots of money for their children to be here. But to me, they're never too pushy. They call me when they need to. But, heck, I think if I was spending this much money I would call too. I tell parents it's an open door policy here. They can come or call me any time.

> Every year you look at your parents and get to know them. Some parents are glad to have their kids here all day, 45 minutes before school and 2 hours after school so they can work and not worry about their kids. Other parents want to be in touch with you continuously, especially at my grade.

> For the most part parents trust us implicitly. Most parents are very open to what you have to say and for the most part they are accepting of what you have to say and for the most part agree with it. The parents here are very involved and I think that's great for their children.

While the other half of the teachers also value the involvement of parents, they are concerned that parents do not always listen, have too much authority and command too much attention from the principal. These participants provided mixed signals about their perceptions of parent involvement. On the one hand they valued the parents' support and on the other hand, they feel the school empowered parents more than was necessary. Several teachers expressed these negative opinions about parent involvement:

I don't think that parents have the power to affect the schooling decisions so much as the individual squeaky wheels affect school decisions.

I have not been here long enough, but I have heard one of the teachers say that she is continually scared of angering a parent or getting a parent upset. I'm young and I'm fresh, but I'm really not scared of them. There must be a subtle pressure that happens over time that you see developing. I'm sure that a lot of people feel it, but I don't really feel it. I have a pretty good rapport with parents and they're still kind of happy that I'm here.

Parent involvement here is really good. I must admit that I don't have too much to do with the parents. That is one of the pluses of my job. I think what we do in the specials is very important, but I don't think that other parents worry about it too much. If parents come in at all, it's because their children are talented and they are looking for other resources.

Sometimes parent involvement can be too much in the fact that they can dictate policy. This whole handwriting business. I can give you the name of a parent who started this whole business. Her complaints, honest to goodness, shortly after this there was this D'Nealian. We had always used manuscript. In my opinion, money counts. I do feel that if you do a good job in the classroom, on the whole, in as much as you are a good teacher and care about the children, and are doing your best and are not incompetent, that you do get supported by the parents. So I feel competent in that sense. Although parents have gone to Mrs Bates and complained about me, I've never felt the pressure.

I do think that parents sometimes have too much say of whether they like a teacher or not. And I think the administration can be influenced, but I don't think I am doomed. No matter how hard you try, you're never going to please everybody. You've just got to develop thick skin and do the best you can because somebody is going to be unhappy.

I had a child two years ago whose parents decided that I had selected their child to persecute for the year. He was biting children, and he was hitting them with the large wooden blocks. He was impulsive and hot tempered and had a volatile mother. We worked together with the curriculum director and principal and finally got the child to a psychologist, who was helping with behavior modification. Very supportive. We do a lot of counseling with parents, and I don't think it falls on deaf ears. But there are times when we realize that there are just certain family situations that are not going to listen to what we have to say.

I had an interesting experience this year where I had a parent who insisted on something. And I felt awful about it and it was against my better judgment and it turned out to be a rather disastrous thing and so I learned. My worst day and that was a case of me not being sure of myself.

In the past ten years, there was so much parent involvement and so many opinions offered by the parents that it could be a real witch hunt. It was almost too much empowerment by some groups. The former principal would return from the coffees at the beginning of the school year and just literally look like he had been beaten because parents would jump all over him about this issue and that issue. But now Mrs Bates and her staff have worked diligently to come to an understanding with parents. As far as I know, there are very few confrontational meetings that transpire these days.

The comments indicate that teachers at Appleman have mixed feelings about the involvement of parents in the school program. The organizational culture in a privatized setting promotes a responsiveness to parents' concerns, and that can produce a strain for teachers. Although parent involvement is perceived as positive, many teachers are concerned about the nature of this engagement and its affect on their ability to teach. While teacher efficacy is often undermined by an inability to engage parents, in this privatized setting several parents appear too involved in policy and curriculum decisions, leaving teachers feeling insecure and threatened. Meeting the needs of parents in the privatized setting can conflict with developing an environment for teacher efficacy. A positive organizational culture in the privatized setting depends upon striking a balance between parent involvement and teacher autonomy.

Teacher efficacy also depends on the role the principal plays in supporting teachers, so they can influence their students' learning. Teachers at Appleman spoke highly of their principal on the whole. Teachers feel that their principal trusts them to make curriculum decisions and is very supportive of their work. None of the teachers commented about the evaluation process that the school uses to assess their effectiveness. There appear to be no common criticism among the teachers of the principal's leadership in assisting the teachers. However, they feel that Mrs Bates has a difficult job trying to keep parents and faculty happy about their role at the school. Teachers noted:

Even though the principal at the public school was a nice guy, he didn't have time for the kids because he was so into the numbers and stuff and keeping the school going. You never saw him. And Mrs Bates, you see her out, you see her with kids. No, I am never intimidated by her. I just respect her so much because she has helped me in so many ways when I'm stuck;

The administration trusts you. They feel you can do your job and if you need to ask her something, her door is always open. I really like that. I think Mrs Bates is offended when you call her your boss. She really wants to be on equal footing with everybody. Her job is the business of the school and our job is the classroom;

Mrs Bates is so together looking and together as a person and all that kind of stuff, sometimes I'm a little intimidated by her. Mrs Bates is intimidating at times. For me, I think it's because she is my boss and this is my first year;

Mrs Bates does not have a background in education *per se*; it's in marketing and business and that sort of thing. Her primary concern is what's good for marketing this school. I understand that she has to sell this school but she is supportive. If you ask people what they remember about this school it's her (Mrs Bates). They remember the sales job. And I think that she genuinely believes in the school, as we all do. If I just sat here and said that everything was perfect, you wouldn't believe me. That's not real. There are problems just like there are everywhere.

In most cases, teachers feel that while their principal is supportive, her priorities are with marketing and promoting the school. Many teachers view Mrs Bates as accessible and responsive to their concerns. Veteran teachers who had worked with another principal feel that Mrs Bates developed a very good rapport with parents, educating them regarding their role in the school. However, the less seasoned teachers find Mrs Bates a bit intimidating and too responsive to parents. Overall, teachers feel their principal supports and trusts them to make autonomous decisions about their curriculum. Teachers feel the principal is helpful in working with students' learning problems, but they believe she could provide more support when difficult diagnostic decisions are made.

Bakersfield School

Of the eleven participants at Bakersfield School, many noted the positive relationship they have with parents and their principal. While Appleman teachers often expressed feelings of discontent the Bakersfield teachers appreciate support from both their parents and principal. Many participants view the principal, Dr Brimming, as a good buffer between the teachers and parents. Dr Brimming is responsible for educating parents about their involvement in the school program and teachers believe her efforts to educate have helped parents understand that it is not their role to dictate curriculum and instructional practices. Only one respondent felt parents were over protective, but even this individual noted that the principal stepped in to assist parents in allowing their children to do their own work. Overall, many of the teachers interviewed feel very efficacious in their ability to teach and affect student learning. They view the principal as supportive and successful in the difficult task of responding to all of the school participants.

All of the Bakersfield teachers feel supported by the principal. In some instances, they even feel they have more power than the principal in working with parents. At least half of the participants describe the principal as a colleague rather than a 'boss', who was open, supportive, and trusting. Teachers expressed the following comments:

> In some ways we have more power. I'm not saying power in a bad way, I'm saying that the language arts in our school has a block of five. If one can't bring up a concern when it's time to do so, one of the other ones can. That is the main thrust here at the school;

> She (Dr Brimming) and I have our differences, that's natural, but I think that Dr Brimming is a wonderful person. I wish I had her language skills. She could talk her way out of anything, I do believe. I tend to get myself into trouble with my mouth. She's a good administrator and she works with you. A couple of times, I've said things that I should have been fired for, but she works with you. I've been in her office several times, because parents did not agree with what I had said to their children and we've worked through it. I know she serves as a pretty good buffer. She has the procedure of calming them (parents), letting them have their say. She rationalizes with parents. That seems to be a large part of her responsibility, being responsive to parents. On the other half, being true to teachers;

> I think we have a really good evaluation process. The administration is very helpful; in that sense, I learn a lot. There are benefits that come out of the process. It's always more constructive positive criticism than negative criticism;

> I think she's a very strong lady. She has to take charge, which is good in her situation. She has to be the one to give the final word and she's real good about making those kinds of decisions. I think it's a little tougher in public schools because the principal may not have as much say;

I would say if there's something that we don't like, it's a little tough because she has the final word;

I think we're all working for the same goal and that makes a big difference. We have wonderful parent support and family support. We have good support, and I know that I've always been able to talk to Dr Brimming anytime. Anytime I needed her she's been there for me. I appreciate that. There are certain things, of course, where she says how it's going to be, but I don't feel it's top down here;

Dr Brimming has given us a lot of freedom here. I think she trusts our judgment. Everybody here is competent and really interested in doing what we can for kids. There is always an opportunity to go to Dr Brimming to voice your opinions. I find that her role is very complex, because at one point she's here in a board meeting where she has to be the aggressor. She has to tell them what's going on; she has to promote the school; she has to confirm to the parents that she knows what she is doing. But then on the other hand with teachers she cannot afford to have that kind of autonomy so then she has to switch to another role where she has to let teachers make the decisions.

With respect to parents, many teachers feel that they are supportive as well as appropriately involved at the school. One participant, who had taught with the school for many years, expressed the opinion that parents are better educated about their role at the school so they are not as vocal as in the past. Teachers at Bakersfield do not view the administration as overly responsive to parents' complaints. They believe that the parents value their professional opinions and appreciate their commitment to the school. Many teachers view parent involvement as instrumental to their teaching since parents do volunteer work and tutor students who need additional assistance. Teachers made the following comments about parents:

Knowing that parents are involved in their children's education is great. They've got a real investment and not just a monetary investment. They're just involved and supportive of what we're trying to do. Basically, we're working together;

The administration steps in when the parents are trying to dictate the curriculum. They would tell the parents that it's not their place to make decisions about what happens in the classroom as far as room assignments. Parents love to say which they want their kids in and we tell them they can't say that. It's not their decision;

I just feel that parents are working for me. They are working for my benefit. I think they appreciate the body of teachers that they have here. I love to have parents in my classroom and have been fortunate with the parents coming in to help me. But I've also gone through times when it wasn't real pleasant and they have stepped over the line. I don't want them (parents) teaching. I just want support. That's usually what you get 99 percent of the time;

It seems they're not as involved in the classroom as they once were. It may be that I am not inviting them in as much. They're interested but I see a difference in parents now. They don't seem to have as much time as they did five years ago;

The good thing about parent involvement is that they really care and are willing to support you totally. They want their children to do well and they'll do whatever it takes in terms of testing and stuff like that. The bad thing is that they are so involved, they can't stand back and look objectively and when testing needs to be done it's very difficult to convince them. They take their children's shortcomings more personally than people who are more distanced from their children.

Thus, teachers at Bakersfield are positive about the role of parents in their classrooms. Teachers are also pleased with the role that the principal plays in dealings with parents. Teachers feel the principal supports them and listens to their concerns. There is no indication that she overreacts to parents. Rather, the principal encourages parents to interact with the teachers thereby enhancing parents' trust. Teachers believe the principal has a difficult role in keeping all the school participants happy. Teachers also feel that the principal trusts their decisions and allows them autonomy in their instructional practices.

Crestview School

The Crestview teachers had responses similar to those of the Appleman and Bakersfield teachers regarding the support of parents and of their principal. Since most curriculum issues are administered by the assistant principal, teachers were very vocal about their interactions with her. Teachers also feel that the principal compensates them for the long hours spent at the school by giving them additional planning time during the school day. Since most of the teachers are very inexperienced, they see a real need for the additional time for curriculum planning and for developing their own program. The principal and assistant principal try to keep meetings and attendance at parent socials to a minimum. Teachers were appreciative of their administrators' efforts to protect their planning time. None of the teachers feels that the school is too responsive to parents' complaints. Indeed, the school appears to balance its response to the needs of parents and teachers. One teacher did comment about the long day at the school: 'You have to be responsive to parents after spending almost ten hours a day with their children. It is very difficult to be responsive to the school's families when you spend so much time at the school.'

Several teachers at Crestview noted that they use parents as a resource to support them in their classrooms. One teacher noted, 'Some parents know about computers more than I do so I call on them to help with the school's technology component. They know about where to purchase things and how to determine the trends for the school.' Another teacher feels that the school is very responsive to its minority parents who help address multicultural concerns in the classroom. The science teacher at Crestview involves parents in their children's education by having them help children with their science projects. Parents with a science background serve as judges in assessing the children's projects. All the teachers feel that parent involvement is important in helping them teach. Because many of the teachers are inexperienced and coping with long school days, they need the support of their principal. They like the principal and the parent involvement but feel the stress of curriculum planning and the length of time to prepare instructional materials.

Professional Community in Schools

Sergiovanni (1994b) views schools as communities which give equal weight to competence and virtue in evaluating professionalism. Because teachers as professionals accept the trust that parents give to them, they must be caring individuals committed to their students. Good teachers work collegially, engaging in interdependent work, sharing commitments for the common good, and developing standards that all can support to enhance their teaching. Professionalism is more than expertise; it is a condition that instills commitment to make a school a place where all children can learn and teachers can work together for the common good.

Louis-Seashore and Kruse (1993, 1995) believe that for schools to become school-based communities there must be specific characteristics and conditions within the organizational context. These characteristics include opportunities for reflective dialogue. In communal schools, teachers are able to discuss problems and work collectively to find solutions. They collaborate, sharing ideas to ensure student learning. In the communal school, teachers are encouraged to pursue ongoing professional development activities that enhance trust and respect among its school participants. The structural conditions include opportunities, such as team teaching and shared curriculum design, that allow teachers to exchange knowledge and techniques to foster student achievement. Teachers have considerable autonomy in developing curriculum and determining instructional practices. This school-based professional community relies on supportive leadership that encourages professional development and establishes a commitment to teaching.

Little (1990) believes that because teacher collegiality benefits the school setting, administrators should encourage collaboration. Students also benefit from teacher collaboration when teachers work together to improve student achievement. Even veteran teachers gain by establishing close collegial relationships. By collaborating, teachers can increase the pool of ideas, materials, and methods that will lead to higher quality instruction. Group problem solving among teachers encourages them to attempt innovative practices in curriculum decision-making and pedagogy. A combination of teacher visibility and shared responsibility in making decisions heightens the influence of teachers on one another. Social support among school members enhances mentoring for new teachers and advances the knowledge of veteran teachers.

Opportunities for teacher collegiality are dependent on the principal and the school structure. These organizational factors, which affect the collegial interaction among teachers, are crucial for promoting professional development among teachers. Administrators can influence the level of socialization among teachers by encouraging discussions about teaching, providing leadership to energize teachers, and supporting collaborative teaching. The principal can also create a workplace that taps the talents of teachers and embraces collaboration and collegiality among them. Principals need to address the organizational capacity to improve teacher performance by accepting multiple solutions to school problems and work collectively with teachers (Hart, 1990).

My notes from faculty meetings and teachers' interviews confirm that the three independent schools in the study emulate many characteristics of a professional-based community. During my year at the three sites and my other yearly visits, I observed an ethos of caring in these privatized settings. Because privatized settings create a commitment to a common mission, an environment develops where individuals feel efficacious about their ability to teach. These teachers willingly put their personal interests aside in order to respond to the students' needs. Whether this evolution of professional community is inherent in the nature of privatization (consumer-orientation, innovative practices, adherence to mission, and teacher autonomy) or due to other causal factors is an issue for further study. Clearly, however, privatization where individuals are given many freedoms provides a framework for examining ways to establish professional community.

Although the research literature of defining and characterizing the professional community is incomplete, my observations and discussions with teachers, parents, and administrators led me to believe that such a community exists at each of the three settings. There was a pervasiveness of collective responsibility and commitment among the participants. Although many quantitative researchers may bristle at this sweeping generalization, on the 'gut level' I knew I was in the presence of a school community. Of course, it is difficult to convey the characteristics of school-based professional community since to do so requires the re-creation of this feeling. To obtain some more objective evidence, I re-examined my teacher interview transcriptions for references to collaboration, empowerment, shared norms and values, deprivatization of practice, and social and human resource conditions as a professional-based community (areas noted by Louis-Seashore and Kruse, 1993, 1995). Commitment and efficacy as noted earlier establish dimensions of professional community, and these elements are extremely apparent in the school-based professional community.

The interview questions, which focused on teacher autonomy, commitment, professional development, and relationships with administrators and parents (see Appendix), do not focus specifically on the dimensions of professional community. Analysis of the teachers' interviews left me struggling with piecemeal data to demonstrate to the reader that these schools emulate the characteristics of professional community. Yet, my observations confirm that these teachers engage collaboratively in discussions about their teaching and share in a mission to enhance student learning. In addition, data from previous interviews allowed me the opportunity to re-identify quotes that gave voice to the teachers' perceptions about their colleagues and their willingness to assume a collective responsibility for learning. The organizational arrangement involving team teaching in all three settings, speaks to the interdependence of teachers who engage in serious conversations about their instructional practices and curriculum. Data from the twenty-eight teacher interviews was reorganized in terms of specific characteristics of professional community. Although the theoretical constructs concerning professional community are difficult to define and to measure, observations, attendance at faculty meetings and interviews with teachers provide insights to suggest that the schools in the study exemplify a community of learners.

Collaboration in Independent Schools

One aspect of professional community is collaboration among teachers who exchange information about their teaching and professional development. Instructional activities such as cross disciplinary teaching, cross grade activities and sharing subject matter concepts with colleagues typify collaboration ventures among these faculty members. In all three settings teachers were dependent on each other as a result of a teaming and mission adherence. Many teachers spoke glowingly of the support that comes from sharing with their colleagues. While many teachers at the three sites spoke favorably of their autonomy in developing curriculum and instructional practices, a review of the tape transcriptions indicates that teachers valued their colleagues' contribution in shaping their own practice and professional growth. The following comments were extrapolated from the twenty-eight interviews at the three settings.

> There seems to be an increasing amount of collaboration among the teachers here at Appleman. I can only really speak for the third and fourth grade levels. This year there was a unit on Columbus in the third grade. The social studies teacher and the third grade teacher spent a great deal of time planning and executing a very effective unit.

Each child wrote a book about it. In the fourth grade there was a unit on land formation and plant study. This was planned by the fourth grade teacher and science teacher. Once again this was a team effort which produced an interesting area of study for children;

Team Teaching is a 'biggie' with two teachers in the room. We split subject areas social studies/science and also teach and support other areas such as reading and writing. There's a great deal of talk between teachers at least at the grade level above and the grade level below. We check new materials with each other or run and tell someone if we see something interesting;

The collaboration with other colleagues is very stimulating, and I would like to see more planning for collaboration during the day with my co-teacher and other grade level teachers;

There is just a real sense of helping each other personally and professionally for the good of each other and the children. There is lots of give and take of materials, subject matter concepts and teaching practices, advice, etc. There is no competition among faculty;

Grade level teachers meet formally once a week and informally every day to share ideas, information and happenings regarding individual students. Subject area meetings occur monthly to share activities and ideas. A lot of effort is put into special scheduling of cross discipline activities and many collaborative efforts are put into special scheduling of these activities as well as joint planning;

I feel that everyone in our school is willing to share any materials or ideas that they have. Since there is no competition between rooms to outdo each other as is sometimes the case in public schools, it is easy to share ideas daily among all of our colleagues.

During my many visits to these schools, it was not unusual to see groups of teachers exchanging ideas and curriculum materials. At one language arts faculty meeting at Appleman in particular, I was amazed at the depth of understanding the teachers showed in articulating their curriculum focus in language arts. Each teacher distributed copies of her instructional materials, identified students' skills, and explained the use of certain literature sets. It was a very collaborative meeting where teachers shared their materials and spoke positively of what each colleague was doing. Bakersfield teachers have similar meetings to discuss subject areas and they, too, recognize the specific expertise of each colleague. These meetings are teacher run and there is an exchange of professional information. There is discussion of how teachers have tried new techniques in their setting. The Bakersfield teachers met weekly to address curriculum issues for the week. Crestview does not do as much teaming, but teachers work closely to schedule activities for the social science portion of the curriculum. Crestview teachers did many cross-discipline activities and worked with the local artists to do many integrated school projects.

All faculty meetings at the three schools are always positive in nature, and teachers seldom argued over issues. Honest discussions are directed toward enhancing both teaching and professional development. There is great respect among the teachers, and petty arguments would not be tolerated by this group of teachers. Most faculty meetings provide teachers with updated information on school and board issues. Student achievement, curriculum, professional meetings, and testing provide topics for subject area meetings and/or team meetings. Teachers seldom discuss instructional practices; instead they focus on teaming, selection of materials, cross disciplinary activities, and exchange of ideas. The teachers rely on their professional exchange as a source of ideas for teaching. Discussions about discipline or problems with low achieving students are seldom necessary because many teachers are quite good at managing the various levels of student learning. Discipline was an area many teachers did not want to address. It was apparent this was a problem and teachers felt uncomfortable addressing it. Discussions of the mismatch between philosophical differences about management was an issue teachers really side-stepped. Problems with team teaching are rare although there were occasional comments from teams about some minor issues. Each school is quick to move if members of a team are not congenial nor supportive; requests for change are honored if necessary when openings occur on other teams. When teachers' philosophies clash, the principal attempts to maintain professionalism and preserve collegiality. For the most part all teachers work collaboratively in an atmosphere characterized by respect.

Teacher Empowerment

Teacher empowerment, a factor in professional community, was examined earlier with respect to commitment and efficacy. Teachers who are committed feel a sense of ownership for student learning and their school's goals. Because they have so much autonomy in their curriculum decisions and ample funds for professional development, teachers feel a collective responsibility for increasing the learning that takes place at the school. When reviewing interview data for evidence of teacher empowerment, the researcher examined factors that allow teachers to have autonomy in developing school policies, selecting staff, determining curriculum and instructional practices, and pursuing professional development. Researchers in the area of professional community note that these elements are important for building reflective dialogue and collaboration among teachers (Louis-Seashore and Kruse, 1995).

Teachers made these comments on their sense of empowerment:

> At Appleman there is a great degree of input by the teacher. Staff selection is handled jointly by the principal and a committee of teachers. We are all encouraged to express our wants, needs and theories concerning curriculum.

> We have input in staff selection, materials, almost completely, and lots of professional development monies that can accumulate for a few years but we have less say in policies but we have the freedom to 'speak' our piece.

> Faculty are asked to chose which hiring committee they would like to join and are included in policy decisions. In my particular area, we develop, refine and explore new curriculum ideas and then we take these ideas to administration. This keeps one refreshed, updated, enthused about our material. I feel empowered and challenged to teach using a methodology which best suits my talents, and the material represents my philosophies. Of course, hiring individuals with similar philosophies is required by school administration, school community and faculty.

> I feel extremely empowered to design and implement a curriculum, change my program, express my opinion, be responsible for my own professional development, use materials that I think are worthwhile in my teaching and try new teaching/learning styles.

> Teachers have the power to determine or change curriculum and also to determine the manner in which it is implemented. We are able to select materials and professional development activities which are most appealing to us. We also have the opportunity to interview perspective team members. Through participation on various committees, we can have input into the calendar, schedule, budget, salaries, development, policies, etc.

These were just a few comments among the many that demonstrate the way teachers feel about being empowered. The teachers were, indeed autonomous in engineering their own professional growth and implementing their own curriculum. Not one of the twenty-eight respondents stated any dissatisfaction with individual autonomy. Seasoned Crestview teachers, however, found the challenge of developing their own curriculum very rewarding. Some of the inexperienced teachers at Crestview were overwhelmed with this autonomy but they felt it was important for them to develop ownership to the curriculum. Teachers feel that the school participants trust their ability to select and develop their own programs. The opportunity to work with other teachers, to share information and emotional support, contributes to a teacher's sense of empowerment. Teachers differed in their views of their input in school policies.

In some instances, although they have little input in some policy decision-making, they feel free to express their opinions. In other instances teachers saw no need for their involvement in board decisions, focusing instead on their teaching and their collaboration with other teachers. It is apparent teachers were given the opportunity to participate in decision making if they felt the need. Some teachers trusted the school to make the right choices so their participation was not needed. The professional community of each setting provides these teachers with mechanisms to improve classroom practice and to develop supportive relationships thereby empowering them as professionals.

Common Beliefs and Shared Values

All of these schools have mission statements that results in common beliefs about how to teach and socialize their students. Schools of choice espouse school missions that prevail in the way teachers use instructional practices, select curriculum materials and respond to the schools' constituencies. Parents select these schools to satisfy an individual student's particular needs and interests or a family preference in general school orientation (Raywid, 1990). To uphold each school's philosophy, teachers work to select new teachers who will 'buy' into the mission. This process of teacher selection results in shared values among teachers concerning the curriculum and the goals for students. This collective focus on student learning based on the school's mission results in higher order thinking activities, inclusion of values in the curriculum, and less dependence on recall-recognition testing. Informal conversations with teachers and comments during the interviews revealed that the school's common philosophy is the driving force in the collaborative teaching environment. Teachers commented on their shared values and the collective focus on student learning:

> We are encouraged and obligated to keep learning about the craft of the profession. I sense some are more interested in truly keeping up and thus they are trying new things in their classroom. I think a big part about the Appleman faculty is there is a sense of community here. In the length of time I have been here, there's been much more concern about student discipline and open dialogue about student learning here. That exists here at Appleman because of the leadership and the tone that's set from on top. I feel trusted and valued and that creates a very positive force and atmosphere;

> We attempt to nurture the whole child which is our philosophy and that often involves special conferences with parents and other teachers. In order to keep our mission strong it is vital for us to talk among ourselves and keep abreast of new findings. Although as a faculty or as team members we discuss discipline we do not have consensus.

147

This happens when teachers of one group of students have different expectations and consequences. This discrepancy is not always a problem, but we do not always agree on how to handle these issues so we don't;

Each student is viewed as a person with special gifts. They are not always visible in their academic accomplishments, but it surfaces in the classroom atmosphere. We try to make the most of the moments and encourage students to realize the value of all people and their own strengths. Consistency in discipline is difficult when the personalities and needs of children vary so much. However, we do have a basic discipline policy with regard to respect. This gives us the foundation for the development of values which help diminish the occurrence of major discipline problems;

We affirm what is our mission here at school in the two day workshops at the beginning of the year. When UE (upper elementary) teachers 'live' with their students during the three day outdoor education program, we try to develop more than academics on a 24 hour basis. On a daily basis our team emphasizes the development of responsibility in each student. Our character curriculum emphasizes other desirable traits in individuals. UE teachers develop set policies of discipline together. We have the students perform a 'community service' when they have done something which has interfered with the cooperative efforts of their community like cleaning everyone's desk when they have made a mess;

I think we all feel the responsibility in our school to help with moral education or should I say character education. The children are with us so much that we do have to be a stable, positive role model for them. When we have a serious discipline problem, this drives me to keep learning and reading, hoping to find a better way to reach the child who is a different kind of learner;

We are committed as teachers to get the best out of each child and provide more that just the academic world-arts, music programs, talent shows, leadership. Collectively, we expect students to behave with respect and a reasonable amount of responsibility;

Most of us expect children to behave properly. We don't always step forward and take charge when children are not in our own domain, however. There is little disagreement about what the standards should be. Enforcement is a slightly different issue. Discipline is a teacher's responsibility and it doesn't seem that the administration is very involved in this.

The comments from the various teachers reflect shared values, grounded in each school's mission, which result in a collective focus on student learning. Teachers are more committed to working collectively in teaching students and feel efficacious in affecting student achievement. Teachers used the mission statement to help define curricular needs, challenging themselves to keep abreast of new ideas, share instructional materials and focus on aspects besides academics.

Structural Conditions for Professional Community

Louis-Seashore and Kruse (1993) believe that structural conditions, such as time to meet and talk, physical proximity, interdependent teaching roles (team teaching), communication structures, teacher empowerment and school autonomy, establish professional communities in school. This observation suggests that schools are complex integrated systems directed toward shared goals. In fact, professional communities are internalized structures of norms and beliefs that work without a regulatory system of bureaucratic control. In addition to structural conditions there are social and human resources that induce teachers to care about their colleagues and their teaching. These abstract conditions include openness to improvement, trust and respect, shared expertise, a sense of efficacy, leadership and socialization. A professional community encourages risk taking and innovation so teachers are willing to reflect upon their practice. Teachers believe that their colleagues respect and trust them. Personal trust can build a sense of loyalty, commitment and effectiveness necessary for shared decision-making. Professional community must be based on effective teaching which involves extensive knowledge of subject matter and sophisticated pedagogical skills. Supportive leadership is also a condition for a professional community. Principals serve as a constant source of relevant information to support teachers in their shared vision of the mission statement.

While comments from teachers at the three sites indicate great respect and support for their colleagues, they do not have as many structured opportunities for informal meetings as they would like. Informal conversations with teachers indicate that they need more time for social opportunities. They enjoyed their professional exchanges but seldom have time to develop social encounters that lead to a more caring, collaborative place. The following comments were gleaned from the teachers' interviews about the structural, social and human resources that create a professional community within these environments:

> The most formal opportunity for exchange of ideas would seem to me to be curriculum committees (language arts, math, etc.). Other committees (board, *ad hoc*, etc.) would provide additional opportunities for this. While some members of the school community readily embrace change, I would say that many faculties have their minds

open to new ideas but their bodies are slow to implement them. Our opportunities for social exchanges are brief and spontaneous. I have found these brief exchanges to be more meaningful than one might expect and they help to establish a rapport with colleagues that can be useful on more formal occasions. Generally there seems to be a high level of trust, respect sharing among the faculty and professional staff. Our leadership is competent, but with issues like discipline our faculty does not feel administration is supportive enough. The administration often seems too lenient and tells parents what they want to hear;

So much time and energy are expended on the classroom and students that we tend to neglect the informal gatherings of staff. We don't have as much time as we would like for sharing ideas but our subject area meetings and division meetings give me an outlet and make me feel comfortable. I believe there is a basic trust and respect for colleagues. For the most part I feel I can dialogue with colleagues about educational issues. I being a person who can easily change and change again if it doesn't work, often feel frustration with the length of time it takes to change. However, my personal preference does make me realize the need for proceeding slowly;

Colleagues are most helpful and listen well, if there are any problems. Leadership is okay unless something goes wrong when they often give ultimatums in which we have no where to turn. There is no grievance committee as in public schools. Our principal tries to keep parents happy even at the expense of staff and teachers' rights and beliefs;

We have ample time for formal communication but little time for informal meetings. Conversations with colleagues only happen if you venture out of your room, which I do not do very much. Our leadership is very supportive and it is a very caring and supportive atmosphere. We try not to have gripe sessions, and I sense trust and respect from relevant colleagues;

Professional exchanges regularly take place at division and subject area meetings and socially we have a dinner at the beginning of the year and several times during the year at conferences and faculty appreciation dinner. We have a wonderful group of caring people and I am pleased to be a part of it;

As colleagues, I guess we respect each other as professional teachers and humans. The leadership of the school is extremely supportive and understanding of the teachers. The social life of the teachers is strictly work and not for much outside socials. We talk about educational issues gained during our professional development and we are willing to make changes if necessary. We listen to parents' concerns and provide them with opportunities to come and observe our classes at any time. We are not perfect at what we do so we will always hear any ideas anyone else has and are willing to change if the ideas are beneficial to all;

Overall, I feel that we trust and respect each other as does the administration. I think everyone cares, but we get caught up in the day-to-day business and sometimes forget there is another world. Change occurs in the school when we are all personally interested in a new method or issue. If it will be effective we are anxious and excited to convert others. The driving force to keep us studying and learning is to find a better more effective way to reach a child or a group of children;

The staff here is so strong — there are only two or three people who I cannot respect. For the most part you can talk to anyone and expect a two-way dialogue. We are lucky at our school because only a few really do not want to change. At my other school none of the faculty got along but here it is really different and supportive;

Although I do not always agree with the discipline strategies chosen by my colleagues, I will always support their decisions and challenge their actions in private. There are numerous judgment calls each day so it is important to know your colleagues will be there to support you. And, hopefully, keep you from making major errors in judgment.

Comments from the twenty-eight teachers indicate that they wish they had more time in their day for informal contacts. Because teachers seek out their peers to exchange information or seek support for the handling of specific situations, they need more time to make these important connections. Each school created an environment where teachers have formal opportunities for exchange of curriculum ideas but inadequate time for daily, informal contact about immediate issues.

School discipline created considerable differences of opinion among the teachers. They feel that other teachers are either too lenient or too harsh. However, my observations indicate that each school appears to have great consistency in handling discipline problems through a positive approach that shows respect for students and allows them to make choices. In the many observations that were made, no harsh words were exchanged between students and teachers. The goal of each school's discipline was to help students accept the logical consequences of their behavior. Even at Crestview where teachers were inexperienced and at the survival stage of teaching, they did not use extreme measures such as screaming or demeaning students. Because classroom management is so individualistic, teachers tended to judge other teachers for their philosophies of discipline producing disagreements among staff members. However, because of the cohesiveness of community, all teachers really try to understand their colleagues and their particular management strategies. This is an area where teachers decide not to discuss. At one point, I asked the three principals if they intentionally hired teachers who had so many commonalities in their discipline practices resulting in the school's collective approach to discipline. Their responses indicated that having a common approach to discipline was the outgrowth of hiring teachers with philosophies similar to other teachers' and a commitment to the school's mission.

Collegiality among teachers leads to a professional workplace. Teachers' professional encounters with one another assume greater importance in helping students learn (Little, 1990). Teachers who are collegial talk about their teaching, share planning and preparation, and teach each other about new ideas and new classroom practices. Louis-Seashore and Kruse (1993) believe that community involves emphasis on broadly shared goals, collective responsibility and increased commitment to school goals, values and caring. Community evolves as a result of commitment to the school and the opportunity to be efficacious in one's professional development.

Teachers at the three settings noted that they feel valued by parents, administrators and other colleagues. Given the responsibility to define their own curriculum and to make instructional decisions, teachers feel they are respected members who are valued for their teaching. Many teachers spoke about their respect for each other and their opportunities to share ideas. Minor disagreements about handling discipline problems are not enough to diminish the caring spirit teachers feel toward each other. While some teachers expressed some concern with the principal's tendency to respond to the whims of parents, they recognize that the privatized setting promotes a responsive context. The veteran teachers learn to live and cope with this tension, but some teachers continue to feel that their autonomy and collectivity are compromised by the knowledge that parents have the upper hand.

Professional community within each school was apparent in my conversations with teachers and through attendance at their faculty and subject-area meetings. There is such a spirit of commitment and of care for the children in everything the teachers do. These settings are not without their problems, such as time constraints and overreactive parents. Adherence to the mission statement results in a collective sense of responsibility where teachers collaborate and support each other to promote student learning. Because principals place value on letting teachers develop their own curriculum and select their own professional development, teachers are encouraged to develop into caring professionals.

Conclusion

In privatized settings a common mission prevailed throughout each school, shaping its practices and resulting in a collective sense of responsibility for student learning. Teachers, parents, and administrators have a 'community of mind', represented in shared values, collectiveness, and reflective dialogue about transmitting the goals of the mission to the students. The culture within these privatized settings transcends the responsiveness to clients that is essential to survival and becomes genuine caring. No rigid, hierarchal structure hampers the teachers' commitment to their practice. The classrooms have a small number of students with several teachers available to assist them. Teachers hold common beliefs about how to interpret the mission statement in relation to their curriculum decisions. Their commitment to teaching extends beyond educating children academically, but working with them to be independent and respectful of others.

Privatized settings such as these independent schools have a mission statement that is reflected in the curriculum. Board members hold the schools accountable for implementing the mission and producing graduates who embody it. Schools in this study have organizational structures that create team teaching opportunities where teachers work collectively to carry out the school's mission. Teachers are also given considerable funds for professional development to enable them to improve their practice and remain current in the field. Teachers are autonomous in defining curriculum and selecting their instructional materials. They are encouraged to become involved on board committees and to voice their opinions on school decisions. Parents appreciate and respect teachers in these settings and often seek their opinions regarding their child's progress. Principals encourage teachers to work collectively and trust their curriculum decisions.

Teachers chose to teach in these settings because they accept the philosophies and feel a deep affiliation. Their dedication creates commitment and encourages them to work collaboratively in implementing the school's mission. My research reveals a high degree of commitment and efficacy among the teachers in these settings. Teachers are committed individuals who care about their students, respond to parents' needs, and participate in policy discussions. They feel valued by parents and colleagues alike. Respect among colleagues develops from team teaching situations with opportunities to discuss subject matter and student learning problems.

Teachers feel a high degree of efficacy in their ability to affect student learning. Organizational variables such as parent involvement and administrative support assist teachers in meeting their instructional goals for their students. Principals in these settings encourage teachers to be innovative in meeting students needs by providing professional development funds and educating parents about their role in the school. Principals encouraged parents to be involved in the school through volunteer work and observations in the classrooms. Teachers feel that parents play an integral part in assisting them in the classroom, serving as resources in such areas as technology, sciences, and arts. Teachers were supported in their attempts to try cross disciplinary activities with other teachers. A collective approach to handling learning problems reduces isolation and provides teachers with support in working with student learning problems.

In spite of their opportunities to be autonomous in curriculum decisions, teachers are still interconnected through the mission statement and through team teaching practices. Although teachers agree in defining curriculum, there are concerns about discipline, particularly with respect to inconsistencies and extremes in managing student problems. However, the rewards of having a collaborative school outweigh the disagreements about discipline. Mutual respect allows teachers to overlook differences in philosophies of discipline. Teachers in these settings are never allowed to fail. There is repeated support from other teachers that enables them to improve their craft. Even teachers who are marginal are supported by a system to improve their teaching through their interactions with peers.

Although teachers are highly committed, some feel that time needed to prepare classes, respond to parents, interact with other colleagues is excessive. Many complained about having to attend so many social and fundraising activities which cut into their personal time. Teachers are also concerned about the amount of collaboration time needed to develop classroom activities. Because they spend so much of their day meeting with colleagues, many long hours at school are necessary. Teachers feel they do not have adequate opportunities for just 'socializing' with other teachers to enhance their own personal lives. Teachers also grapple with compromises they make with colleagues to preserve the mission of the school. They feel that in some ways cooperation ensures uniformity and coherence to the school's mission, but, in truth, very few felt that individual inventiveness and creativity were actually compromised.

Teachers also expressed concerns about the context of privatization. Although supported by the principal and parents, teachers feel somewhat alienated by the school's concern with attracting and retaining parents. Their opinions are heard and valued, but sometimes overruled. In interviews teachers described their principals' waffling when parents complained. While no specific examples were noted, there is a pervasive belief that when parents have a strong influence, teachers' professionalism is compromised. Teachers feel they often act to please parents by making six or more contacts a year, spending long hours in conferences, meeting informally with parents, and going well beyond what they had done in public schools.

These privatized settings are not perfect, the teachers embrace the professional community that they represent, speaking openly about their commitment to teaching and their high degree of personal satisfaction. Even teachers who complained about demands on their time and other problems still 'love' their jobs and believe strongly in the school where they teach. The institutional support for collegiality arises from opportunities to make curriculum decisions, team teaching practices, beginning of the year retreats, discussions about mission and appreciation dinners/luncheons. While many see their colleagues as slow to change, they recognize that support rather than coercion leads to innovation for the good of students (Madsen, 1996). Establishing team leadership in privatized settings is a complex task; teachers must transcend personality differences and avoid complaining about the demands of the job. Because of the professional community, teachers do rise above these concerns and focus on cultivating their talents.

Since being in a setting with so much collegiality was rare for me, I was eager to discover the source for this community. What makes teachers care so deeply about their teaching? Why are they so committed to their school and colleagues? Observation confirmed that to work collaboratively, teachers need a common mission that is prevalent and visible in the school. Organizational structures that focus on team teaching practices and cross disciplinary activities are critical elements in developing a reflective dialogue for improving teaching. In addition, the principal must encourage greater teacher autonomy and instill the importance of professional development for teachers to be innovative and willing to take risks in their teaching. Principals have to promote interaction among the faculty and downplay teacher isolation in establishing goals for the school.

Chapter 5

Parent Engagement through Privatization

Parent involvement has been seen as contributing greatly to student achievement. During the past decade educators have recognized the mutual interests and overlapping influence of schools and families (Epstein, 1992). To understand parent engagement, it is important to assess what parents expect their child to take away from the educational process or what the child will accomplish within that system. Parents who view education as a means of upward mobility have high expectations for their children. Having access to choice (private vs. public choice), parents identify schools that will help them to attain their goals for their children (Schneider and Coleman, 1993). In most respects private schools seem to have an ideal environment for encouraging parental involvement because parents select a school for its mission. The school will assume that its families value education, accept its philosophical tenets, and expect to take an interest in decision-making (Chubb and Moe, 1988).

Many people believe that choice leads to more parental involvement because there is a greater investment. However, whether public and private schools actually differ in the level of parental engagement is debatable (Bauch, 1988). Cibulka, O'Brien, and Zewe (1982) believe that private schools encourage local control and decision-making, thus creating high degrees of parent engagement. By nature, privatization represents a form of parent autonomy since families exercise choice. Membership in a community can result in similar views to educate students.

Although there is considerable research on parent involvement, no clear link has been established between privatization and parental engagement. The intent of this chapter is to examine parent involvement to see how the context of privatization engages parents in the educational process. This chapter also studies how these private schools respond to parents' concerns and expectations and empower them through their involvement in the governance structure. In view of choice, this research examines the decision-making process parents use in selecting an elementary school for their child and why they remain at their school of choice.

Literature That Supports Choice

Parent Efficacy

Parent efficacy is defined as allowing parents to have some control over their choices in order to raise their children in a supportive environment and where they can exchange resources with other parents. Schools that enhance parent efficacy increase the potential for parents to be engaged in the school process. Schaefer (1985) indicates that parents with an internal locus of control are proactive in the educational needs of their child. Parents' self image, their relationships with others, their beliefs about their role in life, and their attitudes toward the future affect their efficacy (Swick, 1988). A positive self image, a sense of support from a spouse, and feelings of mutuality are particularly significant for carrying out the parent's role as educator.

Parents' perceptions of significant others such as spouses, friends, and relatives are highly related to efficacy. Having friends with children in the same school setting contributes to establishing a high degree of parent efficacy. Such support systems for problem-solving, resource-sharing, and social interactions increase the potential for parents to be proactive (Swick, 1988). The validation that comes from a similarity in experience strengthens parents' efficacy.

Watson (1981) found that parents with a high degree of efficacy are more engaged in their children's home learning and more involved with them at all stages of their development. School practices that support parent efficacy include: parent education seminars, home visit programs, parental involvement in school governances, community-wide child assessment, support services for parents, and specialized services (Swick, 1988). High efficacy schools provide programs to strengthen and support the family, such as quality day care settings, family school collaborations, education and inservice programs, and family-oriented work contexts.

Teacher and Parent Expectations of School Involvement

Opportunities for parents to interact within the school can range from the macrolevel, where all parents are asked to attend school functions, to microlevel conferences with individual parents discussing their children's progress (Epstein, 1986). Schools are, after all, social organizations with a tradition of interacting in particular ways which may no longer meet the changing needs of parents. Yet, opportunities for such interaction are extremely important. Positive connections between home and school will lead to improvement in academic skills, positive self esteem, and independence for school-age children. Children perceive that caring people in both environments are investing time and coordinating resources to help them succeed. The child's academic work is legitimized by this process of mutual support (Epstein, 1986).

Despite the value placed on improving parent–teacher relations, the literature on the subject reveals the problems in attaining this goal. Cutright's (1984) survey of parents, teachers and administrators reveals that while there is support for increased parent engagement, parents are often unable to participate in the school. From the parents' perspective, several factors mitigate against productive involvement in school, such as lack of time, minimal opportunities for involvement, and indifferent or antagonistic attitudes on the part of the school personnel (Hoover-Dempsey, Brassler, and Brissie, 1987). Teachers may hesitate to involve parents because of the time investment required for productive parent involvement, the absence of external rewards for efforts to involve parents and problems with low commitment on the part of some parents (Epstein and Becker, 1982). Teachers may fear parents because of feeling incompetent or because a parent may blame them for a student's problem (Power, 1985).

Epstein (1986) surveyed over 1,300 parents and teachers to assess the quality of parent engagement. This study reveals differences in how parents and teachers perceive the role of the school in engaging parents. Overall, parents had positive views of parent involvement but they felt the school could do more. Most parents believed they were excluded from some of the most basic school communications such as phone calls, conferences, problems at school and school programs. Other teachers did not involve any parents unless there were problems with their child. However, in some classrooms, where the teachers were leaders in the use of parent involvement, parents said they were frequently involved in learning activities in the school. Teacher leaders who engaged parents in the educational process assisted these families by providing them with ideas and knowledge about their children's instructional program. As a result, these teachers were rated higher by parents in their interpersonal skills and overall teaching quality.

Epstein's study (1986) also reveals that as a child progresses to the higher grades there are fewer opportunities for parent involvement. Parents in the upper elementary grades were often frustrated because of the inability to help their children with homework issues. Parents' feelings about helping their children are based primarily on their own level of education in relationship to the children's grade level. More parents said they could help if they had more education or if their child were in the lower elementary grades where less specialized knowledge is needed. To keep these parents active in their child's education, workshops or special instruction may be necessary to explain how to help in reading, math and other subjects. Ogbu (1974) points out that a parent's lack of knowledge does not necessarily mean lack of interest. Parents report a high degree of efficacy in working with teachers if they receive ideas about how to help the child at home, believe that the teacher does want them to participate and understand what the child has been taught previously (Epstein, 1992).

Teachers differ in their practice of parent engagement according to grade level and subject matter. Elementary programs have a stronger commitment to parents. Teachers of reading and English involve parents more, while teachers of math and social studies need more assistance in engaging parents in the educational process (Epstein, 1992). In a survey of teachers completed by Becker and Epstein (1982), 65 percent of the 3,698 teacher-respondents reported that they discuss 'with each parent' what they can do at home with their children. But many teachers who discuss helping a child with homework do not discuss the teaching methods that a parent might use.

Most teachers have serious doubts about the success of practical efforts to involve parents in learning activities at home (Becker and Epstein, 1982). Leitch and Tangri (1988) observed that teachers-respondents in their study cited the following barriers to parent involvement: parents' unrealistic expectations about the school's role, parents' attitudes that the school is not important enough to take time from work, parents' inability to help with the school work, parental jealousy of teachers' upward mobility, apathy of long time teachers and their lack of responsiveness to parents, and teachers' resentment or suspicion of parents who are involved. Teachers with the most experience seemed more inclined to describe parent involvement as a reciprocal communication process.

Teachers and parents disagree on whether parents are involved and whether they want to be involved. Parents are not involved in the schools for many reasons, ranging from a lack of interest to insecurity about their own educational background when it comes to assisting their children. Teachers, on the other hand, want parents to be involved but may lack the skills necessary to engage parents in the educational process. While teachers may say they want parents to be involved, they often leave parents with mixed signals regarding their role in the school. Teachers at all grade levels tend to blame parents for their low level of responsibility. Yet, there are teachers even within the same schools who succeed in engaging parents in the school.

Models of Parent Involvement

Many researchers have attempted to classify the various types of parent involvement that occur at the school level. Gordon (1977) and Rhine (1981) have identified six types of parent involvement which include: (1) teacher of own child, (2) classroom volunteer, (3) paid paraprofessional, (4) learner, (5) decision maker, and (6) audience. However, Williams and Chaukin (1989), who also identify parent roles at the school, produce a somewhat different list: (1) audience, (2) home tutor, (3) program supporter, (4) co-learner, and (5) advocate. Hester (1989), defining a very similar model, begins with the idea of communication: (1) communication with parents, (2) parents as teachers, (3) parents as supporters of activities, (4) parents as learners, and (5) parents as advocates.

Henderson, Marburger, and Ooms (1986) summarize the literature on parent involvement, identifying two basic types: (a) parent activities aimed primarily at strengthening the overall school program which indirectly help parents with their own children, and (b) parent activities that involve assisting one's own child. Recently, there has been a shift in models of parent involvement from social activities at school to home site assistance. Schools are doing more to educate parents about their efforts to socialize their children at home both in informal and in school-directed activities. These models of parent involvement have changed over the years to respond to parents' concerns. However, most of these changes have only occurred at the preschool and elementary level. Epstein (1992) notes that her studies indicate that parent involvement declines over time with less engagement of parents at the secondary level.

Greenwood and Hickman (1991) view 'the parent as audience' as the traditional way to engage parents in the school. These parents are considered passive partners in assisting the school program by attending assemblies and parent conferences. But a 'parent as volunteer' concept seems more suited to encouraging commitment and interest. These parents are recruited to help the teacher with all types of classroom responsibilities. They might also serve as guest speakers who share their expertise with a group of children. 'Parents as teachers' is another effective way to develop a partnership with parents in supporting the school curriculum. The school can also serve parents by providing inservice opportunities to address their needs, which might range from language arts theory to 'parenting skills'. Teachers can assist with determining the type of inservice programs that will be of most use.

The most difficult to implement is the 'parent as decision maker', which involves parents in the school governance. Parents are often critical of the limitations the school seems to impose on their ability to have input. Parents often receive mixed signals from the administrative staff, and sometimes feel that their concerns are not heard. However, Greenwood and Hickman (1991) indicate that allowing parents to participate on advisory committees and in parent organizations produces commitment to the school.

Private schools are more likely to create organizational structures that allow for more parent involvement. Empowering parents through choice allows them to have greater control of their child's education. Parents' efficacy is enhanced when parents have opportunities to confirm their choice in other social situations with parents. Thus, privatized settings create an environment of ownership with opportunities to solve problems collectively (Cibulka, 1989). As a result of school choice, parents develop a high degree of efficacy which, in turn, increases the likelihood of their contributing positively to the school. These parents in privatized settings model to their children that school is important. By engaging in the choice process, parents become active players in schooling. As a result, children, too, become engaged in their own learning. Positive engagement between parents and schools assist children with academic skills, self esteem, positive attitudes toward learning, independence and other characteristics. Privatized schools set the stage for parent engagement by being responsive to their concerns and affording the opportunity for parents to take part in the governance structure.

Summary of the Literature

The literature reviewed for this study addresses parent involvement from a variety of perspectives in order to expose what is most unique in the privatized setting. It seems particularly important to define parent efficacy since the private schools seem to cultivate this sense of satisfaction in their parents. Parent efficacy can be defined as empowering parents, giving them a sense of control over their children's education. In addition, efficacy results when schools provide a parent support system of significant others who have similar beliefs about education, encourage parents to participate in the school governance and establish a connection between the school and the child's learning. Privatized settings create many opportunities for parent efficacy because these settings encourage choice, which leads to shared beliefs about education and participation in the governance structure.

Several studies done by Epstein (1986, 1992) reveal discrepancies between what parents and teachers want for the students in their schools. One such discrepancy has to do with the way parents and teachers define parent involvement; these differing definitions affect how teachers and principals respond to parents' concerns. Many teachers doubt that parents want to be involved, while parents feel that schools should do more to involve them (Epstein, 1986). However, in privatized settings these discrepancies are reduced; private school educators tend to expect parental involvement, assuming that the parent is interested in participating in the child's education.

Models of parent involvement have been identified to define ways schools can engage parents in the school. These models can range from parent as teacher to parent as decision maker (Greenwood and Hickman, 1991). In order for parents to have high degrees of efficacy, schools must engage them in the governance structure and go beyond the traditional role of 'parent as audience', where parents only come for special occasions and conferences. A school's engagement of parents is affected by how it perceives parents and how willing the school is to encourage parent participation. Since market-driven schools require responsiveness to parents, these schools encourage various models for parent involvement. Although the 'parent as decision maker' can be the most difficult model to implement, the organizational culture of private schools reflects an effort to create this role for parents. By equalizing the decision-making power, a private school establishes an environment of collaboration and ownership.

Epstein's (1992) conceptual model explores the possibility that efficacy is based on an interactive process involving the overlapping influence of the home and school, which is affected by grade level, age changes, and cultural context. These variables imply that the school sets the tone for how it will respond to the needs of parents by defining the level of involvement. As the catalyst for encouraging teachers to be responsive, the principal creates an environment where the parents feel welcome and want to participate. Without this validation, parents do not achieve high degrees of efficacy and do not feel the school is responsive to their needs. Privatized settings ensure an interactive relationship so parents can feel their concerns are heard. Principals in these privatized settings work to establish a partnership among teachers, parents and school staff, who all are accountable for enhancing student learning.

An Analysis of the Parents

A total of thirty-two parents were interviewed to gain information about their perspective on school responsiveness, school selection practices and their participation in the school governance (see Appendix). Questions were developed after observations and attendance at school socials had enabled the researchers to understand parent involvement in privatized settings. Each principal was asked to generate a list of parents to be interviewed based on criteria established by the researcher. The following criteria were used to identify parents: Parents had to be with the school for at least a year, and involved in the governance structure through either the parent organization representative or board member. Given these criteria, a list of ten to twelve parents from each school were identified. None of the principals knew what parents were questioned to assure confidentiality for the subjects. The parents were contacted by phone about their willingness to participate in the study. In most cases, parents were not aware of this research project and felt pleased to participate. My attendance at school functions, parent conferences, and fundraising activities also gave me opportunities for more informal contacts with parents. Although I was concerned that the principals in each setting would select parents who were not critical of the school, I found the parents, in my discussions with them, to be fair in their perceptions and quite revealing about their school.

At Appleman School, twelve parents were interviewed including nine females and three males. All participants were white except for one female African American parent. Four of the female participants worked either full or part time in professional positions. The parents' average length of stay at the school was four years, with a range of one to twelve years of having children attend the school. Four of the twelve parents had transferred to the school because of discontent with a public school that failed to challenge their child or wanted their child to receive special education services. The other participants (eight) had private school experience themselves and wanted their children educated in the same tradition. Most of the parents had an average of two to three children at the school.

At Bakersfield School the researcher interviewed a total of ten parents. There were three males and seven females. All of the parents were white except for one female African American parent. Most of the female participants were 'stay at home moms' with only two females working full time. The parents had an average of six years of experience at the school with the range of school experience from one to eleven years. Two of the parents transferred from the public schools due to an identification of a misdiagnosed learning problem. Parents felt the public school had made their children feel inferior in their ability to learn. Most of the parents with a private school background (5) had come from Catholic schools and wanted their children to experience religious diversity in another private setting. These parents had an average of three to four children at the school.

At Crestview School ten parents were interviewed, including two males and eight females, three of whom were African American. The average length of stay at the school was 2.9 years, with a range of one to five years of experience. All of the female participants at this school worked full time. Of the ten participants, only two parents were educated in Catholic schools. Since none of the parents interviewed had been exposed to independent private schools, they did not know what to expect from this type of school setting. Only two parents interviewed had more than one child at the school. In fact, many of the parents selected Crestview School because of its high percentage of parents with only 'one' child in the family. The school provided their only child with an opportunity to play with other children younger and older. At least two children of the parents interviewed transferred from the public schools while the other eight parents had been with the school since preschool so their children had never attended a public school.

In all, a total of thirty-two parents were interviewed for this study. Over 25 percent of the participants were male while 75 percent were female. A total of five African American females were interviewed, representing approximately 16 percent of the total number of participants. The average percentage of minority children at the three sites is 28 percent. The largest number of minority children is at the Crestview School, since, of course, this school is located in the city where 50 percent of the city's population is African American. The average length of stay at the school is 4.3 years with Bakersfield having the largest number of parents who had been associated with that school for a longer period. A total of eighteen parents interviewed attended private schools, while the other 56 percent had been educated in the public schools. Approximately 25 percent of the parents interviewed transferred their children to independent private schools due to difficulties with the public schools. Over 43 percent of the women participants worked either part or full time. All of the parents interviewed were either board members or served on the school's parent organization.

Attracting Parents through Choice and Mission Adherence

The whole process of selecting a school for their child is empowering to parents, who match the educational programs to their child's needs. Many parents initiated the school selection when their children were entering preschool. Parents also indicated that their own educational experiences tended to influence their selection process. Parents believe that choice means selecting a school that will be responsive to their needs and have similar views of educating their children. They have a voice in the school's mission and 'vote with their feet and dollars' if the school does not adhere to its program. By providing choice, private schools create an environment of close cooperation and trust among parents and school participants. These private schools naturally adopt a governance structure that encourages parental involvement.

Appleman School

At Appleman School many of the parents interviewed (eight) had been educated in public schools so they initially looked at public schools in their neighborhoods, where, for the most part, they have access to quality public elementary schools in the more affluent school districts in the metropolitan area. These eight parents noted that they did not like their local elementary school because of large classes where their children would become passive learners, open classroom structures, a principal who ignored them during an on-site visit, and a school curriculum that did not focus on building self-esteem or appear academically rigorous. Eventually, this dissatisfaction with their local schools led them to look in the direction of private schools. The other four parents came from independent schools themselves and wanted that same experience for their children.

These parents varied in their reasons for selecting Appleman but used a similar process in identifying this school. After discussions with friends and consideration of proximity to the parent's home, name recognition, and educational philosophy, all twelve of the parents generated lists of private schools to visit. Ten of the parents listed two to three schools, including Appleman and other schools in the same geographic area. The other two parents only considered Appleman and looked at no other schools. All of these parents then contacted the school for a formal visit to discuss the educational program, facilities, faculty and tuition costs. In most cases, all of the parents knew immediately that Appleman was the school for their child. Parents noted a heart-felt response that somehow the school's ethos would be beneficial for them and their children. The choice was intuitive rather than intellectual, generated by what appeared to be a caring environment for their children. At least two female participants visited other schools to validate Appleman as their choice. Only one male participant did any research to find the appropriate program for his child. His decision was based on his experiences with teaching at an independent private high school. He selected Appleman since he viewed its students as the best prepared for the rigors of the secondary school. The other male participant stated that his wife was responsible for selecting Appleman, and he let her make the decision for their children. All of the female participants revealed that they were more active in the process of finding a school for their children than their husbands. (All the schools in this study required that both parents/significant other attend the formal admissions' interview.) While the husbands did play a role in validating the wife's choice of school, they tended to be more concerned with costs and school facilities than with programs and ethos.

All of the female participants, along with their husbands, agreed that the principal was the reason for choosing the school. The principal was perceived as confident and knowledgeable, with the same educational philosophy as the parents. As indicated, husbands tended to focus on the school facilities, concerning themselves with playground equipment, physical plant and gym space. Three of the female participants stated that their husbands liked the school because of the size of the gym and the sports program. Five of the female participants noted that something about the 'community' feeling prompted them to select Appleman School. Almost immediately, the school generated a sense of belonging for families that provided them with an identity they could share with other school participants. The school was not simply an academic program; it created an environment where parents believed there were common values for educating children. At least two female participants noted that the school provided her children with a warm nurturing environment similar to their home environment. The management style of the classroom also influenced parents' decisions. They wanted teachers to be positive in their approach and to reflect the kind of discipline used at the home.

While the selection process to identify a school for their children was similar among the participants, the reasons for selecting Appleman School varied. Appleman is well known for its traditional curriculum, and at least four participants stated they wanted just such a curriculum for their children. One parent said, 'Our family believes in structure within the curriculum along with emphasis on being well rounded.' This rather typical statement illustrated the relationship between the school's mission and the parents' educational desires for their children. Another parent noted that she 'examined schools for curriculum and mission philosophy, and eliminated schools that did not match a traditional curriculum'. Another participant stated, 'Our child needed structure, and Appleman could provide this for us.' One parent who left the public school because her child was not challenged said she selected the school 'because it gave grades and not fluffy reports that we did not understand'. Parents who selected Appleman wanted a traditional educational philosophy that matched the educational goals they believed were needed to educate their children.

Other parents cited the warm and nurturing atmosphere of the school. Two participants liked the idea that 'the teachers eat lunch with the children on a daily basis'. These participants felt the personal element of a warm and caring faculty was important to them. One parent, whose child was identified as ADHD, felt it was important to have an adaptive curriculum with individual planning for some children. This parent also noted that the school had a learning specialist that worked with those children who needed additional special services. The minority participant, who originally put her child in the public school, moved her son to Appleman because of the school's reputation for providing 'a challenging atmosphere in a warm, nurturing environment'.

This parent also felt that her public school located in an urban area was dependent on memorization, while Appleman did many applied learning activities that motivated her child. Another parent also noted that the school had an excellent record for placing students in prestigious secondary schools. Appleman students were well prepared to compete at the college level because of its rigorous program, yet the school had a solid reputation for producing well rounded children.

Bakersfield School

The identification process that Bakersfield parents used to find a school for their child is similar to the Appleman parents. Of the ten participants at least 50 percent came from public school backgrounds while the rest had attended religiously affiliated private schools. Two parents interviewed had their children in Catholic private schools and transferred them to Bakersfield because of its Montessori program and its religious diversity. There were two parents who left the public school because their children had learning problems, and the public school was not willing to meet their needs. In both cases the child was doing poorly and, as a result, developing a poor self-image. Parents felt the public school was not committed to insuring their child's learning needs.

Like the Appleman parents, many of the Bakersfield parents began the search when the child was in preschool. Parents usually generated a list of schools and made school visits accordingly. All of the female participants worked alone, selecting schools based on proximity and name recognition within the community. The three male participants, like the Appleman fathers, said they trusted their wives' choice; they only went along for the final interview with the principal. Again, the male parents were more concerned with the physical plant and the sports program than with their wives' views of the academic program and ethos. In fact, one female participant said her husband was not happy with her choice of schools for their children, but since she is considered the 'sole educator', she made the decision in favor of selecting Bakersfield. After being at the school for several years her husband finally agreed with her choice. This husband did not like the Montessori approach and was put off that the school had no sports program. At least seven participants noted that their selection was similar to the Appleman parents, which was grounded in a 'gut' reaction. This 'gut' feeling was engendered by the mission, set of values, philosophy and ideology that parents wanted for their children. Reporting on her choice, one parent said that as she was talking to the principal, she realized that the principal used to be her first grade teacher. She took this to be a sign that she should enroll her children at the school. Another female participant, who was considering several Catholic schools, was talking to a friend who told her about Bakersfield School. Later that day, she met a teacher from Bakersfield at her aerobics class and took this as a sign that she should consider Bakersfield. But the 'gut feelings' that this environment was appropriate and philosophically similar were cited as the reason for selection more often than these coincidental signs. It was apparent that the school's culture of shared values influenced these parents' decision making. The sense that this school's mission was what they wanted for their children gave parents a connectedness to the school.

In addition to the 'gut feeling', the school's educational program influenced parents' choice. All of the Bakersfield parents identified in the study selected the Montessori program rather then a traditional elementary program for their children. Unlike the Appleman parents, they wanted a child-centered approach rather than a traditionally structured elementary program. In some cases (three) the parents said they did not know anything about the Montessori approach but were already using some of its concepts at home. Those parents (seven) who knew nothing about the Montessori philosophy found the principal so convincing in describing the school's program that they enrolled their children. At least eight parents stated that they selected the school because of the principal and her ability to focus on what the parents wanted from the school program. They found her to be a good listener, with a philosophy similar to their own about teaching children, who was responsive and open to parents' concerns. They also noted that she was very knowledgeable about Montessori teaching methods. All of the female participants at both Appleman and Bakersfield noted they wanted a warm, nurturing environment for their children to learn to be independent and self sufficient. However, the parents' desires for this type of environment received more emphasis at Bakersfield. Parents also selected Bakersfield for the curriculum which emphasizes teaching independence and character development. Two of the male participants noted that the school did more than just teach basic skills; it focused on character development they wanted their children exposed to. One male participant stated:

> Bakersfield has sparked the children's interest where the children really want to learn. I don't want my child to be the smartest person in the world but a person who has integrity; public schools do not do any character building at all. Although not an informed party it is only based on what I hear from others who have children in the public schools. Children can get accelerated classes at the public schools but it is the character side that is most important. If my children are happy and are people of integrity then they will feel good about themselves.

Crestview School

At Crestview School this was the first time parents were exposed to the independent private schooling perspective. Only two of the ten parents interviewed were educated in Catholic schools, while the other parents only attended public schools. Crestview School is located in the heart of a large city, where choices are limited to inner city public schools, city magnet schools and only a handful of other independent and religious private schools. The options for choice are greater in the areas where Appleman and Bakersfield are located. Crestview School recruits in the urban areas where families live in renovated neighborhoods.

Crestview offers a full day of school from 7.00 a.m. to 6.00 p.m. and is open all year long, including holidays, to meet the needs of working parents. In spite of the school's differences with the other schools in the study, the process that the Crestview parents used to select the school was similar to that of the other parents. Many parents were so attracted by the school's focus on working parents that they did not spend their time looking at any other schools. Only two parents noted that they really investigated their options; they only considered city magnet schools or Catholic parish schools. One male parent stated, 'I saw an advertisement in the Sunday paper about the school's hours and decided to take a look at the school.' This single parent, recently divorced, had sole custody of his child and needed his son to be close to his workplace. Another parent (who had a child in preschool and kindergarten at Crestview) was in the process of getting a graduate degree while her husband had relocated to another city. She selected the school because she needed an all day situation where her children would be safe while she completed her studies. She often struggled with child care concerns and felt much like a single parent.

The reasons the parents selected Crestview varied from this 'gut level feeling' to a desire for a school to meet their needs while working. At least four parents discussed the need to find a program that was convenient, met their child care needs, provided a social context and was academically sound. Some parents based their choice on the tangible items of child care and academic quality. Parents felt connected to the school because it met their child care needs by being responsive to working parents. In particular, they noted that the principal was supportive and listened to their concerns. Parents also chose the school for its arts emphasis. Because the school would have their children for such a long period of time, they saw the arts program as necessary to round out the academic focus. All of the female participants stated that they liked the idea that the school provides art, music, and dance lessons since they do not have to worry about taking their children to these activities when they came home from work. With so little time in their busy schedules, the school reduces some demands on these parents and gives them more time to spend at home. They are also pleased to have all of their child care needs met under one roof. The school provides extended day care during the holidays so these mothers do not have to worry about finding people to care for their children during their work day. Parents value Crestview because it meets their immediate day care needs. The other two schools have many nonworking mothers, so child care is not a priority for them.

Crestview's parents view the school as a safe community where their children are provided with academic and social opportunities. Placing their children in such an environment helps them deal with the guilt a working parent feels. A parent stated that she just knew this school was perfect for her and her child because she would be close to the school, and, at the same time, be able to focus on her job responsibilities. Since the school had no playground facilities, the children were often taken to the city park where they were exposed to some unfortunate urban ills like homeless people. Three parents said they are aware of these encounters since the children had talked about homeless people. These parents said they use these conversations to teach their children values and to discuss the human struggles some people face on a daily basis. At least seven parents mentioned that they wanted their children to be open to the realities of life and a protected suburban setting would not provide such an understanding. Most of the parents also noted that they are committed to living in the city and want their children to understand and accept individual differences. Parents at Appleman and Bakersfield, on the other hand, have no desire for their children to embrace urban life. In fact, they selected their private suburban schools because they want a safe environment where their children are protected and shielded from urban problems.

The African American parents who were interviewed (three) stated that they selected Crestview School because of its fully integrated multicultural curriculum. The parents stated that the school's curriculum teaches children to accept individual differences and to value other cultures. They believe the school allows their children to have a sense of self. One parent stated: 'My son can keep his identity and not feel separate from the school. My son has educated me that instead of saying white you say people of noncolor and you should not indicate color.' Another minority parent revealed:

> Here at Crestview the children are taught it is OK to have individual differences. Multicultural is not segregated and it is part of the curriculum. I have found that my children are more accepting of individual differences because of the school's influence. My daughter is fascinated with different cultures and wants to try different foods. The learning process at the school is that everyone contributed to the history of the United States.

At Appleman and Bakersfield, the African American parents also discussed their children's racial identity, but they saw themselves, rather than the school, as responsible for developing that sense of self. These two minority participants selected their school for the academics with the multicultural issue as only a secondary factor. An African American parent commented:

> The school is striving to get to that point and I can appreciate that it is not going to happen over night. The school's role is to give you a sense of confidence but not cultural, and that is the parents' role.

Comments were similar from the other African American parent:

> Raising my child is very difficult but I want my child to be well rounded. I want my child to know what his strengths are and what my child can

bring to survive in the White world. I attended a predominantly black school, and when I was working I had difficulties dealing with the white environment. The school appears to be committed to diversity.

The African American parents are supportive of the academic programs in the three schools in the study but feel the schools should do more to recruit more African Americans. The priority for the African Americans was finding a school that was academically rigorous and challenging. These African American parents left the public schools because the institutions did not have high expectations for their children.

Summary

Parents at the three schools noted that they felt a sense of control in being able to choose the school that was right for their children. Raywid (1985) suggests that schools of choice are popular because their curricular themes are definite, appealing, and distinctive; and their principals and staffs succeed in implementing those themes. All of the participants noted that they select a particular school because its unique character matched their philosophy of education. They believe that the principal has the same education goals that they want for their children and that the teachers and the school will work to achieve those goals and be held accountable. Parents did not use a sophisticated process to find the 'appropriate' school. Most decision-making was based on vicinity, word of mouth, and name recognition. It was not until parents visited the schools did they have any sense of what they wanted. Parents trusted their instinctive response and made decisions in how the school made them feel and if it would benefit their children. These 'gut feelings' were often translated into finding the kind of educational program they wanted for their children. A parent just knew this school was 'right' for them and their children. The match between the school's program and mission and the families' needs ensured a high degree of commitment and evoked a willing partnership. Because they made a choice based on their needs, parents become engaged in the school's mission and develop a sense of belonging. Since private schools attract parents through the appeal of their mission, to remain competitive, they find ways to present a mission that matches the educational needs of parents.

School Responsiveness to Retain Parents

Woods (1993) believes that giving parents choice forces schools to be responsive. Such responsiveness enables parents and teachers to convey their views and take part in the decision-making process which affects the quality of schooling. During the interviews, many parents expressed a high degree of satisfaction with a school that listened to them and tried to balance their individual needs with the good of the whole. While the school could not satisfy every wish, the parents felt that at least the principal listened and offered some solutions for change. While the parents listed many reasons why they remain at the school, it is clear that a school's responsiveness plays an important role in keeping them satisfied. Woods (1992) believes that school responsiveness is not limited to image management; rather it involves substantive changes meant to enhance the mission. It is evident that the privatized settings in the study created a responsive environment with a greater degree of accountability in retaining its mission, implementing its curriculum, using its resources, and maintaining the quality of its graduates into secondary schools.

Appleman School

At Appleman School there were multiple reasons why the parents continued year after year to send their children to their private school. In conversations, the parents noted that they selected Appleman largely for the school's structure and its rigorous academic program. This program, which reflects the mission, also keeps the parents at the school. Parents noted that Appleman's educational program is important in retaining them. Parents spoke highly of the way the school implemented its mission throughout the curriculum, commenting as follows:

Appleman School had less emphasis on drill and practice and the children are allowed to do problem solving kinds of activities;

Appleman School teaches children to think and reason;

Children are taught good study habits and the school has set homework policies; and the teachers are resourceful and plan a challenging curriculum.

Almost all Appleman parents cited the traditional educational program as a primary reason for remaining at the school. Parents believe the school's commitment to its curriculum and the teacher's ability to reflect the traditional curriculum in their instructional practices retains them at school.

In addition to the school's commitment to its mission, the principal serves as a major factor in recruitment and retention, according to the parents. Mrs Bates made parents feel welcome and that she would listen to their concerns about a teacher or a school issue. Apparently, a certain degree of authentic courtesy is extended to the families, and in the atmosphere of respect, parents believe it is their prerogative to share their beliefs and expectations with their principal. All participants noted the responsiveness of the principal. Parents' commented as follows:

> The school was responsive to my work schedule by providing longer school hours and after school enrichment;

> The principal helped my daughter with the sixth grade transition by helping parents with this process. High placement rates are essential to a school;

> The principal made a change in the preschool program from being teacher centered to child centered which has helped greatly with admissions;

> The principal's vision has to be responsible to the clientele who send their children there. It is consistent with the parents' vision and there has been no conflict.

Some parents said they are concerned that the principal may appear too responsive to other parents' concerns, producing continual change. The private school principal plays a precarious role in balancing parents' requests with the overall goals of the school. The principal spends considerable time educating parents about their role in the school and what they can or cannot change. One parent felt that 'the parents listen and take action without waiting to have approval from above; however, the board trusts her vision for the school and supports her decision and not other parents' complaints'. Another parent was concerned that it appeared as if the school might be out of control because of its responsiveness, but she did not see it as a problem. She noted, along with other parents, that the principal educates parents about their role in the school and parents soon learn the process for complaints: 'You go to the principal about school issues, but the board is not the place.' Because parents can visit the school at any time, they acknowledge their role in keeping the school accountable. Another parent expressed similar sentiments about the fears that the school may be overly sensitive: 'The school is responsive but doesn't allow parents to get out of control. Parents feel the need to have a say about the school but understand their limits.'

Mrs Bates spends much of her time in educating parents about their degree of control in defining the school program. She helps parents see when the general good must transcend individual interests by focusing on the intent of the educational program. In this privatized setting with its shared aims and goals, all school participants work together to promote the school. Parents in these settings become partners, willing to put individual needs aside to support the ethos of collaboration in the school. Appleman, much like the other schools, struggles to create an environment that equalizes power among a committed group of families, focused on similar goals.

Overall, the parents interviewed were very positive about their input in the educational process of the school. Each school, in its mission, affirms the importance of parents in educating children. The schools spent considerable time educating parents about how they are empowered, but the need to use the appropriate procedures for change. Because they believe in the mission, parents endorse the educational program and support the goals of the school. Constituencies never work at cross purposes since all of the participants want the same things for the children at Appleman. Any disagreements noted were not about the mission, but about the process of implementing the mission. In the interviews two participants mentioned that a handful of parents are unhappy with disciplinary practices at the school. Although these participants were not directly involved, they felt compelled to tell me that some parents had left the school over student discipline problems. These parents feel their children's classrooms are not well managed because certain children are allowed to disrupt the learning of others. However, none of the participants cited the problems as their own; instead they noted that 'other parents' were concerned. Discussions with the principal at Appleman identified concerns with management and curriculum; she admitted that she cannot always address everyone's needs. She believes that the school is committed to all children, and as a result a few parents will be unhappy. Responsiveness, she noted, must be general rather than particular so it is not just the 'squeaky wheel' that gets the 'grease'.

Teachers were also recognized for their ability to respond to parents' concerns. Parents felt the principal was instrumental in ensuring that Appleman's teachers were responsive and assessable. Parents' comments indicate genuine respect for the teachers and their methods:

Children are not allowed to fail at this school;

All things are available to help parents with the child. The teachers have high expectations and boost the child's self esteem;

Parents are encouraged to call on a regular basis with the bad and good news;

Parents can call the teacher at anytime, but it is not abused.

At least eight parents noted that the school keeps them well informed about their children's progress. These parents never encounter 'surprises' at conference time. They feel the school makes every effort to reach out to parents by encouraging teachers to call them. Conversely, teachers noted in their interviews that parents are very involved at the school. In some cases teachers are unhappy about the amount of time involved in working with parents. However, for the most part, teachers view parents as a great asset in fostering their child's learning. An apparent partnership between teachers and parents results in a school community that reflects its mission.

Bakersfield Parents

At Bakersfield School parents expressed similar satisfaction with the principal, the teachers and the school's adherence to its mission. The school's mission, based on the Montessori philosophy and includes a character development curriculum, is also important in retaining parents at Bakersfield. Parents view the school's curriculum as 'less dependent on rote learning'. In addition, they note, 'The children are given opportunities to make choices in their schooling.' According to parents, 'the school teaches the children to be independent and promotes learning through higher order creative thinking activities.' The school program at Bakersfield allows for cross disciplinary activities which many parents view as a strength. One parent stated that 'the school does many cross activities with science and social studies which the kids love'.

The parents interviewed at Bakersfield noted the responsiveness of their school's principal. One male participant noted that when he pays tuition, he continually evaluates his reason for sending his child to the school. He believes that commitment to the mission statement fosters a sense of community where all participants want the same thing for their children. He particularly respects the school's principal and her ability to make all the families happy:

> The principal is very responsive to all parents; she does not want one family to be unhappy with the school. She tries to make families happy through compromise, but she will not sacrifice the overall quality of the school.

Other parents voiced similar views regarding the principal:

> The principal is willing to listen and parents are a priority;

> I was able to convince the principal that there needed to be one more teacher in my child's classroom;

> I was concerned about the reading program since my child was having problems with reading comprehension so the principal reviewed the overall reading comprehension at the upper elementary level;

> The principal responded to my concern about the number of African Americans at the school so she developed a board committee to address this issue.

In spite of this positive identification, parents often disagreed with the school about discipline. One parent said, 'I am concerned about discipline at the school, but the principal is not receptive to dismissing children.' Another male participant feels the school should not dismiss problem students; in fact, he respects Bakersfield's commitment to all children. He noted, 'Besides, children need to be exposed to all kinds of children to show them the realities of life.' Many of the male participants feel that the school supports teachers in dealing with discipline problems so they can help children. Discipline remains a major area of conflict because the school does not have clear guidelines for acceptable behavior. Because the principal is committed to working with all children, the school works to accommodate all children with severe behaviors rather than asking them to leave. Some parents, who do not support this philosophy, feel helpless and alienated from the school. However, they remain at the school because of the other values that the school represents to them, such as the mission, the quality of teaching and the community atmosphere. Only one vocal parent spoke with dissatisfaction about the principal. This parent noted a personality conflict between herself and the principal, with whom she frequently 'butted heads'. When asked why she remained at the school, she said, 'Although we do not always agree about the process, we both want the same thing for our children.'

The teachers were also cited as being responsive to parents' issues. Many parents talked about calling teachers to discuss problems their children were having at the school. While most parents believe they can call the teachers at any time, they do not feel that they abuse this access. The teachers do not make them feel guilty for calling; instead they listen and offer suggestions. Several parents mentioned that they make many visits to the classrooms to ensure that the teacher provides a positive learning environment. Parents have a very strong attachment to teachers and seek their opinions. Many parents feel the teachers model positive ways to interact with their children. By observing in the classroom parents feel they also develop good communication with their children about what occurs at the school. Parents believe their presence keeps the school accountable and ensures the school's mission.

Crestview School

At Crestview the parents' reasons for staying at the school differed from the reasons parents reported at Appleman and Bakersfield. Recognition of the needs of working parents was cited as the primary reason many parents remained at the school. Parents praise the educational program for its sensitivity to the students' concerns and view the school's long hours as a positive response to their needs. Parents also cite the unstructured facility, accelerated learning, varied approaches to teaching and testing, multiage activities, creative projects, and focus on library skills as elements that attract and retain them. In addition, since all of the participants work, several parents felt that the school provides a 'family atmosphere in conjunction with academics', that provides a 'sense of security', and an opportunity to 'develop self-esteem'. Many parents believe the school provides a sense of community or support which allows them to focus on their work without guilt. This perception of family that many Crestview parents addressed in their interviews was seldom mentioned at the other two schools. For the working and many single mothers, who make up a high percent of the Crestview parents, this family atmosphere seems to fill a very significant need. Parents can participate in school activities that fit in with the demands of their busy schedule. They also enjoy the opportunity to meet other parents who have similar needs and concerns.

Because the principal had come from a school where working parents were an after thought, she decided that her school needed a philosophical base that took employment into account and made working parents a part of the school. Many Crestview participants appreciate her commitment and her efforts to incorporate parents' work schedules into the school activities. The principal is 'always willing to listen and tries new things for the working parents'. Parents feel the school provides an atmosphere where parents can voice their needs and the school listens. The teachers, also recognized for their concern about working parents' needs, are always available when parents come to pick up their children after work. The school organizes the curriculum to provide after school enrichment so when parents leave at the end of the day, they need not take the children to additional after-school activities. Instead, they are free to spend family time together when the day is over. In addition, two parents commented on the progress of one particular child who had a learning disability. The assistant principal, who has a special education background, often made modifications for a number of students who are identified as learning disabled. These parents noted they are impressed with the way the Crestview teachers provide for children with disabilities. The growth of these special needs children made many of the parents realize how responsive the school really was.

Summary

Overall, all the parents interviewed for this project remain at their chosen school because the school's philosophy matches the learning needs of their children. The school's ability to implement its mission, the curriculum, and the instruction are important in retaining parents at the school. Parents feel that the principal sets the tone of responsiveness by listening and reacting to parents' suggestions. Parents believe their suggestions are strongly considered and the school makes an attempt to see where a parent's idea may fit in the mission. Because parents are educated about the goals of the educational program, they work cohesively to meet the school's needs. They feel their ideas are given very strong consideration, and they feel free to talk with teachers and the principal. Retention of parents forces these schools to react to parents by allowing them to express their opinions in an environment where they had involvement in the governance and long range planning.

The principal, in each school, also stimulates teachers to communicate with parents about their children's progress. This policy encourages teachers to make contact with parents to ensure a degree of responsiveness that makes the teachers accountable for the students' learning. With the mission in view, the principal creates an environment where parents and teachers work together. Teachers are receptive to parents' concerns and communicate with them about classroom activities. When parents are upset about a teacher's practices, the principal serves as a sounding board by responding to parents' concerns. In the ideal, the principal satisfies parents while providing support for teachers preventing inappropriate parental involvement.

Meeting Parents' Needs for Their Children

While most parents help their children at home, they do not always know whether they are doing the right things (Epstein, 1992). Yet, parents want to know how to help their children at home and want to stay involved in their education (Epstein, 1992). Although teacher's efforts to involve parents in the classroom decline and vary as the child progresses through school, parents of all children at all grade levels want the school to keep them informed about the educational practices occurring in the classroom (Epstein, 1992). Parents have different needs throughout their childrens' education. Parents of younger children tend to feel that they can help them, but parents of older children may need clear and sequential guidance from teachers (Epstein, 1986). Parents have a high degree of commitment when they know what the school expects and feel they can help their children or request changes to improve performance (Swick, 1988).

Interviews with parents indicated that they have various needs in relation to grades in raising their children. The school keeps abreast of those needs through parent education seminars, curriculum changes at the various grade levels and teacher responsiveness. In each of the three independent private schools, parents noted similar needs at particular stages. Parents of children in the lower grades are concerned with management and parenting skills, the middle grades raised concerns with teaching independence and study skills, and children in the upper grades caused parents to focus on secondary school decisions and career assessment. Parents believe their school recognizes an appropriate role for parents to meet their children's developmental stages.

Appleman School

At Appleman School parents noted that the school's educational program is structured to meet their needs at various grade levels. Five parents who had been with the school five years or longer were in tune with how the school supported them as their children went through the various grade levels. They described the various stages as follows:

> In the early years (preschool–second grade) they needed assistance with discipline and ways to 'provide a warm and nurturing environment'.

In the middle grades (third-fourth grade) they needed help with 'teaching their children to be independent, organized and responsible for completing homework'.

Finally the last years of elementary was the process of selecting a secondary school that 'would meet their children's needs and abilities'.

One parent who was with the school for twelve years and had three daughters go through the school's program also described the developmental progress.

I think the teachers are much more nurturing and huggy. Once the children hit the third grade they have to be responsible for their actions, by the 6th grade if the child is not secure and does not know where they want to go it is traumatic and it affects the parents more than the children.

Another parent noted that while the assignments become more sophisticated with each grade level, the children are provided assistance for the increasing rigor:

I have noticed each year that they are beginning to integrate the different subjects. Their homework assignments are more parallel and they are integrating all the material so it flows. This seems to relate to more projects especially in literature where they do a report.

Parents whose children are in the lower elementary grades commented on child rearing practices at this stage. Most parents need support with discipline and suggestions for reading to their children. Parents also noted that in the early grades they observe the teacher using good management practices they can practice at home. In addition, they learn what developmental skills are appropriate for reading readiness. One parent with one child in preschool and another in kindergarten stated:

Teachers have been very helpful with my son's discipline, he got into a fight and I did not know how to handle this so the teacher helped by talking to my child.

Many parents with children in the middle years noted that the 'independent stage' is quite stressful. Parents commented as follows:

I did the nurturing environment at home but now they are at a point where they are teaching the children to be independent.

The teachers have a structure in place — a structure for each grade — third grade is more organized — they have homework to do and they have to have it done.

Finally, the 5th–6th grade transition poses a challenge for parents as they face selecting secondary schools and career preparation:

> My son is going to be in the upper school next year and they do a lot of that prepatory foundation. The philosophy here is that you are a big kid and the oldest in the school and you should act that way.

> Everything at that age is in turmoil and you have to make decisions that will affect the rest of their lives or at least at the sixth grade.

Most parents appreciate the way teachers and administrators respond to their needs at the different grade levels, although some feel they have a right to this guidance. Through the school's support, parents are able to respond to their children's needs. While parents are vocal about the school's obligation to provide direction for them, they are very positive about the school's response to their needs. Parents stated:

> At each stage the school has various expectations for the children and parents are expected to go along;

> The school's organizational structure provides an equal basis of parent and teachers working together;

> Making children independent is a commitment to the curriculum;

> Children leave the school with good academic grounding to be able to compete at the secondary schools;

> Parents do not do homework. Teachers work with us to manage our own children's home work.

> The school works with parents for the 5th and 6th grade transition and the school minimizes the stress.

Parents believe the school listens to their demands and, in fact, implements meetings with parents to provide them support throughout the grade levels.

Bakersfield School

At Bakersfield School parents voiced similar needs for particular kinds of support at the various grade levels. Many of the participants who had more than five years experience at the school had a great deal to say about transitions from preschool to sixth grade. Bakersfield parents were not as perceptive as the Appleman parents in defining the early and middle grade stages, but they were quite vocal about the sixth grade transition. According to the principal, the school makes great efforts to educate parents at the lower, middle, and upper grades. These efforts may explain why parents don't feel the same anxiety as the Appleman parents experience in the early elementary grades. Parents stated:

> My child had a difficult time while in the fourth grade but by 6th grade she knew what she wanted. My child has made the transition to the junior high but her friends from the public schools are struggling because they were not forced to do homework and being responsible for completing homework;

> My child did well transition wise. The school spent a great deal of time educating us and our children about the move to the secondary level. I am confident that a Bakersfield student can go anywhere but I let my daughter make the decision within the alternatives of choices, and as a parent of a third grader I already feel the pressure to find the best place for my child.

Noting that the school is responsive and accommodating, parents described a video tape, prepared by Bakersfield, that addresses their concerns at each grade. The teachers and students put together a videotape that shows in detail the trials and traumas of a specific grade. The school also moved the 4th–6th grades into a separate section of the building and established lockers to create a middle school philosophy. The school also does cross-age activities with the first and sixth graders to ensure the transition for the younger children. Teachers hold meetings at the end of the year to inform parents about the expectations for the next year's grades. These meetings address concerns about independence, homework, and preparation for the secondary schools. Teachers met individually with mothers and fathers of children in the sixth grade to discuss their options for secondary schools based on their child's ability.

The needs of parents at the various grade levels are addressed through parent seminars which parents cited as evidence of the school's responsiveness. Bakersfield School succeeds with smaller meetings where parents gather in their children's classroom rather than in large group meetings. The other schools, Appleman and Crestview, use large group meetings to work with their parents. Bakersfield, however, holds small group meetings twice a year for each grade level.

Crestview School

At Crestview, parents cited similar needs as their children progress through their various grade levels. Because Crestview parents had a limited experience about independent schools, they were often confused about their role in assisting the school. Because of its newness, Crestview lacks the traditions of parental involvement that work so well at the other two schools; as a result these parents feel a bit uneasy about their interactions with teacher and school personnel. Since the school is just confronting the experience of placing students in secondary schools, there is great anxiety about this transition. Because the children are grouped by age-appropriate behaviors rather than by grades, the parents are very concerned about the sixth grade students' ability to function at the secondary level. Appleman and Bakersfield schools, on the other hand, have strong traditions for preparing students for the rigors of the secondary curriculum. Even at the preschool level, there is some confusion among Crestview parents who were ambiguous about their needs because of their inexperience with independent private schools. (At least five of the parents interviewed were new to the school and only recently had put their child in the preschool program.)

Due to an unequal distribution of too many preschool parents and only a few upper elementary students, more parents need help in the areas of discipline and school readiness, and issues associated with preschool and lower elementary students. Thus, Crestview tends to focus its parent education on preschool areas rather than on parents whose children are graduating to the secondary level. The school justifies this focus because it fosters retention for the bulk of its preschool parents. Crestview personnel believe a focus on recruiting preschoolers will attract more parents and younger children to the school's program. Of late, because the school has problems with parents leaving at the upper elementary grades, more energies are spent working to educate new parents about the benefits of remaining at the school the full six years. Parents who have children in the lower grades are happy with the school, while parents with children in the fifth and sixth grades are less content.

Crestview parents with children in early grades report that they need help with discipline at home and with teaching readiness skills. Five parents stated that they talk frequently with the principal and the preschool teacher about their children. One parent stated:

> I will have different needs but I know there is a point that once they learn to read you are not as concerned about where they are. Then you look into their interests and how the school can support these interests.

Another parent described the middle grades, as designed 'for weaning the children into independence'. She spoke of 'the development of moral fiber and academics throughout . . . their schooling'. Lower-grade parents overall are happy with the school and its ability to meet their needs. Crestview has not quite succeeded with its sixth grade parents. At least four parents interviewed expressed their concerns about the school's ability to assist them with this difficult transition. This parent was rightfully concerned about this transition:

My son will be going to a school similar to Crestview, but there are issues of him leaving his friends. I am worried about moving to the secondary schools since there have not been many who have graduated to see how well they will do. By the time he goes from 6th grade at Crestview he has only three or four students but when he gets to junior high then maybe he will be overwhelmed from going to a few to many.

Many parents are worried both about the school's ability to ensure that their children will make a successful transition and about the preparation of their children for secondary schools. Because Crestview does not have a tradition of successful secondary school placements, many parents are hesitant to enroll their children in school. Yet, the school itself does not seem worried about their upper elementary students since retention is no longer an issue. The Crestview principal focuses her energies on the lower grades in order to retain those parents. Of course, many parents who have children in the upper grades feel the school needs to be equally responsive to their secondary school transition needs. My conversations with the Crestview principal indicated that she too feels uncomfortable that students may graduate from the school and not succeed. However, the Crestview principal sees her energies as better spent in recruitment of parents rather than retention.

Even with the school's problems, many parents still support Crestview for its multiage activities and its ability to prepare the children to get along with other children. Parents noted:

Here my child is able to interact with babies and older children. As my child gets older she has learned to communicate with all ages of children;

The teachers promote social skills and this is an important development;

This school creates a well rounded individual and the influence is not just academics.

The school itself is experiencing many growing pains as it confronts parents' needs at the secondary school transition. In summary, many of the parents who have younger children feel the school responds to their needs about discipline and readiness skills, but at the upper level, parents feel very isolated from the school as they face secondary school selection.

Summary

Parents at various times through out their children's schooling have specific needs. At all three sites the parents indicated that their needs varied as their children went to a different grade level. The parents with children in the lower elementary grades feel they need assistance with discipline, reading readiness skills and ways to provide a warm, nurturing environment. However, either due to the school's rigorous curriculum or parents' desires for secondary school preparation, parents with children in the middle elementary grades search out techniques from teachers to encourage children to bring home and take back their book bags and to complete homework. Parents are frustrated by their inability to motivate their children to complete and return the homework to the teacher. The most difficult transition parents worry about is the move to the secondary level, in terms of academic preparedness, social skills, making friends and finding the right school in relation to the child's ability. Many parents worry about their children's ability to make the middle school transition and adapt to the rigors and social stresses of secondary school.

In spite of their worries, parents feel that their schools provide them with inservice education and opportunities to talk with their children's teachers and the principal about these changes at each grade level. Each school provides formal (parent meetings) and informal (regular, daily contacts at school) opportunities for parents to talk. The three schools establish many social activities for parents to communicate their concerns about each grade level. All three schools provide support to parents through parent education programs, social opportunities to meet with other parents, and specific one-on-one contacts with teachers. The community atmosphere at each school makes parents feel comfortable in vocalizing their needs and wants. Parents have a high degree of expectations for the school regarding secondary placements. To retain parents, these schools are accountable with respect to mission adherence, secondary placement rates, and student achievement.

Each school approaches their parent groups differently, but the contents of the meetings have many commonalities. Appleman and Crestview use large parent group meetings to address parents' issues while Bakersfield cultivates more intimate family contacts at the different grade levels. Appleman School only holds small group meetings at the beginning of the school year and at the fifth and sixth grades when parents face secondary school placement. Each school uses parent meetings to support parents with their needs and to engage them in their child's learning. The schools have collaborative relationships with parents based on mutual respect. Because these schools are motivated to retain parents, they must work to support them. Parents respond to the school, interacting with school participants to gain a better understanding of the school's intent and instructional practices and of their own role in facilitating the education of their children.

Parent Efficacy in Decision-making

According to one of the models of parent involvement, parents may function as decision makers, taking roles in school governance through the PTA, school advisory committee, or parent council (Greenwood and Hickman, 1991). Schools have an important role in communicating the importance of home–school collaborative decision-making and in encouraging parents to voice their perspective on the educational program at the school. It is the role of the parent to be knowledgeable about school governance in order to support the school mission. Schools assist by training parents to be leaders and representatives, developing their decision-making skills and their ability to communicate with the parents they represent (Epstein, 1992). Woods (1992) feels that schools are only beginning to develop systematic planned ways of facilitating parental feedback which can influence school policy-making. Much of the site based management literature on parent advisory councils cites the difficulty of educating parents to serve as observers rather than participants in the school's governance. However, this type of site-based management generates involvement, but it does not empower parents (Malen, Ogawa and Kranz, 1990).

Each school in the study has very sophisticated procedures for engaging parents in decision-making through the parent organization and board structure. The parent organization serves many purposes such as fundraising, staff appreciation activities, family get-togethers, school volunteers and curriculum enrichment support. The parent organizations at each setting are similar in creating a supportive relationship between the home and school. Parents are strongly encouraged to participate in the parent organization activities which support their children's learning. At Appleman and Bakersfield schools, the parent organization is primarily involved with fundraising and providing social events that enlist the parents' talents. At Crestview the parent organization supports the school curriculum with social activities and more direct parental involvement in the school. Each school's parents consider the parent organization as the vehicle that enables them to decide how they will support the school. The parent organization helps determine the role parents play in providing financial and curriculum support for their school. The parent organization has considerable power in determining how the money they raise will be distributed. All school participants view the parent organization as a necessity in raising funds for the school. These schools' parent organizations are important in subsidizing the school budget and since 'money is power', the parent organization wields considerable influence.

Parents are also empowered by serving on their school's board of trustees. Board responsibilities include developing and executing school policies and overseeing the financial stability of the school. A significant board function involves overseeing the school's long-term financial status and security while the day-to-day school operations are the sole responsibility of the principal. The board determines if the principal administers the school program in accordance with the mission and the long range plan. The three schools shape their board committee structures to fit their particular mission. At Appleman and Bakersfield, a representative from the parent organization reports to the board about parent activities and fundraising events while at Crestview the parent organization has no representation on the board. However, Crestview does have a parent representative who serves as a liaison position between the board and parents. Each school's board has a nominating committee which makes decisions about the type of representation that the board needs. Nominating committees look to the parent organization first to see if there are individuals who can provide the expertise that they need. These parents, who are selected for board positions, contribute knowledge of a particular sort, but they do not represent other parents' concerns. All three schools spend considerable time educating trustees about their role as decision makers in determining school policy. Board members understand that they are to contribute their expertise for board purposes and not to represent parent complaints.

Of the thirty-two parents who were interviewed for this study over 44 percent either presently serve on the school's board or had done so in the past. Parents with board experience were interviewed to gain understanding of their involvement in each school's governance. Appleman and Bakersfield provided a number of parents with board experience for the study, while at Crestview, only two parents interviewed had such awareness. Both of the board presidents at Appleman and Bakersfield schools had their children in the school and were interviewed for this study. Because the board president at Crestview had no children attending the school, parents viewed her as an outsider with little connection to them. The current presidents and a past president of the parent organization also were interviewed for this study. Parents were questioned for their understanding of the role of the board and their opportunity to shape the school through their involvement in the governance.

Appleman School

Many of the parents at Appleman view their board as very connected to parents when governing the school. Parents believe they understand the role of the board, and, in fact, many described the board's responsibility in the same way: 'The role of the board is to set policy and not curriculum. A good part of the board is financial, more policy making than day to day operations. The board clearly sets policy.' One parent who was on the board stated:

> The board's role is policy making. I feel that as a whole we want to make sure we do not make the tiny decisions, like who can chew gum or shoes to wear and what kind of textbooks, but good decisions about how the school is going to work. What kind of school do we want to present to the community? How do we want to be involved and what do we stand for? The board feels it is a policy making body and so unified; there is no descension.

Overall, the parents interviewed understand that their questions about curriculum and staff should be addressed to each school's principal rather than the board.

Four parents feel the school might do more to disseminate board information since there is no formal vehicle for communication, no open discussion of board issues and no regular distribution of minutes. For the most part, parent organization meetings serve as forums for parents to find out about new school policies and board decisions. When the board makes particularly important decisions, the principal sends personal letters home to parents. The school also uses a weekly newsletter to inform parents of school activities. While parents are concerned about board decisions, they view the school's governance structure as an excellent way to involve parents in the decision making of school policies.

Parent board members know how to respond to parents' complaints, directing them to the principal. If parent complaints present a majority and share common elements, board members take up the issue with the principal. At Appleman's board meetings, the principal keeps members abreast of issues that concern parents that might affect the school's stability. The board, in keeping with its role, remains detached. Parents at Appleman are happy with the direction the board takes at the school, and they often note with pride their own involvement in shaping the school's mission.

Bakersfield School

The parents at Bakersfield have the same feelings toward their board. As one parent stated:

> The board does not work with the day to day operations. Its function is to govern, plan, financial review and be in tune with the school. The principal oversees the day to day operations, curriculum, and implements the policies.

Many Bakersfield parents feel the committee structure of the board works well, giving them an opportunity to participate in decision-making. One parent expressed confusion regarding the education committee of the board, since the role of the board is policy making. This parent sees the education committee as a place to vent their concerns about curriculum without threatening the school's control of its academic program. Three parents stated that the board of Bakersfield keeps the principal, parents, and teachers in agreement about their vision for the school.

Bakersfield over its thirty years has grown tremendously. Partly because of the principal's leadership, the school has progressed from a small Montessori preschool to a sophisticated academically strong multipurpose school. Since the principal has many years of service, many parents feel strong ties to her. Parents who have been with the school for a long time witnessed the board governance change from a reserved and tentative involvement to a sophisticated understanding of its role in defining school policy. Over the years, the principal worked very hard to prepare her parents to serve as board members. Now that Bakersfield board parents finally understand their role, they express mixed feelings about the relative strength and weakness of the board in relation to the principal. Parents commented as follows:

The principal has a strong personality so in some years when you have a weak board her controlling comes through;

The principal is knowledgeable but the board is firmly in control and their own interests come first;

The board (members) used to be puppets but as the school has grown the board has become stronger. The board sees themselves as more than just room mothers;

The principal and the board president set the agenda, and this is a cohesive venture but there have been times when there are weak and strong boards. The principal has a change in leadership based on the personalities on the board. If you have weak committees then the meetings begin to ramble and meetings last longer, then the principal has to step in and guide the board.

The parents at Bakersfield support for the board's structure. Like Appleman parents they believe the board's structure gives them opportunities for input into policies. Parents who do not serve on the board receive information via the principal, through the school newsletter, and on the school radio station. However, board meetings at Bakersfield are open, and parents are encouraged to attend. Parents feel their views are represented through the board structure, and they trust board decisions because of the significant parent representation.

Crestview School

Crestview School presents a different profile in the relationship between the parents and the school's board. The board insists that parent participation should be limited because the school's unstable financial situation requires confidentiality. Over time, the number of Crestview parents serving on the board has increased, but the board is driven, for the most part, by community members from outside the school. At least seven of the parents interviewed are unhappy, wanting more parent representation on the board. Parents stated:

It bothers me that board meetings are closed. There is no publicity coming from the board and I hear from a parent representative on the board about what is going on;

> It is frustrating but it has become a little clearer for me. It is a little mysterious what the board does. I am not sure why the president of the parents' organization does not sit on the board as a representative.

The Crestview board has a parent representative who talks with parents and serves as a liaison to present their concerns. In theory, a parent's representative on the board talks with the school's families and then shares their thoughts with board members. However, for a variety of reasons the exchange of information has been inconsistent, leaving parents feeling left out. While many parents at Crestview are knowledgeable about the board's role in defining policy and resolving financial issues, there is much confusion about their exclusion from the board governance. Parents stated:

> The board serves the financial side and determines salaries and tuition increases and in charge of some financing;

> There are a lot of mixed messages about how fundraising is supposed to be divided; back and forth between the board and parents and there is tension as the organization grows.

Several parents view the school's communication with parents as poor, resulting in a lack of trust in how the board works and what its role actually is. The principal makes it very clear that she and the teachers are responsible for the school program while parents provide support for the educational goals through the parent organization. Only hand-picked parent representatives identified by the board are allowed to attend board meetings. The principal informs parents that they can bring their issues to the board's attention through their parent representative. However, due to conflicting work schedules, it is often difficult for parents to make contact with their parent representative. Many parents reported that while they know who the parent representative is, she seldom attends any school or committee meetings. It seems clear that parents and board members are not well connected, and the result is distrust of the board's role. Crestview parents vary in their understanding of the board's role and their own position in the governance structure. It is difficult to tell if this confusion results from the parents' first exposure to independent private schools or from a limited board that does not value parent representation. The school's financial instability precipitated closed board meetings, which, in turn, limited parents' opportunities for input.

Summary

Generally, at the three sites parents feel their individual perspectives are represented and respected in the governance of the school. Each school structures its board and governance according to the parents' level of expertise and the school's needs. The board and parents display considerable deference to the principal's leadership and judgment. Discussions with the three principals revealed that they work hard to educate parents about their role in the school and about the function of the board. Understanding the board's role enables parents to see how the school functions and remains accountable. Engaging parents in the governance of the school creates a community where participants all work toward the same mission. Parents interviewed for this study noted that the board structure holds the school accountable and empowers them to set the direction for the school. Parents also see the principal as leading the board in determining the vision for the school. In each school parent participation is defined according to the context, with its particular norms and rituals. Crestview does not encourage parent participation in the governance structure, while Appleman and Bakersfield actively engage large numbers of parent representatives. By providing opportunities for parent involvement in the governance, the school forms strong ties with their participants.

Conclusion

Privatization, by its nature, creates a context of choice, openness, competition and accountability. This consumer-orientation gives rise to an organizational structure where parents and schools make a reciprocal agreement to support a particular educational mission. Advocates of choice note that a market-driven system will improve schools as a result of competition and a greater degree of autonomy in defining their mission. In addition, privatization results in a school community where faculty develop a sense of ownership and parents participate in the governance structure. Bryk, Lee, and Holland (1993) believe that the concept of 'market-responsiveness' is not what drives schools to be sensitive to parents' concerns. Instead, such sensitivity results from a 'voluntary community' with a communal ethos. Private schools have a greater degree of autonomy, and a voluntary supportive relationship between faculty and parents in the interest of students. The voluntary community in these privatized settings leads to greater commitment and engagement to the school.

The terms 'choice' and 'privatization' are so entwined that at times their definitions seem synonymous. But choice alone does not necessarily create a 'voluntary community'. Privatization, the outcome of choice, results in environments that are responsive in order to retain school participants. Focusing on mission adherence and doing that well becomes essential for attracting parents. It is not the market but mission that forces these schools to focus on what they do well. The privatized institution runs on 'social capital' contributed by all participants who hold membership in a functional community united by an educational mission. The privatized organizational structure functions well by reflecting on mission, emphasizing its implementation, greater student accountability and efficient use of resources. These schools value parent participation, creating meaningful dialogue regarding the intent of the school. Decision-making in these settings evolves from positive interactions involving all participants.

A mission-driven educational setting cannot ensure parent engagement without the development of a sense of community. To create this environment, the school must be accessible to parents so they can make connections to teachers, observe in the classroom and address academic issues about their children. Privatized settings encourage parent involvement in the governance structure and make connections to their constituencies. The mission statement serves parents as both a reason for commitment and a test of quality. Parents choose a particular mission that they feel reflects what they want for their children. What sustains a parent's commitment to the school is its successful implementation of the mission and its ability to reinforce the value of the initial choice through interactions with others. Parents' personal growth and self awareness emerge as a result of the communal existence in the school. Open communication between teachers, parents and students takes place in an authentic atmosphere of courtesy. A privatized setting enhances a collective sense of identity that responds to individual needs while it balances personal priorities with the collective life of the school.

At all three of the schools in the study parents said they selected their school because of its curriculum and mission. Each school designed itself so that its mission is reflected throughout the school program. This commitment to the school's curriculum and accountability of student achievement leads to the retention of parents. At Appleman School the families want a structured, traditional academic program; at Bakersfield School the families choose a Montessori approach; while Crestview is unstructured and focused on the arts. The parents and school staff members in each case are pursuing goals that reflect the mission they have chosen. Most parents did not use a sophisticated process in locating a school for their children. The majority of the female participants said they selected the school in response to a 'gut level feeling' that this was the school for their children. This 'gut level feeling', based on their sense of comfort often reflected their own educational background. Discussions with parents indicated that they selected schools by recalling what they liked or did not like about their own schooling. In some cases, parents wanted a nonreligious school because they themselves had attended a religiously affiliated school. Or, if as children, they attended a school that was very structured, they assessed whether such an environment would make their child happy and eager to go to school. Such considerations led some to select the Montessori approach for the freedom it allowed their child. Given choice, parents are compelled to reflect on their own experiences to determine what they want for their children.

Parents also view themselves as respected in the school environment because they can voice their concerns and elicit a response. Each school provides opportunities for fruitful discussions based on mutual respect and openness. Several parents cited specific examples of presenting ideas to the principal and then seeing those ideas implemented. This kind of response makes participants feel connected and powerful in the school environment. Parents also feel that the teachers, who are always available, even at home, react to their questions in a positive manner. Several parents do feel their school listens to their concerns regarding discipline. The schools face a dilemma of too much responsiveness which means undermining teachers. In addition, the schools are unwilling to abandon their commitment to children with behavior problems just to satisfy a few parents. Although these parents are not happy about the schools' philosophy of discipline, they usually agree that the school should take the leadership role in this area. Those parents who are unhappy about discipline issues do feel free to voice their concern to either the principal or other parents. However, those who remain dissatisfied usually leave the school for another setting. Here again, the positive element of choice allows for parents to voice their complaints, and then, if the school does not respond accordingly, they have the option to leave. Private schools provide outlets for parent discourse. Principals and teachers, always accessible for discussions, can make compromises when doing so does not undermine the mission or the educational program.

Parents have a voice in defining the goals and objectives of the educational mission through the governance structure. Parents and the school use a collaborative management to govern a cohesive community of individuals who share a similar philosophy. Parents value their ability and power to shape school policy through their involvement in the school's governance. The board structure holds the school accountable for how it teaches children and uses its resources. Parents see the school as responsive by allowing them participation in the governance structure. Parents contribute to the mission and long range planning which insures their input.

Parent support for the school is further enhanced by the sense that the curriculum meets the children's demands at each grade level. Regular exchanges between teachers and parents about classroom expectations ensure this mutual support. Each of the schools in the study demonstrated an ability to meet the needs of parents, with the principal serving as a catalyst in encouraging communication between parents and teachers about a child's progress. Parents noted different needs as their children progress through the elementary grades. In the early grades they need assistance with discipline, teaching readiness skills and providing a warm nurturing environment. By the middle grades they face the task of teaching their child to be independent and organized and in the upper grades they need assistance with the transition to the junior high.

Through encouraging parent–teacher interaction, principals establish an overlapping influence that works for the good of students. The principals at the three sites encourage parents to interact with teachers either through phone calls or on-site visits. Many parents noted that conference time offers no surprises since teachers are continually contacting parents with positive or negative updates about their children. Teachers communicate regularly letting parents know what occurs in the classroom and how they can assist. Supportive of the teachers, parents value their opinions in dealing with the parents' own children. If parents have a problem with a teacher the principal suggests that they talk with the teacher first. Parents note that the principal is deliberate in her process of handling complaints about teachers. Many of the parents noted that the teachers at the school encourage them to ask questions about their children's progress during conference times. Parents feel they are able to call teachers at any time and to visit the school often to discuss their concerns. Many of the parents noted that the teachers make them feel comfortable in their interactions. Teachers are highly solicitous of their concerns, treating them as equals. In some cases parents even cited subtle cues from other teachers that prompted them to make a visit to address a problem with the teacher.

The context of privatization can be enhanced through the leadership of a principal who envisions parents as helpful facilitators in a school partnership and not as a threat. A private school principal has greater freedom in selecting a team of teachers with values and beliefs that match the school's mission. In this study all of the parents noted that the principal in their school is pivotal in defining their level of involvement. The principals encourage them to participate in the school as volunteers, decision makers, advocates, or members of an audience. Parents feel the principal empowers them to act as advocates for their children, encourages them to be proactive in talking with their children's teachers, and supports social interactions by providing parents a place to meet at the school. These principals do not perceive parent involvement as a threat to their authority or control. Each principal encourages parents to be actively involved in the school to keep the school accountable. Each parent feels substantial autonomy within his or her own sphere of expertise since the principal encourages the use of that knowledge base in supporting the school.

During the study it was noted that the principals are very familiar with the families in their school. During the interviews with administrators the three principals stated that they spend considerable time getting to know parents and listening to their suggestions or thoughts. The principals use discussions with parents to promote a context for interaction, exchange of ideas, and mutual respect. Parents provide feedback that principals use to plan inservice programs for parents, to identify modifications in the educational program and to select teachers who can contribute to the school mission and assist parents.

Because these schools have to compete for students, they must continually improve their programs. Thus, privatized schools are motivated to improve their curriculum, teaching methods, and school goals to retain parents. Responsiveness, which creates the interaction between parents and the school, also fosters retention. The element of choice begins the initial engagement of the parent. What retains the parents is the responsive environment created by the school's accountability to the mission, efficient use of resources, participatory decision-making, and consumer-oriented organizational structure. Parents need continual affirmation regarding the investment of time and resources directed to their school choice. When parents choose a particular school, they are in part choosing the type of educational program they hope to reinforce or instill in their children. When their input is valued and meaningful dialogue leads to school changes, parents become committed participants in the school community. Before schools can engage parents, a context of choice must exist to give them autonomy. Because school privatization involves an ongoing belief in free will and choice, these schools seek to establish goals that facilitate identification and reciprocation among the school participants.

Chapter 6

Student Engagement through Choice

Schools organized as communities exhibit a set of common understandings among the members of the organization. Bryk, Lee, and Holland (1993) define a 'communal school organization' through three critical components: a set of values shared among the school community, a set of shared activities of both an academic and nonacademic type and a distinctive set of social relations among the faculty, parents and students. Because parents have selected the independent school for its particular educational program, members of the community share a common belief in what students should learn, how students and teachers will interact, and how the students' academic and social behavior will reflect the intent of the school. As a result of this common agenda, reflected in the curriculum and in the teachers' commitment, the school participants work cohesively, facilitating personal ties to the school. Due to this, students share similar academic and social experiences that bind them to the school's traditions and its future.

In privatized settings, the commitment to student learning, based on a common set of beliefs, creates an environment for improving student achievement. Research in privatized settings indicates that mission driven schools enjoy high achievement rates. Choice creates a high degree of engagement on the part of both staff and students because of the match between family preference and philosophical mission. In these environments it is easy to upgrade the curriculum to enhance student learning and produce uniform quality. Curriculum decisions in these settings come from the bottom up as teachers are given considerable freedom in ensuring mission adherence. The result is a coherent curriculum and a content-oriented school, with a structure for continued improvement, where students' individual needs are addressed. Parents become part of the child's learning cycle because the school expects parents to support the mission to enhance the child's learning. Because parents have the option to leave students do not feel coerced into a mission. Instead they identify with their school, becoming active participants in their learning and working with the school toward similar goals.

Student Profiles

In order to understand student engagement in privatized settings, students were interviewed regarding their views about schooling. They were questioned about their allegiance to the school, the school's instructional practices, empowerment opportunities, discipline and secondary school preparation. In conjunction with the interviews, students were observed throughout the research period in situations involving discipline, and in their interactions with teachers. The researcher also attended several student-run meetings to understand their opportunities for empowerment and participation in the school's governance structure. Most of the students interviewed were fifth and sixth graders who had been with the school for several years. Interviews were conducted in groups so students were comfortable with the interviewing process. Participants were informed about the study and asked to give honest responses to the questions.

A total of thirty students were interviewed for the project in groups of five to six students. At Appleman School, a total of ten students from the sixth grade participated in the project. There were two groups of five students with approximately 50 percent from each gender. 50 percent of the students interviewed had attended Appleman School for five to eight years. The other half of the participants had less than three years experience at the school having previously attended public schools in their neighborhood. These students left their public schools for various reasons, among them the large classes and unstimulating learning environment. At Bakersfield School a total of eleven children were interviewed with an almost equal number of male and female students. There were two groups of sixth graders with five or six students in each. 54 percent of the total number of students had been with the Bakersfield School since its preschool program; the other participants (46 percent) had fewer than five years experience in local public schools. At Crestview School a combination of nine fifth and sixth graders were interviewed in two separate groups. Each group contained almost equal numbers of male and females with most of the students having less than three years experience at the school. Only one Crestview student had been with the school since kindergarten; most of the others transferred to the school from public schools. Many of the Crestview students were quite verbal in discussing their negative experiences in their public school settings.

At Appleman School the interviews took place during the students' art classes. While other students were working on their art projects, participants were questioned. At Bakersfield School, where sixth grade students attend a weekly meeting with the principal to address their graduation and secondary placement needs, students were pulled from the meeting to participate in the project. These students volunteered for the project and were encouraged by their principal to give honest responses to the questions. Crestview students were interviewed during their art and music classes. These students had recently returned from a field trip and were quite active during the interviewing process. All students participating in the project were responsive to the questions and seemed pleased to participate. The students were very positive about their schools, viewing them as good places for them to learn. Students did complain about the lunch program and, in some cases, their school's dress code.

Students' Allegiance to their School

Students were asked why they like their schools. Responses indicate that they view the school as small, very personable, and a caring place. Students also noted that their teachers know how to help them to succeed and the school creates a family atmosphere. Many of the students feel that their school provides them with a sense of tradition and academic preparation they are expected to uphold. They feel their school offers challenges that prepares them for the secondary schools. They also believe their teachers care about them not only as students but as individuals. As members of a community of learners, these students build authentic relationships with their school and other students.

At the three schools, students noted that their teachers listened to them, remained positive in their discipline, and encouraged them to do their best. Observations in the classrooms confirmed a caring relationship between teachers and students. Even when discipline is required, students still feel respected by their teachers. Treated with fairness at all grade levels, students are given considerable freedom in making decisions about their learning. Students' work is displayed throughout the school, along with family and individual student pictures and the work of previous students. Each school presents a homey environment that demonstrates its focus on the students' well being, their achievements and their contribution to their school's tradition. Each child who graduates reflects the school's philosophical intent. Students are educated about the school's history and its traditions.

With teachers, students develop a relationship with an adult that involves greater emotional distance than the relationship with their parents. Children soon learn what is appropriate in dealing with teachers who are evaluating their academic progress. Students come to understand that their success rests upon what they can do rather than who they are. Children are taught that to succeed in school, they must learn the norms for independence and achievement and come to recognize that their well-being depends not only on social membership but on their ability to meet the school's standards of achievement (Smith, 1993).

Appleman School

The students noted that their parents selected Appleman because they just liked the school. The students themselves did not have much input regarding their choice of school. Those students who had attended public school prior to Appleman noted a difference in how the teachers cared about the students, individualized their learning and provided outside help. Students indicated that they really like their school and look forward to coming everyday. Students also feel that the school really prepares them to compete at the secondary school. In some cases, a sister or brother had done well at a secondary school, because they attended Appleman School. Most of the students interviewed had been with the school since the preschool program and knew of no other setting. However, those students who had been in public schools recognized a significant difference between the two settings noting that their public schools did not seem to care about them and they were not academically challenged.

Students made many comments to explain why they had such a strong allegiance to Appleman School. They spoke highly of the caring atmosphere and teachers:

The teachers here are really nice. They only yell if the students are really bad. They help the students to understand stuff;

The teachers are really here for the students, trying to help everyone be independent. Also, the way the teachers teach isn't a lecture; it makes school fun;

The school is sort of like a family, because everyone knows everyone's name;

My teacher told us [the students] that if we get too bored with any one way of learning, like outlines, she will change the process because she does not want the students hating to do any one particular thing;

The teachers go further here; they do things like geometry and French and stick with it for about two weeks. In my other school (public) they stick with something for a very long time and it gets boring. It is never boring here;

I like the academics; teachers are nice as long as you get your homework done. If you forget your homework, they get very upset;

I like the school because I like the fact that its hard but it's fun too. They don't make everything really hard where all you do is sit around and listen. We draw on the boards, do games, lots of challenges, and the food is pretty good, too.

Many students believe that the Appleman teachers have very high expectations for them. They also noted that on several occasions they had called their teacher at home. Students are encouraged to call, them if they need help or have missed assignments. At least three students said they call regularly and feel their teacher is receptive to the call. Several students feel Appleman has prepared them for the transition to the secondary level. Their social studies and science teacher 'had taught us how to take notes, how to study, what pace to set, and how to avoid cramming for exams and how to do outlines'. Students noted that their public school friends seem jealous of the things they are able to do. While many of the Appleman students resent the dress code, overall they feel that their school is a caring place.

Bakersfield School

Comments made by the Bakersfield students were similar to the Appleman students' responses. They view the school as family oriented, with a support system that allows them to excel. Bakersfield students were very sophisticated and quite articulate for their grade level. It was evident that they know what they want from their learning and what they expect from their school. Bakersfield students stated that they enjoyed learning and view their school as a challenge. These students were more articulate about the school's instructional practices while the Appleman students were more vocal about the caring environment at that school. Bakersfield students offered the following comments about their school and the benefits that it offers them:

I like how the teachers don't come into class and tell the students to open the textbook, do these pages. The teachers really help the students and help everyone work at their own pace. I also like how they approach learning, its not just read the material. They have interesting ways of showing students, not just telling the students. The school being so small helps;

The people here are also warm and caring because the school is so small and everyone gets along and knows everyone else. No one has to worry about walking into a place and not knowing any one;

I like the fact that the students work at their own pace and that we don't have to be doing what everyone else is doing;

In the younger grades, our teachers would put us in groups and I was put with two people and we worked on activities together. I also like how we can move at our own rate of how we can learn. I think the environment is different. My friend thinks her school is really boring; she would finish assignments and have to just wait. But here we are able to go onto our next assignment or do certain games;

I have been to my cousin's public school, even though I was two grades ahead of her. The material was boring and I could have walked out of the room when the teacher had her back to me. Here, the teachers pay attention to the class and know when students are leaving. But at that school, the teacher just sat at her desk and people were walking out of the room and not coming back.

The students at Bakersfield appreciate the interesting way their school presents information. They believe their teachers are insightful in meeting individual learning needs. For example, students who are either ahead or behind in their learning are given individualized instruction. Students describe their school as a very caring place where teachers show respect for students. However, Appleman students were more vocal about the responsive nature of their teachers, who allow students to call them at home. Appleman students see their school as family oriented, while the Bakersfield students note a very strong connection to their peers rather than an association to the entire school. Bakersfield students were vocal about the school's ability to make them accountable for their learning and expressed great appreciation for the opportunity to attend Bakersfield.

Crestview School

The Crestview students, in their responses, focused on the opportunity for freedom in their setting. Crestview School has a large open setting, divided into pods. Each pod, sectioned by sound proof room dividers at each corner of the room, represents a specific grade level where the teachers present their various subject areas. There are no desks in the pods so students sit on the floor during specific classes. The teachers used the soundproof pod areas for small group instruction. When students are assigned seatwork, they return to the large open setting to work with other students. Students may sit at their assigned seats or in other areas of the room as long as they are quiet and they complete their work. There is minimal supervision in the open setting. However, students are held responsible for completing the assigned work before they engage in other activities. Students apparently enjoy the child-directed setting and expressed feelings of autonomy in their learning. Students are encouraged to articulate their academic needs and let the teacher know how to help them. They are pleased to be treated as individuals whose teachers give them much attention. Because of the freedom and the caring teachers, students enjoy attending Crestview. They made their feelings known:

> I had a choice between two schools, this school and City Elementary (another independent private city school). I chose this school because I hadn't ever been in an environment like this (Crestview) and I figured it would be worth a shot.

> I was in the public schools, and it was too strict and the teachers were kind of mean. So my mom and I visited it here and really liked it. We looked at other schools but I realized we have a lot of freedom here and my mom let me choose which school I wanted to go to;

> The freedom feels so good because it doesn't feel like being trapped in a cell. When I was at the other schools, I felt like we were only there to learn and do what we had to do and there was no freedom or fun. We just sat around and did work.

Many of the students expressed their discontent with public schools. Since most of Crestview's students transferred from the city's magnet schools, their comments reflect upon conditions in these particular institutions. Many students noted that they did not have books, that teachers were mean and impersonal, and that the classes were very large. One student also expressed concern about the safety of their school, noting that she was afraid on several occasions in public school but felt safe at Crestview. Students at Crestview, much like those at the other schools in this project, expressed great support for their teachers. They feel their teachers treat them like adults and really care if they learn and complete their work. Crestview students believe that the strength of their school lies in having freedom to make decisions about their own learning. The school's curriculum is based on project learning and cross disciplinary activities that ensure the students' involvement in their learning. The teachers work collaboratively to facilitate group dynamics which allow the upper grades to assist the lower grades. The school is very small so teachers know all the students very well. In some cases students feel that familiarity is detrimental because, 'we cannot get away with things'.

Students at all three schools have a strong allegiance because of their connection to teachers and the instructional program. Their comments on the particular way their school's curriculum benefited them demonstrated their awareness of the school's mission. Crestview students noted that their school gave them considerable freedom and trusted them to make appropriate decisions for themselves. Crestview's mission also suggests that the curriculum should foster independence and group learning. At Appleman the students feel that the school offers a very nurturing environment, while it prepares them for the rigors of the secondary level. The implementation of Appleman's mission is apparent in the classroom where teachers prepare students to take notes and become independent. Bakersfield with its Montessori program focuses on strong academic preparation and its connection to the students' well being. While Bakersfield students eloquently described their school as a warm, friendly place, their emphasis was on the teachers' use of various instructional methods and individualized learning. Bakersfield teachers are responsible for setting the pace and ensuring student accountability in connection with the school's goals.

In these privatized settings, students value their caring teachers and the strong emphasis on academics. Parents listen to what their children have to say about whether the school is appropriate for them. Teachers are held accountable for student learning as it relates to the school's mission. Students know what is expected of them and feel that their teachers help them to achieve their goals. Teachers at each setting encourage their students through various means. The Appleman students, for example, feel they can call their teachers at home, while Bakersfield students can request individualized instruction. Crestview students are encouraged to work independently but teachers are always available to them. Observations in these schools verify the positive interactions that exist between the teachers and students at each setting. Students are challenged by stimulating questions and independent learning activities. Because students are never idle there is little time for behavior problems. Transitions are minimized so the students' instructional time is never wasted. The teachers' ability to instruct their students is maximized because students know what is expected of them. Given the strong commitment to the mission through the instructional program promotes a strong allegiance by the students.

Students' Responses to Instructional Practices and Secondary Preparation

Because these privatized settings emphasize mission adherence, many students and parents hold the school accountable for student achievement and engagement. Teachers are expected to show respect for students and to develop activities for the various levels of achievement. Standardized testing serves to ensure accountability in each school, where children are expected to perform in the upper percentiles. Test results, which measure student achievement, are shared with board members and parents. In fact, students in these settings usually perform above the national level, but each school is sensitive to the scores and open to change. Board members and parents recognize that test scores do not tell the whole story since the school's mission is not strictly academic. Because parents are familiar with each school's intent, they hold the school accountable for instructional practices as well as academic performance. Teachers are expected to emphasize character development throughout the curriculum and the implementation of a values curriculum.

The secondary school surveys provided another means of accountability. Each school, except Crestview, sends letters to secondary teachers while their graduates attended to determine the quality of their students' preparation for secondary school. Parents are concerned that each school prepares their children for successful experiences at the secondary and college level. Because each mission focused on strong academic preparation, schools were held accountable for secondary school placements. Parents want to be certain that by the end of the elementary years, their children will have the opportunity to select among the most academically rigorous secondary schools and make a successful transition to college. To these schools, secondary school placements are as important as test scores. Recruitment and retention are at stake if these schools are unable to ensure successful secondary placements and smooth transitions to the secondary level. Each school believes it is important that their classroom and curricular practices embody the mission of the school. One important way to verify the school's achievement of its goals involves having parents in the classroom confirming their choice. Students seem aware that the schools should promote what they say and insure their transition to the secondary level.

Appleman School

Appleman students noted that many of the curriculum practices reflect a theme orientation and provide them with options for assignments. Students who were interviewed spoke highly of the school for preparing them for the rigors of secondary schools. Several students feel the school teaches them successful study strategies that will enhance their success at the secondary level. According to the students, their teachers hold them accountable for their work, pressuring them to excel. However, some students view the pressure to do well academically as self imposed for some students. Students spoke highly of the social studies teacher and her willingness to let them do individualized projects. This teacher establishes various projects and allows students many options for doing assignments. Students cited numerous examples of advanced math and reading assignments that took them beyond their grade levels. While students complained that the school requires too much homework, they saw it as a good way of building their study skills for future use. Comments from the students emphasize the quality of instructional practices and the rigorous preparation for secondary schools:

> We just finished a neat project about working on a newspaper for the Civil War, working on an editorial, feature story. We had to choose a battle and find information about it, then type it up on the computer into a newspaper form;

> Last year we had a medieval feast and chose things like witchcraft, the Black Death, the plague, and the Crusades. We got dressed up and decorated the room and desks. We had a feast in the middle of the room and went around and presented our projects;

> I like the projects we do in social studies. The teacher helps, but she makes the projects more independent and students have to figure out a time schedule for themselves. It helps us to learn self-discipline, learn how to pace ourselves. We do many long term projects like making a book;

> I liked the aviation project; we saw movies, took field trips, and did projects we presented. [I liked] the explorer project because we made a magazine and told about explorers.

All the students cited many different projects that they found valuable for their learning. They particularly liked the social studies curriculum and the many independent activities.

The topic of secondary preparation elicited many responses. However, all eventually agreed that they are well prepared for middle school. Students commented as follows:

> Lots of the specialty teachers like social studies and science have taught us how to do notetaking, how to study, what pace to set. One of our teachers really helped prepare us and cram. She (teacher) has given us some of the circumstances she has been in, like a 60-page report. I think we all have developed a lot of good study skills here;

> The teachers make sure you really understand. And they don't just call on one person. The teachers call on all students, even the ones who don't have their hands raised. They make sure everyone understands;

> The advantage of going here is the reading program. The classes read three or four books a month, so reading skills have really gone up;

> Students can read whatever books they want every night, thirty minutes every night. We interview after reading each book with specific questions like, title, author, illustrator, setting.

Because of the large amount of assigned work, students soon learn to manage their time and perfect their study skills. Three students noted that their sisters who had graduated from Appleman did well at their secondary school because of their school's preparation. Appleman's philosophy for its sixth graders is to prepare them for the rigors of secondary schools in order to reduce the anxiety of the secondary school transition. Appleman stresses academics so its students have confidence in their ability; this confidence makes for one less worry during the transition from elementary to secondary school. Clearly, this philosophy works since many parents and students interviewed feel that Appleman's strength is its strong academic preparation and successful secondary school placements.

Bakersfield School

Because many of the Bakersfield students emphasized that they like their school for its instructional practices, these students focused more on secondary preparation. Students believe the school's strength is its rigorous program and its emphasis on reading. Students are positive about being able to select their own reading to suit their interests. The school emphasizes a writing program that encourages students to express their ideas. Like Appleman, Bakersfield is held accountable through its test scores. However, the principal at Bakersfield works to educate the families and board members to recognize the limitations in using test scores alone to evaluate a student's abilities and the school's success. Bakersfield, like Appleman, uses secondary placements as another measure of its success. Bakersfield does extensive follow up of graduates and interacts with parents who have gone through Bakersfield's program to see what changes should be made. Many parents are actively involved in the classroom as volunteers or observers. While parents often observe several times a year at the preschool and lower elementary level, parents with children in the upper grades do not make as many visits. Teachers appreciate the work of parent volunteers, and there is positive interaction between the two groups. Students feel good about the school and the support that it offers them. Students made the following comments about the program and their friendships with other students:

> Our class is good at leaders and followers. We can have a meeting without a leader and someone may start the meeting. But, we can just say what we think when one person is done speaking;

> More than half the class is going to the same school which is a big advantage. It is kinda up to us to know if we are ready;

> Our teacher had us read these certain chapters of books to get us ready for seventh grade. They were certain literature books. There were also other books in the class that we can read, like short stories, and we write a lot, too;

> Here there are sort of groups of friends, not really cliques, everyone is one group. But some people are better friends with some people, no one excludes anyone but some people have closer friends.

Bakersfield students believe they are well prepared for school. They also regard their friends as a good support system. While students speak highly of the challenging learning atmosphere, they place less emphasis on their secondary placements than the Appleman students. Bakersfield students appear more relaxed about their options for secondary schools and are more carefree about their ability to succeed in these settings. My observations indicate that the Bakersfield principal is responsible for reducing these secondary school 'anxieties'. She meets weekly with the students to prepare them for the transition and to respond to their concerns. She prepares for the sixth graders secondary school interviews, and taking the placement tests. The Appleman principal handles the sixth grade transition through the sixth grade teachers and parent meetings. Both schools work to calm students and parents about the secondary school transition.

Crestview School

Because only two students had graduated during the schools six year history, Crestview places less emphasis on secondary preparation. However, the school had contacted the parents of the two graduates regarding their education at Crestview. In both cases, the students were accepted into the city's more prestigious private schools and parents felt their children were doing better than their peers. The two parents who have children graduating within the next year are concerned that their children will have a very difficult transition to a larger middle school because of Crestview's size. In spite of their anxiety, the school's emphasis is not on its secondary placement; rather Crestview focuses on the needs of its lower elementary population since the bulk of Crestview's student population is in the lower elementary grades. Parents with children in the upper grades have asked the principal for more help with this transition, and she recognizes the need for the school to be more accountable for its secondary placements. The students believe the school is a good place for them because it gives them considerable freedom to develop their own interests. Students commented on the school's program and the interesting way it is organized. Most of the comments focused more on instructional issues rather than the secondary school preparation. Students noted:

I like it here because we do lots of different things like go swimming and other things;

I like it here because the kids have nice manners; the teachers are nice, but sometimes crabby. I like swimming, too. I like all of the different activities we do. And I like the field trips and participating in things;

We have these races with soup cans; we used a table to prop them up. We had cream of broccoli and chicken noodle soup; we learned that they can go faster if they just have broth in them;

We did a project on colors, we used colored staples and things and put them in a little jar, and we dumped it on the grass and tried to pick them up. Then we made a chart to see what colors we found the most and least of. We didn't find the green but actually the green actually stood out;

We do some creative writing, like fairy tales, fictional stories;

We also have a newspaper we do every month which has different articles like sports, news, editorials, etc. Everyone gets assigned something and has to go around interviewing and taking notes.

To meet the needs of the children of working parents, Crestview had to design a program that is both academically sound and enriched by after-hours activities. The academic program takes a hands on approach and involves trips to the downtown museums and public institutions, made possible by the small number of students. Students often traveled throughout the city using the mass transit system for field trips related to their studies. Observations in this setting revealed a rather large open space with children engaged in multiple activities involving noisy interactions among them. While the environment appeared very distracting, students were on task and involved in their learning. They are encouraged to develop their own projects yet, work in small groups while completing their work. There was much emphasis on cross disciplinary activities and research for their projects.

The school's mission involves a hands on academic approach with a strong emphasis on the arts. Students take music, art, and dance classes from actual performers in the community. It was interesting to watch the 5th and 6th grade boys participate in the dance program without concerns about their masculinity or the reactions of others. Parents like their children to be involved in the school's arts program so they did not have to take their children to additional enrichment classes on weekends and evenings. When parents pick their children up from the school, they have their evenings free from additional lessons. Providing this service is important for the school which promotes the idea of a partnership between the home and school. Children spoke highly about the school's role in keeping them 'occupied' while waiting for parents to pick them up after work.

All three schools view the mission as the driving force for the school's academic goals and curriculum. All three schools promote academics as the heart of their mission which determines instructional practices shaped, in turn, to promote learning. Each school is held accountable for the quality of its program, measuring its success with standardized test scores and secondary school placements. Crestview School does not emphasize its secondary placements at present, but to attract and retain parents in the future the school recognizes the need to promote its program with the secondary schools. These privatized settings design their educational programs to reflect their mission and to meet the learning needs of their participants. Each school is held accountable for implementing the mission and keeping students engaged in their learning. Observations indicate that these students stay on task, that transitional times are minimized, and students make choices that reflect their own interests. These students like the way their school prepares them for the secondary settings and believe that learning is important.

Student Empowerment and Discipline

Student engagement in education seems directly related to important variables such as voice in school governance and control over student behavior.

Community in school is maintained through the deliberate cultivation of a social order based on norms and values rather than formal rules and regulations. Schools that promote a caring environment spend considerable time communicating the school's expectations and promoting a positive learning atmosphere. A strong community is maintained through an organizational culture that promotes humane treatment of individuals and collaboration in the pursuit of goals. The school does not create a custodial environment or impose a confining structure; rather students are treated as learners who, may need reorientation to the school's ethos of caring and not as candidates for punishment (Smith, 1993). Schools encourage children to accept their norms through instruction and induction into the social milieu. These settings teach children new patterns of interaction with adults from whom they are expected to learn. Students assimilate into the school's community, and their success is dependent on their complying with the school's expectations.

Although private settings have the opportunity to remove difficult children, many do not because of their commitment to the student and their willingness to work with the family. This commitment to retain difficult children can cause other families to leave because of discipline concerns. Each principal noted that it is difficult to retain children who represent management problems and, at the same time, to meet the needs of other parents who have children in the same classroom. Each principal stated that they seldom ask children to leave unless the behavior is so extreme and the school cannot meet the child's needs; in such a case, the school has no other choice. However, when there are student discipline problems, parents are contacted and informed about how the incident was handled. If a child is asked to leave, parents are informed that the school's program is not what the child may need. They are educated about alternatives and encouraged to find other programs that support their child's disability. (This metropolitan area has several independent private schools that serve children with severe emotional and learning disabilities.) In making the difficult decision to expel a child, independent schools must recognize that disgruntled parents can directly influence other parents who are considering the school.

Appleman and Bakersfield schools' discipline policies promote the school's expectations for their students' behavior. The policy for each school involves showing consideration for others and respect for teachers and other students. Each policy lists consequences for misbehavior, which may include calling parents. The direct consequences range from taking time out, making retribution, and staying in during recess. In cases where the behavior is considered severe, students are sent to the principal's office or expelled for a period of time. Both principals stated that they have suspended students, sending a message to parents that the student's behavior will not be allowed. Once parents realize there is a possibility of expulsion, they are more receptive to working with their child's behavior. The school tends to set behavioral expectations that must be met if a student is to remain at the school. The Crestview School, which does not have a discipline policy, shows greater tolerance of students' behaviors, due perhaps, to the open setting and a larger number of students with disabilities, Crestview's teachers are more flexible and more open to students' difficult behavioral problems.

Teachers who were interviewed at each setting find students respectful and parents supportive in changing an unruly behavior. However, Appleman and Bakersfield teachers feel that as a whole their colleagues do not agree on the consequences for discipline. These teachers are in agreement about a positive approach to discipline, but they disagree when it comes to consistency, consequences and determining the severity of the behavior. Each school promotes a positive environment where children are treated in a fair manner and with respect. Observations indicate a respectful manner between the teacher and students. Teachers' comments to students are never demeaning, and they avoid screaming at children for their behavior. (Although at Crestview, there were times when the noise of the open classroom resulted in teachers yelling at students to 'shut up'.) All schools handle problems like talking, off task behaviors, and student aggression in positive nurturing ways.

Appleman School

When the Appleman School children were interviewed about discipline, they spoke highly of their teachers' positive approach. Many noted that teachers put their names on the board if they misbehave, talk to them in private about their behavior, and use an honor system in the upper grades. Teachers are free to design their own system and style since no management practice is dictated from above. As it works out, each teacher treats each child with respect and encourages him or her to make choices about behavior. Many students view the discipline as handled fairly. Students know they are in serious trouble when their teacher asks them to see the principal about their behavior. Students noted these issues about the school's management practices:

> The teachers here never say shut-up. They say be quiet so I can teach you in a calm voice;

> Like if someone is talking and she tells them to be quiet once or twice, and they still keep talking, they will have one last chance. Your name goes on the board when homework isn't done;

> Hardly anyone gets sent to the office. The principal is nice, no one could imagine her getting mad, but she does;

> The fourth graders were in a lot of trouble last year for making fun of each other, so she [the principal] came over once a week to talk to them;

It's good that a principal will come to talk to kids, it gives her a chance to know them [students] and do things with the principal.

When asked about their opportunities to have a voice in the school, students cited their many options for making choices. Students noted that they can decide what books they want to read and write about. More broadly, the school works hard to establish open lines of communication between the staff and the students. There is a student council that offers opportunities for their empowerment. Student council gives Appleman students freedom to identify community projects they can do and to select, for each grade, once a month a favorite lunch. Student council assists the student body in selecting a theme for student council week. During this special week, students are allowed to pick how they will dress. This week, instituted because students were unhappy with the dress code, gives them some control over their appearance. The school also provides the students with a choice week when they are encouraged to make good choices regarding their studies, television watching and food selections. Students like choice week, and the teachers have an opportunity to encourage good decision making. In addition, the curriculum director encourages teachers to provide students with more choice in assignments and projects. Appleman's mission is to encourage its students to be independent and to promote a healthy lifestyle through good choices. The students noted that the school listens to them and they can talk freely with school personnel about their issues.

Bakersfield School

The Bakersfield School uses a very positive approach in working with discipline issues. The school has established procedures for discipline that incorporate timeout for most problems. However, if the behavior continues the child is sent to the principal and parents are called. If the behavior is severe the student might be suspended for three to ten days depending on the misbehavior. Students who commit minor infractions are assigned community service tasks such as cleaning desks, washing lunch tables or helping in the gym. Students revealed that the principal was very helpful in solving their problems. Students feel that the school's discipline is fair and the teachers respect them as individuals. Students talk about the community service as a way to improve their behavior and, at the same time, support the school. Students made the following comments about discipline in the school:

We have something called community service which means you wash desks after lunch or something. I have visited other schools and I was amazed at how much less discipline there was at the other schools. Here the teachers are in control of what is going on in the classroom rather than the students;

At public school the teachers will put checks or send them to the principal's office right away. But the teachers here try to work with the students to find out what is wrong and help them with their problems. Sometimes the teachers will call on students when they aren't paying attention which can be embarrassing, but the person will probably never do that again;

If we do something bad we get sent to the principal's office. I think that's OK because we learn from our mistakes and if we go to the principal she talks to us about helping with our problem and not criticizing. I know I've been there and she helps to fix the problem;

I've never been sent there (principal's office), but last year I wasn't paying attention so I had to do community service. The teachers give warnings instead of yelling and if we do it again we have to stay after school.

Bakersfield School takes a very positive approach in working with children with discipline problems. A few parents who were interviewed feel that the school could be stronger in handling serious discipline problems. However, the principal insists that the school is committed to all students and believes that children should be involved in controlling their own behavior as a way to handle their problems. The community service was established so that students know there are logical consequences for their behavior. This mode of discipline allows students to give back to the school in some capacity as the school demonstrates its commitment to teaching independence. Some parents noted that parents left the school because of the lack of discipline and its impact on other students' learning. However, the principal stated that because the school is committed to all children, it is important for everyone to work together in solving discipline problems.

Because the school's mission promotes independence, students have many opportunities for choice. In each grade, students are given more responsibility and greater representation. The emphasis on independence is most noticeable at the upper elementary level where students assume the responsibility for the school's store. Students actually select items for the store and decide how the profits will be used. Fifth graders write persuasive letters applying for specific store positions. The graduating sixth graders then select the fifth graders for the various school store responsibilities. In addition, the school uses many cross age activities where upper-grade students have freedom to design their interactions with the lower grades. Students have pen pals in different grades. They also develop videotapes presenting their grade level so incoming students know what to expect when they reach the same grade level. The principal meets weekly with sixth graders to assist them with the secondary transition and to work with them on their graduation speeches. The school promotes student empowerment by giving students opportunities to choose how they will interact with each other. Many students stated that the school is a caring place because everyone tries to make them feel as if they belong.

Crestview School

Due to the open classroom environment and inexperienced teachers, there are more difficulties with discipline at Crestview school. The philosophical intent of the school is about making choices and giving students more autonomy. The setting is often noisy, full of distractions that make it difficult to keep students on task. This environment fosters behavior management techniques such as 'bribing' students to be good through a rules and consequences approach. Students noted that while they have many freedoms in their setting, at times teachers are pushed to their limits because of the room set up and the noisy activities. Although students complained a bit about the behavioral constraints, they believe the school really cares about them. Because the school has no written formal policies for behavior there are many inconsistencies at the various levels. The preschool program is geared to a choice orientation while the other elementary teachers use a more behavioral approach. The students noted that the freedom they have at the school allows teachers to treat them as individuals when dealing with behavior problems. Students' views varied regarding discipline and the way the school works with them on their behavior. Students noted the following:

> Some teachers are really strict like our gym teacher. She makes us get in a straight line and face the back without moving a muscle;

> I don't think this school is all that different from other ones. They give us freedom but when we don't act right, they don't really discipline, they bribe;

> In one class our teacher said if we didn't finish an assignment we wouldn't be able to go on this field trip;

> The younger kids try to get the other students upset. They do sneaky things and get away with it; we don't.

It appears that the school has no philosophy behind its approach to discipline and, as a result, the teachers resort to punitive consequences. Their philosophy of personal autonomy is often undercut when students misbehave. Teachers appear conflicted in their desire to allow children to make good choices and their knowledge that students have difficulty behaving in an open, distracting environment. Because many Crestview teachers are inexperienced in this type of setting, they have difficulty managing the students. As a result children are often unruly creating an uncooperative relationship between the students and teachers. Students mentioned that teachers often yell at them, but, at the same time, they recognize that their behavior warrants this reaction. In my observations, the teachers were often frustrated because of the length of time spent with the child. Teachers know that the setting creates distractions that children find difficult to ignore. However, teachers work with students in a positive manner.

Due to the low number of upper elementary students, there are few choice options for them. The school does not have any student government programs, and students have no input into the school as they have at Bakersfield and Appleman. The philosophical intent of Crestview involves allowing children to be independent by giving them opportunities to sit where they want, freedom to play with other students, and a choice in free time activities. Because of the small number of students there are more freedoms than at the other two sites. With all these freedoms, it may seem that the students do not need more autonomy. In fact, students do have considerable freedom to choose projects that they want to pursue. Students value the freedoms at Crestview and believe that the school is committed to enhancing their personal autonomy.

Discipline and choice options are unique features in these privatized settings where students are treated respectfully and behavior has logical consequences. Because they are treated with respect, students show respect for their teachers and the school. In each setting students are given personal freedoms to make decisions about their behavior. Parents facilitated this atmosphere by encouraging children to be responsive to their teachers and by supporting the school's discipline policies. The schools work with parents to ensure that they deal with inappropriate behavior in a positive manner and allow children an outlet to change. The schools seek student input and encourage them to voice their concerns. Students appreciate the positive relationships they have with their schools and believe the schools are committed to helping them.

Conclusion

In these privatized settings there is a commitment to learning that is articulated throughout the program. This commitment to mission adherence underlies a coherent curriculum that is content driven. Students feel connected to the school and identify with its traditions. As a result, students are respectful to the teachers and committed to their learning. They are motivated by learning experiences that give them choices in selecting the projects they are interested in pursuing.

Students have a strong affiliation to their school because of the good learning environment and the responsiveness of teachers. Teachers are always available and flexible to meet their learning needs. The teachers have high expectations, but students know that the teachers care about their success in future settings. Students have positive feelings about a setting that focuses on their learning. When discipline problems occur the teacher treats students fairly and consistently. There are clear expectations regarding appropriate behavior and consequences if students do not behave. Teachers promote logical consequences for inappropriate behavior. Because they respect their teachers, students are responsive in their interactions with the school.

Because privatized settings must maintain a positive learning environment to retain parents and students, they work to create a community of learners. Students feel an identification with the school which they view as a caring, family-oriented place. Students know that teachers care about their learning by providing a challenging environment that ensures their success at the secondary level. There are clear expectations about their behavior and academic achievement. Students benefit from having a collaborative environment, an innovative curriculum and a commitment to student achievement. Collaboration among teachers allows for an evolving curriculum and a creative approach to management concerns. Students and parents benefit from a comprehensive and flexible program that they respect and understand. Market-driven schools like these attract and retain students through their comprehensive programs which insures accountability and responsibility.

Chapter 7

Lessons for All Schools

As the restructuring movement looks in the direction of decentralization, schools can expect to take more authority in administering the quality of its practices. Facing a range of educational programs, parents will enjoy the freedom to choose a school that is appropriate for their children's learning. Choice empowers parents and schools and challenges them to be more creative in defining what educational program will benefit the children it serves. While the assumption that market competition will improve schools is unproven, there is substantial data to suggest that choice and other school privatization enterprises involve parents in an interactive partnership. A decentralized choice plan creates school flexibility and accountability and provides alternatives for parents. In this era of school reform, a strategy of choice combined with other advantages associated with privatization, can revitalize schools and deregulate the monopolistic bureaucracy of public schools. Choice can no longer be dismissed as a myth or unattainable for public schools.

Before 'choice' can be implemented, public schools have to determine how they are going to define their authority and their relationship with parents. Choice results in each school creating a 'school worth choosing'. District-wide decentralization goes well beyond developing a few magnets or charter schools which offer limited access to choice. Instead, public school deregulation creates a context where individual schools have considerable authority in determining how to provide educational services. Thus, before districts can be decentralized, each school of choice must demonstrate the educational effectiveness of its mission and provide information about students' academic progress and attendance, parents' involvement and school climate. Each school must define how it will share power, responsibility, and ownership with various constituencies in the educational process. A self-governed school should cultivate a responsive dialogue between parents and school participants who define shared goals. Since such a relationship may be new to schools the transition to decentralization requires a process of education where schools are 'readied' to be self-sufficient.

Presently, there is limited research to support schools undergoing radical decentralization. Schools are building their planes as they fly into decentralized territory. Although the charter school movement provides a context for self-governance, this information has not proven useful to schools. No clear guidelines define the process of school reorganization. Kean (1994) has iden-tified several models for implementing school autonomy. While these models address mission definition, they provide no leadership for the actual deregu-lation process. The London schools which are experimenting also with decen-tralized models in their grant maintained schools have encountered their own problems. Clayton (1994) noted that some British principals were resistant to the change in their traditional administrator role. Other principals also lacked the management and leadership competencies to cope with the burdens of self-governance. While there is little data about the success of this endeavor, schools coped fairly well in spite of the difficulties. In fact, principals who were autocratic oriented became increasingly more analytical and critical of their roles.

While there may be a few studies in the literature that document the process of decentralization, there is a wealth of information available from another source. For public school decentralization to be successful, there be-comes a rationale for studying private schools. These settings can serve as models in this process because they are autonomous, compete for students, engage families and remain accountable to their constituencies. Data found in this book provides a context in order to assist public schools with this evolu-tion. This chapter gives the reader a framework for school decentralization grounded in the independent school model which is built on a record of success. This prototype of 'school autonomy' can provide direction for schools facing a major transformation as they redefine their missions for serving stu-dents. The valuable lesson we learn is that mission, not market, lends itself to school improvement. Efforts to continually evaluate the quality of schooling is based on collectively developing a long range plan.

Lesson One: Mission Adherence

The mission of each independent school provides the mechanism for estab-lishing a cultural linkage within the school community. Members of the com-munity continually examine what the school means, what the child who leaves the program represents, and how the mission is reflected through the educa-tional program. The school's marketing theme centers on the way the school reflects its mission. The mission determines long range planning and allocation of resources, and creates a linkage with the participants. The curriculum, parent organization and board agendas revolve around the school and its treatment of students. Teachers implement the mission through their instructional prac-tices and define their professional development in relation to how the school might benefit from new practices. School participants embody the mission in their practices. The mission keeps each school centered so that there is a struc-ture in place for school improvement.

Common themes found in each school's mission reflect a commitment to academic rigor and to spiritual development through promoting personal values, and to preparing children to become life long learners. School missions are important in defining the context for how children should be educated. While the commitment to mission remains constant, evaluation of school goals must be ongoing. The mission fosters a community bound by emotional ties to the school. Each school continually seeks validation through its interactive relationships with parents and school participants. Parents who choose a particular mission for their children will ensure that their children will act in accordance with the school's goals. Parents support the school by maintaining its mission through their interactions with their children.

Because the mission shapes how a school promotes its agenda, each school needs an established process for evaluating its achievements. Every five years, each individual school reviews its mission and long range plan. In addition, a school improvement agenda brings participants together to evaluate the future direction of the school. School members believe all participants can contribute to the mission of the school. Evaluation of the school's focus calls for an assessment of future needs but maintains its traditions and beliefs. Accountability and responsiveness to how parents view the school's priorities provides a partnership for ownership. As the school surveys what the participants want, it uses this input to foster collective responsibility, with an eye to maintaining traditions and preparing for the future.

To begin the decentralization process, individual schools and their participants must identify educational goals for their students. Since mission definition establishes a cohesive structure that motivates and shapes the behavior of the participants, the participants' responsibility is to agree to what the school should become and what the students' should reflect. Then, participants work collectively to define how the instructional program should be implemented throughout the curriculum. Parents and school staff, working together, build a framework to meet the future needs of the school.

As this study shows, these schools have a clear vision rooted in their educational program. The strength of independent schools lies in their ability to pull everyone into the dialogue in defining the purpose of schooling. To ensure accountability, parents and school personnel evaluate how the mission is reflected in its graduates. Evaluation of the long range plan implies that constituents value the mission and expect to see its impact. The three schools in the study used several methods for renewing their missions and ensuring their accountability. The following recommendations are derived from techniques they used to begin their five-year evaluation cycle. These recommendations are not to be perceived as a recipe for decentralization, but they are suggestions based on success. Schools facing decentralization should:

- identify the participants involved in defining the mission of the school; then develop a process for consensuses where everyone will have a voice. Small focus groups are a good way to encourage a collective voice.

- rather than reinventing a wheel, review other school missions and visit these schools to examine the connection between mission adherence and the educational program. Those with an independent school in the vicinity may want to develop a partnership to share strategies.
- encourage teachers to focus collectively on curriculum themes and instructional practices that will emulate the school's practices. An assessment of the future direction of educational trends should provide good insights for school improvement.
- pursue discussions with past graduates to collect vital information about the way these individuals view the school. Alumni at various stages in their lives bring depth to what they envision for the future generation. The school should do a follow-up with the secondary students to identify the strengths and weaknesses of the school's graduates.

The mission becomes the blue print for shaping the school's program. It defines the type of student and parent that the school will want to attract and retain. The school's curriculum shaped by its goals serves to recruit teachers who embrace a similar philosophy. When like-minded participants are engaged through the mission, a vital culture evolves; this culture, in turn, allows individuals to work collectively to solve problems and set goals. If you build and maintain a quality school, it will attract students. It is not about competition or marketing. School privatization is mission adherence and how schools engage parents into their governance structure.

Lesson Two: Organizational Structure

Each independent school revolves around a board structure composed of representatives from the school. The board is the governing nucleus of each school. This structure for self-government implements the long range plan as defined by its participants. By setting goals, the board holds the school accountable and establishes procedures for school improvement. Schools have autonomy to make decisions at the building level to benefit the participants. Board participants, identified for their expertise and their potential contribution to the school are not just advisory; rather they contribute to policy-making and to school governance. They are assigned to committees, like other members of the school, and are held accountable through goal setting.

For successful school decentralization, various constituencies — parents, teachers, and administrators — must be represented on the board. The schools themselves set policies regarding representation, term limits, committee composition and board duties. Educating board members about the governance structure become a necessary administrative function for successful board representation. Board members are selected to meet particular needs rather than to represent a constituency of parents. When a board position is available, a nominating committee determines which individual, connected to the school, might provide the necessary expertise to assist the board with implementing its policies or long range plans.

The board executes its long range plan through its committee structure. Individual board committees, using the long range plan, determine their objectives for the year and establish a time line for completing their goals. Although all board committees contribute to the school's mission, some carry more authority than others. The executive and finance board committees are the cores of the administrative structure of school. By refusing to provide a forum for parental complaints, the board retains its focus on the executive duties for administering the school. A commitment to implement the long range plan supersedes responding to the day-to-day complaints which fall quite rightfully to the administration of the school.

The ideal board members understand their roles and the way their expertise serves the school's mission and long range plan. Board members must detach themselves from the parent role and make decisions that will benefit the entire school. Board members support the principal and staff in their responsibility for implementing the school's educational goals. Because board members provide an expertise that supports the school's mission, the success of school governance rests with the quality of its board members. A board member's knowledge and his or her ability to work collegially can enhance the school's ability to implement its goals.

Because the board structure is pivotal to the success of self-management, schools undergoing decentralization must have a thorough understanding of the way parent involvement in the governance structure is valued and practiced. The board's ability to visualize the school's future and implement its long range plan becomes the vehicle for school improvement. The board's focus is on the future needs not the day to day problems that plague the school. The success of a school's board structure ultimately rests with the board members. They provide the wisdom that will allow the distribution of power; they hear individual voices, but they work toward the collective good.

Lesson Three: Parent Organization

The parent organization plays an important role in establishing cultural linkages between the school's traditions and its future. Through fundraising, social interactions, and its voice to the board, the parent organization establishes the culture that interacts around the school's goals. A partnership grows between the parents' organization and the school because they are united by the mission and their mutual interests. The parent organization serves as a place for parents to interact with other school participants in establishing an open climate.

For the parent organization to be successful in decentralized settings, clear policies must define its role in the school. These policies should facilitate a connection to the board through the parent organization representation on board committees. Parent organization officers need time on the board agenda to insure a role for this constituency in the governance of the school. Because the parent organization is critical to parent engagement, the board should support its activities and encourage parents to become involved in the school. The role for the parent organization is to promote the school's goals through fundraising activities. Established fundraising and social activities become the traditions that compliment the social connection with parents and other school participants.

In addition to fundraising, the parent organization should serve two functions. First, it ensures parent commitment through social activities. Parents are involved in school traditions such as appreciation dinners, school auction, parent night and cookie exchange. They welcome opportunities to affirm their choice of school through their interactions with other parents and school personnel. United by a common mission and long range plan, parents work cohesively to ensure the success of social activities. The second function of the parent organization is parent education. Given the need for parent leadership on board committees and in the school's governance, the parent organization serves as testing ground for socializing parents for their involvement in the school's governance structure. Participation in the parent organization activities fosters the understanding of the school's ethos. Parents come to understand other parents' needs and the role of the parents in creating a cohesive structure to support the school's goals. Given this understanding, parents become suitable candidates for board membership. Involvement of parents through the parent organization is pivotal to socializing parents in their commitment to the school. Parents need to be educated to recognize what skills and abilities they can contribute to enhancing the school's community.

If schools are to redefine their governance structure, the parent organization provides a pool of candidates to assist with the decentralization process. Parents involved in the parent organization have been 'readied' to assist with defining and governing the school's mission and long range plan. These parents know what other parents want and value the school's traditions. The parent organization is vital to the successful implementation of school choice since it prepares an able educated group of parents to contribute to the school.

Lesson Four: Leadership and Management Skills

The organizational structure of the Board found in independent schools provides an integrated process for policy-making, planning, resource allocation, and evaluation of the school's goals. The success of the school's self-governance is dependent on the leadership and management of the principal. The principal's administrative behavior requires him or her to balance his or her authority with the participants' wants and needs. Principals cultivate a coalition for change and politically negotiate the interaction among the participants. Responsive to both parents and teachers, these principals become active listeners who facilitate collaboration and community, creating an environment where parents continually affirm their choice and commitment to the school.

Leading the self-managed school requires that the principal mold a coalition for change in order to create a common vision. Because each decentralized school must define its mission and long range plan, the principal must be a political negotiator who builds a community. Leaders in these settings must be risk-takers who can draw consensus and be willing to seek the advice of their constituencies. Active listeners, these principals balance the needs of a vocal few with the good of the 'whole'. They provide leadership to the school by continually educating the board about educational trends and the direction the school should take. Good leadership in a decentralized setting, where the power is equalized, creates a strong institutional culture which empowers individuals to participate in the decision-making process and equips them with the knowledge and skills to support the school's educational goals. Such administrative leadership involves the ability to act as a consultant who educates participants so they can become empowered in finding solutions for school issues.

Given the fluidity of choice, principals must respond to a constituency who share power and hold them accountable. Principals in decentralized settings are less concerned with controlling what people do and when they do it, and more concerned with managing the accomplishments of the board and meeting school participants' demands. Such management requires an ability to keep various constituencies happy, even as the 'playing fields are leveled'. Facilitating everyone's needs while maintaining authority places new demands on principals in deregulated settings. These principals must foster ownership to ensure participatory decision-making. They work to create opportunities for teachers to work collaboratively so the school mission becomes a reality. Principals act as advocates for both parents and teachers to ensure an equal partnership and commitment to the school's intent.

Traditional management used to administer public schools is not effective for running self-managed schools. Deregulated settings, where principals draw constituencies together behind a common vision, requires a collaborative management style that builds coalitions to support and monitor program goals. The principal empowers school participants so they can solve problems collectively and work with the board and the administration to define goals that will realize the school's vision.

In decentralized settings, the principal must facilitate an environment that fosters autonomy in participants. Principals support the participants by giving them voice, honoring their needs, finding resources, and responding to their suggestions and problems. Such responsive leadership is the key to attracting and retaining school participants. Principals must use their leadership and management skills to empower the school participants either by providing resources and information. If schools are to be self-sufficient, the principal must lead a diverse constituency toward a shared vision based on an educational mission shared by all. Principals in privatized settings can provide much insight for the public school principals undergoing decentralization. The private school principals understand the need to be responsive to all participants and to build coalitions. They understand shared governance and view themselves as the glue that bonds the constituencies. Private school principals are leaders who envision change rather than manage a centralized bureaucracy.

Lesson Five: Professional Community for Teachers

The organizational culture in independent private schools gives teachers input into the governance structure and offers them professional development opportunities and greater autonomy in their curriculum and instructional practices. A professional community evolves when participants share responsibility for enhancing students' learning and pursue innovative practices to accomplish goals. Teachers in autonomous settings have a shared philosophy for educating the children in their school. Working in teams seems to meet their professional needs. By collaborating, teachers share their ideas, materials, and methods reinforcing their commitment to teaching.

Lessons from the privatized settings have taught us that teachers respond very positively to an opportunity for input into the mission and the long range planning. Such participation establishes ownership, which strengthens commitment to developing curriculum and instructional practices that supports the mission. Teachers feel empowered to share their views of what the school should mean to its participants. As participants in the governance, teachers develop personal efficacy and commitment to the school's mission. When school authority is equalized, teachers feel empowered in their practices. They view their principal as a colleague because she helps them address their needs. Individuals are evaluated based on a process of cultivating teaching that promotes goals, not prescriptions. These teachers believe they have control over their professional lives, and they are sustained by professional growth opportunities shared with their colleagues.

A healthy environment is critical for cultivating a professional community. The school's commitment to its mission and long range plans is instrumental in supporting the teachers' goals for educating their students. Principals encourage teachers to grow through their interactions with other teachers by providing structural conditions for autonomy. Organized into teams, teachers profit from dialogue and support as they experiment with curriculum and instruction. They talk collegially about student achievement and take responsibility for students' learning. In this environment, teachers shape curriculum to support the mission. They get the most from the school's resources because they work together. The kind of isolation that leads to dissatisfaction is reduced by the team approach in these schools.

Parents support their teachers' professional goals though the choice process. A common agenda is established that leads to a partnership between parents and teachers. Parents are viewed by teachers as a support network because of their involvement in the school. Parents serve as volunteers to sustain teachers' goals. They also provide expertise that can be incorporated into the school's curriculum. Teachers in these settings feel valued by parents. Parents provide appreciation dinners, contribute resources for teachers' needs through fundraising, and seek out teachers' views about the school. Parents work very hard to insure that the teachers who work with their children are fulfilled in their teaching.

Schools of choice, where teachers are valued and given professional growth opportunities, provide models for other decentralized settings. The teachers' involvement in the school's governance and freedom to define their curriculum establish a professional community. These settings work to ensure that principals do not reduce teaching into a prescriptive set of improvements. Instead, principals encourage a teacher's professional goals and establish an organizational structure that supports teaming. Principals ensure a balance between supporting teachers and meeting the demands of parents. A principal who is overly responsive to parents' concerns destroys teacher commitment and diminishes teachers' professionalism. Thus, the principal is crucial in supporting a professional community that is required to sustain teacher efficacy. The administrator establishes an environment where teachers have time to plan to exchange ideas, to function as professionals, to contribute to the mission through constant professional interaction.

Lesson Six: Parent and Student Retention

When given the opportunity for choice, many parents feel a sense of control in defining the educational program that best meets the needs of their children. The parents' educational experience tends to influence their selection of schooling for their children. As a result of the selection process, the school can assume that its families accept its philosophical tenets and expect them to participate in decision-making. Membership in a community can lead to a unified concerted effort for parents to educate students about their performance and role in the school. This fellowship of school participants develops an environment where parents are willing to remain, knowing that the school represents the best interests of their children.

Parents often select schools in response to a 'gut level' feeling engendered by an environment that matches what they need and seems to offer what they perceive as necessary for their children's learning. Parents feel that the school they select for their children reflects a high degree of commitment to excellence in education and to a strong partnership with parents. Since schools of choice attract parents through the appeal of their mission, to remain competitive, these settings must find ways to market an educational program that supports parents. To maintain that appeal such schools are bound to respond to parents'concerns, building a partnership through the implementation of the educational goals.

Schools that are intent in retaining parents attempt to understand their needs as their children progress through their grade levels. The school keeps abreast of parents' needs through parent education seminars, board education committees, and parent organization meetings. Parents articulate their needs and the school implements strategies to answer them. The school provides parent education to assist with their children and opportunities to talk with their children's teachers. It establishes a social context where families can interact with other families to address common concerns. Thus, parents have informal outlets for approaching teachers and the principal about their problems at each grade level. The community atmosphere gives parents a forum for addressing their needs and for understanding the school's intent and their own role in facilitating the education of their children.

Involving parents in the governance structure requires that the school takes a role in educating them. Parents must see that they are to provide expertise to support the school mission rather than represent their individual interests. The focus on mission allows parents to work collaboratively with school officials to implement the school's long range goals for improvement. Understanding the board's role enables parents to see how the school functions and remains accountable. Engaging parents in the governance of the school creates a community where participants trust and respect each other.

Choice creates a high degree of engagement for both staff and students because there is a match between family preference and philosophical mission. Retaining students is tied to the school's success in implementing its mission. Schools are held accountable for their treatment of students and their achievement rates. Students value their caring teachers and the strong emphasis on academics. They identify with the school which they view as a family-oriented place. Collaboration between teachers and parents promotes a stimulating environment where there is a comprehensive program committed to preparing students for the rigors of the secondary schools.

Final Notes

This book presents a study of privatized settings which functions as models of decentralization for schools to emulate. Independent schools tested through their years of existence have maintained stable communities based on tradition and commitment to their mission. Keenly aware of their competition, these schools are challenged to define their intent. A mode of governance that empowers participants to shape the context of the school seems essential to their success. Because participants are solicited for their views regarding the school's curriculum and practices, they are committed to the successful implementation of the mission.

It remains to be seen whether the lessons of independent schools can be implemented in a public school framework involving choice. The private schools in this study are stable schools with a high degree of parent engagement. Is it possible to create an educational communities like those in this study when there is no tradition of parent involvement and when schools face a variety of social concerns? Will legal guidelines be necessary to ensure equal opportunity and to limit and define school missions? These and other issues for school decentralization face the public schools as they move toward decentralization. The fact that the practice of self governance is foreign to many schools creates further problems. Relying on parents' leadership to shape the school means the school must accept the challenge of educating parents. Parents and school participants must understand their shared role in determining how they will educate their students. Policy implementation issues of the independent school model will impact the success of using this model in many schools.

Independent schools provide many lessons for school reform. For many decades these schools have embraced shared governance where the focus is on long range planning. These schools set an agenda for improvement knowing that they must attract and retain students. The notion of competition is apparent when these schools focus on what they want to offer students and parents. They are not concerned with who their competition is but how they can attract students who will benefit from their mission. These schools work toward improving their mission knowing that if they do not meet parents' needs they can leave. By focusing on what the school should be, it retains parents and moves in a school improvement direction. The long range plan defines a process for school reform that unites all participants behind a collective responsibility for school reform based on a common mission.

Appendix

Research Questions

Teacher Questions

Structure/Organization of the school day
Curriculum decision making — Curriculum emphasis
Salary, benefits, leave, professional development
Academic freedom/Selection of materials
School committee involvement/Level of input
Classroom organization/Variation of instruction
Evaluation/Supervision by head
Engagement of parents/Response to parent concerns/Support of parents
Assessment of students/Report cards/Conferences
Use of positive/negative rewards/Discipline
Administrative structure/Place within the hierarchy
Empowerment of teachers/Administrative response to teachers' concerns
Budget/Supplies/Textbooks
Student academic problems/Special education concerns
Promotion of multicultural education/Diversity/Community projects
Interaction with students
Perks — Parents/School
Faculty rapport/Team teaching/Cohesiveness of the school organization
Private/Public school experience/Level of education/Years teaching
Computer/Technology

Student Questions

Reasons for attending the school/Likes–Dislikes
Student involvement in governance
Input with school administrators
Empowerment of students within the school
Curriculum emphasis/Specialty areas
Private/Public school attendance
Motivation/Reinforcers by teachers/Administrators
Community involvement activities
Input for school choice

Parent Questions

Decision making for selecting your school
Contentment with decision
Positive/Negative about the school
Opportunities for input/Response by school personnel
Curriculum/Academics/Social concerns for children
Discipline concerns
Tuition costs/Extended day care/Lunch/Additional costs
Public/Private school experiences
Minority recruitment/Diversity concerns/Participation in governance
Level of involvement with school governance
Selection of board and committee members

Administrator Questions

Staff evaluation and supervision/Percentage of time in classrooms
Rapport with parents/Response to parents' concerns/Parent involvement
Written communication to parents/Teachers
Curriculum decision/Involvement of teachers
Problems of discipline/Academic problems/Special education
Budget/Fundraising/Salaries
Support system/Board relationship
Support for teachers
Training/Experiences/Professional development
Student recruitment/Minority recruitment/Scholarships
Organization of the school day
Administrative structure of the school/Who reports to whom
Committee structure/Different committees: parents, teachers, board
Perks/Salary/Benefits
Rapport with teachers
Role of assistant director/Development director
Average time spent per week with school activities
Agenda development for board and faculty meetings
Selection of board members/Issues of gender and minority parents
Preparation for junior high/Selection of schools for sixth graders
Follow-up on graduates

Bibliography

AITKEN, H.P. (1993) 'NAIS project on pricing and affordability,' Paper presented at the Annual Meeting of the American Education Research Association, April, Atlanta, Georgia.

ANDERSON, G.L. and DIXON, A. (1993) 'Paradigm shifts and site-based management in the United States: Toward a paradigm of social empowerment', in SMYTH, J. (Ed) *A Socially Critical View of the Self-managing School*, London, Falmer Press, pp. 35–49.

ARCHBALD, P.A. and PORTER, A.C. (1994) 'Curriculum control and teachers' perceptions of autonomy and satisfaction', *Educational Evaluation and Policy Analysis*, **16**, 1, pp. 21–39.

ASHTON, P., WEBB, R. and DODA, C. (1983) *A Study of Teachers' Sense of Efficacy*, Final Report, Executive Summary, Gainesville, University of Florida.

BACHARACH, S.B., BAMBERGER, P., CONLEY, S.C. and BAUER, S. (1990) 'The dimension of decision participation in educational organization: The value of a multi-domain evaluative approach', *Educational Administration Quarterly*, **26**, 2, pp. 126–67.

BACHARACH, S.B., BAMBERGER, P. and MITCHELL, S. (1990) 'Work design, role conflict, and role ambiguity: The case of elementary and secondary schools', *Educational Evaluation and Policy Analyses*, **12**, 4, pp. 415–32.

BAUCH, P.A. (1988, Winter) 'Is parent involvement different in private schools?', *Educational Horizons*, pp. 78–82.

BAUCH, P.A. (1989) 'Can poor parents make wise educational choices?', in BOYD, W.L. and CIBULKA, J.C. (Eds) *Private Schools and Public Policy: International Perspectives*, London, Falmer Press, pp. 285–309.

BEARE, H. and BOYD, W.L. (1993) *Restructuring Schools: An International Perspective on the Movement to Transform the Control and Performance of School*, London, Falmer Press.

BECKER, H.J. and EPSTEIN, J.L. (1982) 'Parent involvement: A survey of teacher practices', *The Elementary School Journal*, **83**, 2, pp. 85–102.

BERNINGER, S.M. and RODRIGUEZ, R.C. (1989) 'The principal as catalyst in parental involvement', *Momentum*, April.

BIMBER, B. (1993) *School Desegregation: Lessons from the Study of Bureaucracy*, Santa Monica, CA, Rand Publication Series.

BOLMAN, L.G. and DEAL, T.E. (1994) 'Looking for leadership: Another search party's report,' *Educational Administration Quarterly*, **30**, 1, pp. 77–96.

Bibliography

Boyd, W.L. and Kerchner, C.T. (1988) *The Politics of Excellence and Choice in Education*, London, Falmer Press.

Boykin, W.A. (1986) 'The triple quandary and the schooling of Afro-American children', in Neisser, V. (Ed) *The School Achievement of Minority Children*, Trenton, NJ, Lawrence Erlbaum Associates, pp. 64–71.

Bridges, D. and McLaughlin, T. (1994) *Education and the Market Place*, London, Falmer Press.

Brown, D.J. (1990) *Decentralization and School-based Management*, London, Falmer Press.

Brown, F. (1992) 'The Dutch experience with school choice: Implications for American education', in Cookson, P.W. Jr. (Ed) *The Choice Controversy*, Newbury Park, CA, Corwin Press, Inc.

Bryk, A.S., Holland, P.B., Lee, V.E. and Carriedo, R.A. (1984) *Effective Catholic Schools: An Exploration*, Washington, DC, National Catholic Educational Association.

Bryk, A.S., Lee V.E. and Holland, P.B. (1993) *Catholic Schools and the Common Good*, Cambridge, MA, Harvard University Press.

Caldwell, B.J. and Spinks, J.M. (1992) *Leading the Self-managing School*, London, Falmer Press.

Campbell, D. and Crowther, F. (1991) 'What is an entrepreneurial school?', in Crowther, F. and Caldwell, B. (Eds) *The Entrepreneurial School*, Sydney, Australia, Ashton Scholastic, pp. 13–21.

Chapman, J. (1990) *School-based Decision-making and Management*, London, Falmer Press.

Chiara, S. (1991) 'The rules of the marketplace are applied to the classroom,' *The New York Times*, pp. 1, 39.

Chubb, J.E. (1988, Winter) 'Why the current wave of school reform will fail,' *The Public Interest*, pp. 28–49.

Chubb, J.E. and Moe, T.M. (1985) 'Politics, markets and the organization of schools', Unpublished paper presented to the Annual Meeting of the American Political Association, September.

Chubb, J.E. and Moe, T.M. (1988) 'No school is an island: Politics, markets, and education', in Boyd, W.L. and Kerchner, C.T. (Eds) *The Politics of Excellence and Choice in Education*, London, Falmer Press, pp. 131–41.

Chubb, J.E. and Moe, T.M. (1990) *Politics, Markets, and School Performance*, Washington, DC, The Brookings Institution.

Cibulka, J.G. (1989) 'Rationales for private schools: A commentary', in Boyd, W.L. and Cibulka, J.G. (Eds) *Private Schools and Public Policy*, London, Falmer Press, pp. 91–104.

Cibulka, J., O'Brien, T. and Zewe, D. (1982) *Inner-city Private Elementary Schools: A Study*, Milwaukee, WI, Marquette University Press.

Clark, B. (1983) 'The organizational saga in higher education', in Baldridge, J. and Deal, T. (Eds) *The Dynamics of Organizational Change in Education*, Berkeley, CA, McCutchan Publishing Company.

Clayton, R. (1994) 'Diversity in state education: The grant maintained option,' in BRIDGES, D. and MCLAUGHLIN, T. (Eds) *Education and the Market Place*, London, Falmer Press, pp. 40–54.

CLUNE, W.H. (1993) 'The best path to systemic educational policy: Standard/centralized or differentiated decentralized?', *Educational Evaluation and Policy Analysis*, **15**, 3, pp. 233–54.

CLUNE, W.H. and WHITE, P.A. (1988) *School-based Management: Institutional Variation, Implementation, and Issues for Further Research*, New Brunswick, NJ, Rutgers University, Eagleton Institute for Politics, Center for Policy Research in Education.

CLUNE, W.H. and WITTE, J.F. (1990) *Choice and Control in American Education, Volume 2: The Practice of Choice, Decentralization and School Restructuring*, London, Falmer Press.

COLEMAN, J.S. (1987) 'The relations between school and social structure', in HALLINAN, M.T. (Ed) *The Social Organization of Schools: New Conceptualizations of the Learning Process*, New York, Plenum, pp. 104–28.

COLEMAN, J.S. and HOFFER, T. (1987) *Public and Private Schools: The Impact of Communities*, New York, Basic Books.

COLEMAN, J., HOFFER, T. and KILGORE, S. (1982) *High School Achievement,* New York, Basic Books.

COLEMAN, J.S., SCHILLER, K.S. and SCHNEIDER, B. (1993) 'Parent choice and inequality,' in SCHNEIDER, B. and COLEMAN, J.S. (Eds) *Parents, Their Children and Schools*, Boulder, CO, Westview Press, pp. 147–82.

COLTON, D. and UCHITELLE, S. (1992) 'Urban school desegregation: From race to resources', in CIBULKA, J., REED, R. and WONG, R. (Eds) *The Politics of Urban Education in the United States*, London, Falmer Press, pp. 134–47.

CONLEY, S.C. and SCHMIDLE, T. (1988) 'Teacher participation in the management of school systems', *Teachers College Record*, **90, 2**, pp. 259–80.

COOKSON, P.W. (1992) *The Choice Controversy*, Newbury Park, CA, Corwin Press.

COOPER, B.S. (1989) 'The politics of privatization: Policy-making and private schools in the U.S.A. and Great Britain', in BOYD, W.L. and CIBULKA, J.G. (Eds) *Private Schools and Public Policy*, London, Falmer Press, pp. 245–68.

CUTRIGHT, M. (1984, November) 'How wide open is the door to parent involvement in the schools?', *PTA Today*, pp. 10–11.

DEAL, T.E. (1985) 'The symbolism of effective schools,' *The Elementary School Journal*, **5**, 85.

DEMBO, M.H. and GIBSON, S.C. (1985) 'Teachers' sense of efficacy: An important factor in school improvement', *Elementary School Journal*, **86**, 2, pp. 173–84.

DOWNES, P. (1994) 'Managing the market place,' in BRIDGES, D. and MCLAUGHLIN, T. (Eds) *Education and the Market Place*, London, Falmer Press, pp. 54–65.

ELMORE, R.F. (1987) 'Reform and the culture of authority in schools,' *Educational Administration Quarterly*, **23**, 4, pp. 60–78.

ELMORE, R.F. (1988) 'Choice in public education', in BOYD, W.L. and KERCHNER, C.T. (Eds) *The Politics of Excellence and Choice in Education*, London, Falmer Press, pp. 79–98.

ELMORE, R.F. (1990) *Restructuring Schools: The Next Generation of Education Form*, San Francisco, Jossey Bass Publishing.

EPSTEIN, J.L. (1986) 'Parent reactions to teacher practices of parent involvement', *The Elementary School Journal*, **86**, 3, pp. 277–93.

EPSTEIN, J.L. (1992) 'School and family partnerships,' in AIKIN, M. (Ed) *Encyclopedia of Educational Research* (6th ed.), New York, MacMillan, pp. 73–87.

EPSTEIN, J.L. and BECKER, H.J. (1982) 'Teachers' reported practices of parent involvement: problems and possibilities', *The Elementary School Journal*, **82**, pp. 103–13.

EPSTEIN, J.L. and DAUBER, S.L. (1991) 'School programs and teacher practices of parent involvement in inner-city elementary and middle schools', *Elementary School Journal*, **91**, 3, pp. 289–309.

ERICKSON, D.A. (1989) 'The communal ethos, privatization, and the dilemma of being public,' in COHEN, S. and SOLOMON, L.C. (Eds) *From the Campus: Perspectives on the School Reform Movement*, New York, Praeger, pp. 136–53.

FINN, C.E. and WALBERG, H.J. (1994) *Radical Educational Reforms*, Berkeley, CA, McCutchan Publishing Corporation.

FIRESTONE, W.A. and PENNELL, J.R. (1993) 'Teacher commitment, working conditions and differential incentive policies', *Review of Educational Research*, **63**, 4, pp. 489–525.

FIRESTONE, W.A. and WILSON, B.L. (1994) 'Bureaucratic and cultural linkages: Implications for the principal,' in SASHKIN, M. and WALBERG, H.J. (Eds) *Educational Leadership and School Culture*, Berkeley, CA, McCutchan Publishing Corporation, pp. 19–40.

FULLER, B., WOOD, K., RAPPORT, T. and DORNBUSCH, S.M. (1982) 'The organizational context of individual efficacy,' *Review of Educational Research*, **52**, pp. 7–30.

GIBSON, S. and BROWN, R. (1982) 'Teachers' sense of efficacy: Changes due to experience,' Paper presented at the Annual Meeting of the California Educational Research Association, Sacramento.

GOLDMAN, P., DUNLAP, D.M. and CONLEY, D.T. (1993) 'Facilitative power and non standardized solutions to school site restructuring', *Educational Administration Quarterly*, **29**, 1, pp. 69–92.

GORDON, I.J. (1977, December) 'Parent educational and parent involvement: Retrospectional prospect', *Childhood Education*, pp. 71–8.

GREENWOOD, G.E. and HICKMAN, C.W. (1991) 'Research and practice in parent involvement: Implications for teacher education,' *The Elementary School Journal*, **91**, 3, pp. 279–88.

GUBA, E.G. and LINCOLN, Y.S. (1981) *Effective Evaluation: Improving the Usefulness of Evaluation Results through Responsive and Naturalistic Approaches*, San Francisco, Jossey Bass Publishing.

GUTHRIE, J.W. (1990) 'The evolution of educational management: Eroding myths and emerging models', in MITCHELL, B. and CUNNINGHAM, L.L. (Eds) *Educational Leadership and Changing Contexts of Families, Communities and Schools*, Chicago, University of Chicago Press, pp. 210–31.

HALL, E. and HORD, S.M. (1987) *Change in Schools Facilitating the Process*, Albany, NY, State University of New York Press.

HANNAWAY, J. (1993) 'Decentralization in two school districts: Challenging the standard paradigm', in HANNAWAY, J. and CARNOY, M. (Eds) *Decentralization and School Improvement: Can We Fulfill the Promise?*, San Francisco, Jossey Bass Publications, pp. 135–59.

HANNAWAY, J. and CARNOY, M. (1993) *Decentralization and School Improvement: Can We Fulfill the Promise?*, San Francisco, Jossey Bass Publications.

HART, A.W. (1990) 'Managing school performance: The role of the administrator,' in REYES, P. (Ed) *Teachers and Their Work Places: Commitment, Performance and Productivity*, Newbury Park, CA, Sage Publications, pp. 241–77.

HENDERSON, A.T., MARBURGER, C.L. and OOMS, T. (1986) *Beyond the Bake Sale: An Educator's Guide to Working With Parents*, Columbia, MD, National Committee for Citizens in Education.

HESTER, H. (1989) 'Start at home to improve home–school relations', *NASSP Bulletin*, **73**, pp. 23–7.

HILL, P.T. and BONAN, J. (1991) *Decentralization and Accountability in Public Education*, Santa Monica, CA, Rand Publication Series.

HOLMES, M. and WYNNE, E. (1989) *Making the School an Effective Community: Belief, Practice, and Theory in School Administration*, London, Falmer Press.

HOOVER-DEMPSEY, K.V., BRASSLER, O.C. and BRISSIE, J.S. (1987) 'Parent involvement: Contributions of teacher efficacy, school socioeconomic status, and other school characteristics', *American Educational Research Journal*, **24**, 3, pp. 417–35.

HOWE, W. (1994) 'Independent schools: Reflections on uniqueness', An unpublished manuscript.

HOY, W.K., PODGURSKI, T. and TARTAR, C.S. (1991) 'Organizational health inventory for elementary schools: The development of an instrument,' Paper presented at the Annual Meeting of the American Educational Research Association, Chicago.

HOY, W.K., TARTAR, C.J. and KOTTKAMP, R. (1991) *Open Schools/Healthy Schools: Measuring Organizational Climate*, Beverly Hills, CA, Sage Publications.

HOY, W.K. and WOOLFOLK, A.E. (1993) 'Teachers' sense of efficacy and the organizational health of schools', *The Elementary School Journal*, **93**, 4, pp. 355–72.

JOHNSON, S.M. (1989) 'School work and its reform', in HANNAWAY, J. and CROWSON, R. (Eds) *The Politics of Reforming School Administration*, New York, Falmer Press, pp. 95–112.

KANE, P. (1986) *Teachers in Public and Independent Schools: A Comparative Study*, New York, Esther A. and Joseph Klingenstein Center, Columbia University.

KANE, P. (1989) 'Public boarding schools for gifted support', *Education Week*, p. 36.

KEAN, H.T. (1994) 'Three privatization models for public schools', in HAKIM, S., SEIDENSTAT, P. and BOWMAN, G. (Eds) *Privatizing Education and Educational Choice*, West Port, CT, Praeger Publishers, pp. 91–105.

KIRST, M. (1990) 'Accountability: Implications for state and policymakers', *U.S. Department of Education*, Report No. 1590–982.

KRAUSHAAR, O.F. (1972) *American Nonpublic Schools: Patterns of Diversity*, Baltimore, Johns Hopkins University Press.

LEITCH, L.M. and TANGRI, S.S. (1988, Winter) 'Banners to home–school collaboration,' *Educational Horizons*, pp. 70–4.

LIEBERMAN, A. (1990) *Schools as Collaborative Cultures: Creating the Future*, London, Falmer Press.

LINDLE, J.C. (1989, October) 'What do parents want from principals and teachers?', *Educational Leadership*, pp. 12–14.

LITTLE, J.W. (1990) 'Teachers as colleagues,' in LIEBERMAN, A. (Ed) *Schools as Collaborative Cultures: Creating the Future Now*, London, Falmer Press, pp. 165–95.

LOUIS-SEASHORE, K.S. and KRUSE, S.D. (1993) 'An emerging framework for analyzing school-based professional community', Paper presented at the Annual American Educational Research Association, Atlanta.

LOUIS-SEASHORE, K.S. and KRUSE, S.D. (1995) *Professionalism and Community: Perspectives on Reforming Urban Schools*, Thousand Oaks, CA, Corwin Press.

LOUIS-SEASHORE, K.S. and SMITH, B. (1990) 'Teacher working conditions,' in REYES, P. (Ed) *Teachers and Their Workplace: Commitment, Performance and Productivity*, Newbury Park, CA, Sage Publications, pp. 23–48.

MADSEN, J.A. (1994, April) 'Parent efficacy in independent private schools: Lessons for public schools', Paper presented at the Annual American Educational Research Association, New Orleans.

MADSEN, J.A. (1994) *Educational Reform at the State Level: The Politics and Problems of Implementation*, London, Falmer Press.

MADSEN, J.A. (1996) 'Developing a professional based community', *Private School Moniton*, **18**, 2, Winter.

MALEN, B., OGAWA, R.T. and KRANZ, J. (1990) 'What do we know about school-based management?: A case study of the literature, A call for research,' in CLUNE, W.H. and WITTE, J.F. (Eds) *Choice and Control in American Education, Volume 2: The Practice of Choice, Decentralization and School Restructuring*, London, Falmer Press, pp. 289–342.

MARSH, C.J. (1990) 'Managing for total school improvement,' in CHAPMAN, J. (Ed) *School-based Decision-making and Management*, London, Falmer Press, pp. 147–61.

McCARTHY, M.M. (1995) 'Private investment in public education: Boon or boondaggle,' *Journal of School Leadership,* **5**, 1, pp. 4–19.

McNEIL, L.M. (1988) 'Contradictions of control, part 1: Administrators and teachers,' *Phi Delta Kappan,* **69**, 5, pp. 333–9.

MERRIAM, S.B. (1988) *Case Study Research in Education: A Qualitative Approach,* San Francisco, Jossey Bass Publications.

MICHAELSEN, J.B. (1989) 'A public choice perspective on private schooling,' in BOYD, W.L. and CIBULKA, J.G. (Eds) *Private Schools and Public Policy International Perspectives,* London, Falmer Press, pp. 63–72.

MILES, M.B. and HUBERMAN, A.M. (1984) *Qualitative Data Analysis: A Source Book of New Methods,* Newbury Park, CA, Sage Publications.

MURPHY, J. (1992) 'School effectiveness and school restructuring: Contributions to educational improvement,' *School Effectiveness and School Improvement,* **3**, 2, pp. 1–20.

MURPHY, J. and HALLINGER, P. (1993) *Restructuring Schooling: Learning from Ongoing Efforts,* Newbury Park, CA, Corwin Press.

NAISMITH, D. (1994) 'In defense of the educational voucher,' in BRIDGES, D. and McLAUGHLIN, T. (Eds) *Education and the Market Place,* London, Falmer Press, pp. 34–40.

NEWMANN, F.M. (1993) 'Beyond common sense in educational restructuring: The issues of content and linkage', *Educational Researcher,* **22**, 2, pp. 4–13.

NEWMANN, F.M., RUTTER, R.A. and SMITH, M.S. (1989) 'Organizational factors that affect a school's sense of efficacy, community, and expectations,' *Sociology of Education,* **62**, pp. 221–38.

NODDINGS, N. (1984) *Caring: A Feminine Approach to Ethics and Moral Education,* Berkeley, CA, University of California Press.

OGBU, J.U. (1974) *The Next Generation: An Ethnography of Education in an Urban Neighborhood,* New York, Academic Press.

PAULU, N. (1989) *Improving Schools and Empowering Parents: Choice in American Education,* Washington, DC, U.S. Government Printing Office.

POWELL, A.G. (1988) *'The Conditions of Teachers' Work in Independent Schools,'* Draft of a Paper written for the Center for Research on the Context of Secondary Teaching, Stanford University, Stanford, CA.

POWER, T.J. (1985) 'Perceptions of competence: How parents and teachers view each other', *Psychology in the Schools,* **22**, pp. 68–78.

RAYWID, M.A. (1980, November) 'Restoring school efficacy by giving parents a choice', *Educational Leadership,* pp. 134–7.

RAYWID, M.A. (1985) 'Family choice arrangements in public schools: A review of the literature', *Review of Educational Research,* **55**, 4, pp. 435–67.

RAYWID, M.A. (1988) 'Community and schools: A prolegomenon', *Teachers' College Record,* **90**, 2, pp. 16–28.

RAYWID, M.A. (1990) 'Rethinking School Governance', in ELMORE, R. (Ed) *Restructuring Schools: The Next Generation of Educational Reform,* San Francisco, Jossey Bass Publishing, pp. 155–205.

Raywid, M.A. (1993) 'Building community in schools', in Smith, G.A. *Public Schools That Work*, New York, Routledge, pp. 10–16.

Reitzug, U.C. (1994) 'A case study of empowering principal behavior,' *American Educational Research Journal*, **31**, 2, pp. 283–307.

Reyes, P. (1990) *Teachers and Their Workplace: Commitment, Performance and Productivity*, Newbury Park, CA, Sage Publications.

Rhine, W.R. (1981) *Making Schools More Effective: New Directions Follow Through*, New York, Academic Press.

Rosenholtz, S.J. (1989) *Teachers' Workplace*, White Plains, NY, Longman Inc.

Sarason, S. (1971) *The Culture of the School and the Problems of Change*, Boston, Allyn and Bacon.

Sashkin, M. and Egermiller, J. (1993) *School Change Models and Processes*, U.S. Department of Education, Superintendent of Documents, Washington, DC.

Sashkin, M. and Walberg, H.J. (1994) *Educational Leadership and School Culture*, Berkeley, CA, McCutchan Publishing Corporation.

Savas, E.S. (1987) *Privatization: The Key to Better Government*, Chatham, NJ, Chatham House Publishers, Inc.

Schaefer, E. (1985) 'Parent and child correlates of parental modernerity', in Sigel, T.J. (Ed) *Parental Belief Systems: The Psychological Consequences for Children*, Hillsdale, NJ, Erlbaum, pp. 106–32.

Schneider, B.L. (1989) 'Schooling for poor and minority children', in Boyd, W.L. and Cibula, J.G. *Private Schools and Public Policy: International Perspective*, London, Falmer Press, pp. 73–91.

Schneider, B. and Coleman, J. (1993) *Parents, Their Children and Schools*, San Francisco, Westview Press.

Sergiovanni, T.S. (1994a) *Building Community in Schools*, San Francisco, Jossey Bass Publishers.

Sergiovanni, T.S. (1994b) 'Organizations or communities?: Changing the metaphor changes the theory', *Educational Administration Quarterly*, **30**, 2, pp. 214–26.

Shakeshaft, C. (1987) *Women in Educational Administration*, Newbury Park, CA, Sage Publications.

Sizer, T.R. (1984) *Horace's Compromise: The Dilemma of the American High School*, Boston, Houghton Mufflin.

Slaughter, D. and Schneider, B. (1986) *Newcomers: Blacks in Private Schools*, Final Report to the National Institute of Education (ERIC Document ED 274 768 and ED 274 769), Northwestern University.

Smith, G.A. (1993) *Public Schools That Work*, New York, Routledge.

Smylie, M.A. (1992) 'Teacher participation in school decision making: Assessing willingness to participate', *Educational Evaluation and Policy Analysis*, **14**, 1, pp. 53–67.

Smylie, M.A. and Brownlee-Conyers, J. (1992) 'Teacher leaders and their principals,' *Educational Administration Quarterly*, **28**, 2, pp. 150–84.

Smyth, J. (1993) *A Socially Critical View of the Self-managing School*, London, Falmer Press.

SPINKS, J.M. (1990) 'Collaborative decision-making at the school level,' in CHAPMAN, J. (Ed) *School-based Decision-making and Management*, London, Falmer Press, pp. 121–45.

SWICK, K.J. (1988, Fall) 'Parent efficacy and involvement: Influences on children', *Childhood Education*, pp. 37–42.

SWICK, K.J. and GRAVES, S. (1986) 'Focus of control and interpersonal supports as related to parenting,' *Childhood Education*, **63**, pp. 26–31.

SWICK, K.J. and TAYLOR, S. (1982) 'Parent–child perceptions of their ecological context as related to child performance in school,' *Instructional Psychology*, **9**, pp. 168–75.

SWIDLER, A. (1979) *Organization Without Authority*, Cambridge, MA, Howard University Press.

SYKES, G. (1990) 'Teaching incentives: Constraint and variety', in LIEBERMAN, A. (Ed) *Schools as Collaborative Cultures: Creating the Future Now*, London, Falmer Press, pp. 103–27.

TIMAR, T.B. (1989) 'The politics of school restructuring,' *Phi Delta Kappan*, **71**, 4, pp. 165–75.

TUCCI, L. (1992, September) 'Spinning ivy into gold,' *St. Louis*, pp. 38, 42.

TUCCI, L. and RAMI, T. (1993, January) 'An affordable Catholic education,' *St. Louis*, pp. 24–35.

VALLI, L. (1992) *Reflective Teacher Education*, Albany, NY, State University of New York Press.

WALLER, W. (1945) *The Sociology of Teaching*, New York, Wiley.

WATSON, T. (1981) 'The relationship between home support and neighborhood support and the achievement of children entering first grade, Unpublished doctoral dissertation, University of South Carolina, Columbia.

WEILER, H.N. (1990) 'Comparative perspectives on educational decentralization: An exercise in contradiction?,' *Educational Evaluation and Policy Analyses*, **12**, 4, pp. 433–48.

WELLS, A.S. (1991) 'The sociology of school choice: A study of black students' participation in a voluntary transfer plan', Unpublished doctoral dissertation, Teachers College, Columbia University.

WHITE, K.R., TAYLOR, M.J. and Moss, V.D. (1992) 'Does research support claims about the benefits of involving parents in early intervention programs?,' *Review of Educational Research*, **62**, 11, pp. 91–125.

WHITE, P.A. (1992) 'Teacher empowerment under "ideal" school-site autonomy,' *Educational Evaluation and Policy Analysis*, **14,** 1, pp. 69–82.

WILLIAMS, D.L. and CHAUKIN, N.F. (1989) 'Essential elements of strong parent involvement programs', *Educational Leadership*, **47**, pp. 18–20.

WOODS, P.A. (1992) 'Responding to the consumer: Parental choice and school effectiveness', *School Effectiveness and School Improvement,* **4**, 3, pp. 24–54.

WOODS, P.A. (1993) 'Competitive arenas in education: Studying the impact of enhanced competition and choice on paper and schools,' Paper presented at the American Educational Research Association Conference, Atlanta, GA, April.

WYNNE, E. (1989) 'Developing school climate', in HOLMES, M. and WYNNE, E. (Eds) *Making the School an Effective Community: Belief, Practice and Theory in School Administration*, London, Falmer Press, pp. 233–51.

YIN, R.K. (1989) *Case Study Research: Design and Method*, (Revised Edition) Newbury Park, CA, Sage Publications.

Index